The
Game Bird Hunter's Bible

Robert Elman

DOUBLEDAY

NEW YORK LONDON TORONTO SYDNEY AUCKLAND

PUBLISHED BY DOUBLEDAY
a division of Bantam Doubleday Dell Publishing Group, Inc.
1540 Broadway, New York, New York 10036

DOUBLEDAY and the portrayal of an anchor with a dolphin
are trademarks of Doubleday, a division of Bantam
Doubleday Dell Publishing Group, Inc.

Library of Congress Cataloging-in-Publication Data

Elman, Robert
  The game bird hunter's bible/Robert Elman.—1st ed.
       p.   cm.
  ISBN 0-385-42383-7 (paperback)
  1. Upland game bird shooting.   I. Title.
SK323.E58   1993
799.2' 42' 0973 -- dc20   93-2387
                              CIP

November 1993

10   9   8   7   6   5   4   3   2

This book is dedicated to
my family—Ellen, Catie, Dan, and Tom.

ACKNOWLEDGMENTS

I wish to express my gratitude to four wonderful friends—John Falk, Lennie Rue, Art Scheck, and the late Sid Latham—not only for their photographic contributions to this book but for their unforgettable companionship, sportsmanship, and laughter in all kinds of weather.

Contents

Introduction

Our prehistoric ancestors were hunter-gathers who killed birds as well as other creatures for subsistence. They may well have enjoyed the pursuit of their prey (just as many nonhuman predators appear to), and our love of the hunt is probably based on an atavistic urge. However, relatively small, swift birds would have been difficult to kill with primitive weapons, and they were seldom worth the effort since they provided far less meat than larger animals and no fur-covered skins to provide warmth and bodily protection. Little wonder that anthropological digs have uncovered far more mammal bones than bird bones in the caves of our ancestors.

The ancient Greeks and Egyptians hunted birds as well as mammals, but contributed little to the traditions of sport hunting as we know it. Hunting dogs were used to run down mammals, and possibly to locate hidden birds which could then be trapped by netting—or on rare, lucky occasions killed with an arrow, spear, or stone. There is evidence that the Romans brought hunting dogs to the British Isles, but

they wrought little change in the methods of the hunt. Falconry appears to be almost as ancient as the use of dogs, but has no bearing on the kind of hunting under discussion here.

In medieval Europe, as in Asia, the objects of the hunt were more often mammals than birds, although game birds and waterfowl were netted and were also lured into funnel-shaped traps. Significantly, serfs and vassals hunted in order to get meat and did so clandestinely, often under threat of death by the feudal lords who owned the land and all creatures dwelling upon it. Hunting as a sport was the prerogative of nobility, a popular pastime of the lords. Often, however, the actual hunting of the most desirable game, such as deer and boar, was done by servants, with the master merely riding in for the kill.

As early as the 16th century, some firearms were used to kill birds and were known as fowling pieces. Those old fowling pieces, however, were extremely heavy and enormously long (a very long barrel being required to burn the

SHOOTING FLYING

S. Gribelin Sculptre

The earliest known English illustration of wingshooting, or "shooting flying," this 1686 etching appeared in *The Gentleman's Recreation*, by Richard Blome. Game bird hunting at that time was still a diversion of the aristocracy, not a sport of the common people.

crude black powder then in use), and they were slow to fire, unreliable, and inaccurate. They were so difficult to hold and swing from the shoulder that they were often propped on shooting stocks or rested on other supports. Birds were seldom killed as they flew, but rather as they rested on water, land, or tree limbs.

With the exception of turkeys, game birds today are killed "on the wing"—as they fly—and that has become a distinguishing character-istic of both waterfowling and game bird hunting—the only acceptable, or sporting, way to go about it. This tradition originated hardly more than a couple of centuries ago, for it had to await the advent of light, short, fast-firing, relatively accurate bird guns. During the first half of the 17th century, many gunsmiths, particularly in England, began making "long fowlers" that were not quite as long or heavy as the older fowling pieces, and in the 1630s Pilgrim shooters astonished the Indians by picking off crows in flight. That sort of feat was a stunt, but during the next century gun weight was reduced, barrels shortened, balance improved, and by the early 1700s fine single-barreled "field fowlers" could be found throughout Europe. Wingshooting, or "shooting flying" as the English called it, was becoming a popular diversion of the wealthy. It remained a diversion of the wealthy for more than a century, both in Europe and America. After all, hunting as pure *sport* rather than necessity requires leisure time and at least a small expenditure of money.

Game bird hunting remained a somewhat esoteric sport until a revolution in flintlock gun design occurred in 1787 when Henry Nock, one of England's finest gunmakers, designed a new breech. Until then, the flash from the priming powder had ignited the main charge at one corner of the breech, and the flame then spread forward gradually, slowly producing the expanding gases that propelled the missile or missiles. Nock's breech employed a little chamber filled with powder behind the main charge. The priming set off this smaller charge, which sent a spurt of flame through the center of the main charge, igniting it all more or less at once. This propelled the ball or pellets much faster and harder, with the result that barrels as short as 30 inches or so could be efficient.

Shorter guns were far more maneuverable, and with efficient combustion and faster propulsion a shooter could be confident of hitting more distant targets. Moreover, it was no longer necessary to lead a moving target by as great a margin as previously.

Multiple barrels were nothing new, but in the past they had resulted in very heavy, cumbersome guns unsuited to wingshooting. With Nock's innovation, short double-barreled guns began to appear, and they were no heavier than the older single-barrels. Then, in 1806, Joseph Manton patented the elevated sighting rib that rested between the two barrels and proved to be an enormous advantage in tracking a moving target.

During the next century, the percussion system of ignition replaced the flintlock and was itself replaced by breechloading systems utilizing self-contained ammunition. Further inventions came with relative speed. Repeating gun actions were perfected, most significantly the pump-action and semiautomatic. These have never fully replaced double-barreled shotguns— neither side-by-sides or over/unders—but they have become more numerous than the classic doubles. Black powder gave way to modern smokeless powders, and in this age of sophisticated plastics, chemistry, and metallurgy, further improvements in shotgun shells have been both drastic and frequent.

The changes in technology have been accompanied by slow changes in customs and attitudes. The lesson of the passenger pigeon was at first lost on American conservationists and sportsmen. A century ago, bobolinks were shot as game birds, woodcock were hunted throughout the summer, and bag limits were in some cases nonexistent and in others so large as to be almost meaningless. As recently as a couple of decades ago, virtually every sportsman believed that no game species had ever been depleted by sport hunting. Market gunners were given exclusive blame for the extinction of the passenger pigeon and the heath hen, although historical records prove beyond dispute that unregulated sport hunting contributed to their demise. The decline of bobwhite quail and woodcock more recently was blamed entirely on a combination of habitat loss and toxic pollution such as the indiscriminate use of DDT for many years. Those factors did, indeed, have a devastating effect, but when bird populations were declining we took some time to realize how ridiculous it was to claim that a continuation of overgenerous seasons and bag limits did not further reduce the diminishing numbers.

At last we seem to have entered an age of

environmental consciousness and conscience, with sportsmen in the forefront of the movement to conserve wildlife. We have organizations of conservationists-sportsmen devoted in some cases to the welfare of wildlife in general and in others to the welfare of such favorite game as turkeys, grouse and woodcock, quail, and pheasants (see Appendix III). Even those organizations that focus on a single kind of game are proving to be of tremendous benefit to wildlife in general through expansion, improvement, and maintenance of habitat. The essence of conservation has become the essence of sportsmanship as well. It's this and only this that allows us to go afield with a light heart and an expectant excitement, knowing that the game birds are still out there for us and will be out there for our grandchildren.

1

Shotguns

Many years ago in Ontario, I hunted Hungarian partridges with a farmer who supplemented his small income by working as a guide. His shotgun (which he used for all game from the little "Huns" to pheasants and even geese) was a battered 12-gauge Harrington & Richardson break-open single-shot. Most of the bluing had worn off long ago, leaving the barrel more or less gray, and a split in the stock had been mended with a long wood screw. He had learned to shoot with that gun, and he seldom missed. Yet he looked with envy upon my pump-action Ithaca with its five-shot magazine, and he had good reason to do so.

An old theory declares that a gun holding but one shotshell is best for learning the art of wing-shooting, because it discourages any impulse to fire prematurely or aim carelessly, and the knowledge that there's only one chance to bring down a flying target is a psychological incentive to practice and to master marksmanship. I used to believe the theory. My older son's first gun was therefore a 20-gauge Winchester single-shot. His instruction went as follows: thorough drills in safe gun handling and firearm safety in

general; practice in mounting the (unloaded) gun properly, pointing it at stationary targets and swinging it through the path of moving targets—dry-firing without jerking or stopping the follow-through of the swing; firing several shots at stationary targets (set up at about 30 yards with a safe backstop) to get the feel of actual shooting—the trigger's let-off, the recoil, the noise; and finally, a lot more shots at hand-thrown tin cans and at clay targets flung by a hand-operated trap.

A pheasant on a game preserve gave him his first chance at a live flying target. A setter pointed the bird, invisible in a thick patch of ragweed, and I walked in to flush it. But instead of flying, it ran—as pheasants often do—and the dog broke its point to give chase. I could see the strain of blended frustration and hope on Tom's face as he waited, with the gun safely held at port arms, while the pheasant raced nearly 30 yards through tall grass before becoming airborne. At last it rose in a low, sweeping arc, almost straight away but veering slightly to the right. My son tracked it with his gun, swinging until the muzzle almost blotted it out, with the

American Arms Gentry

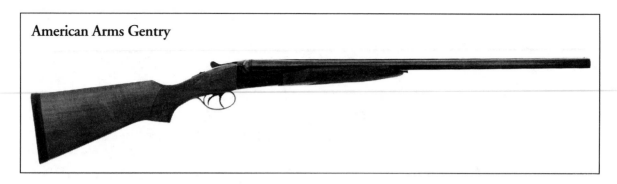

Ruger Red Label

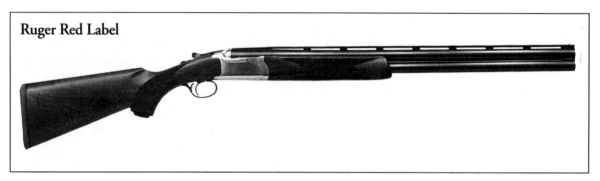

Remington Model 870

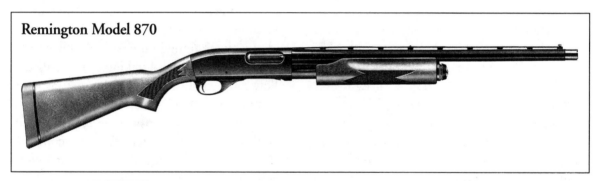

Browning Field Grade Auto-5

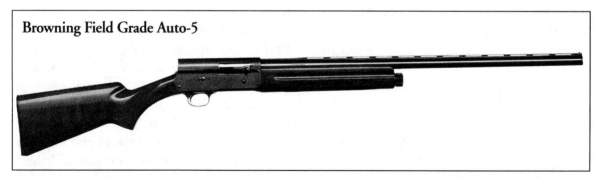

Here are four examples typifying the shotgun actions generally used in hunting game birds. They are (from top): a side-by-side double, over/under double, pump-action repeater, and semiautomatic repeater. The side-by-side model shown here has two triggers, but such guns are also built with a single, selective trigger.

upper part of the target seeming to rest atop the bead—but he waited until the bird was a good 15 feet up, high above the leaping dog so there would be no chance of a stray pellet's hitting the setter. When Tom finally fired, the distance to the target was at least 45 yards, and it fell from the air like a stone.

One shot, one bird bagged, an excellent beginning—and yet, if Tom were a boy again, I'd prefer to start him with a pump-action or a double-barreled gun rather than a single-shot. The advantages of learning wingshooting with a single-shot can easily be duplicated by enforcing a rule that (at first, perhaps for the first season) the gun must be loaded with only one shell. Before very long, it's time to learn how to make follow-up shots, an art in itself since there's a natural tendency to stop the gun swing instantly after the first shot or to lift one's cheek from the stock—either of which will probably cause the second shot to miss.

Very often in wingshooting, the first shot misses and the second brings down the bird. And with many kinds of game (most notably quail, pheasants, doves, chukar and Hungarian partridges, and some varieties of grouse) it often happens that two or more birds flush or fly by simultaneously. A wingshooter can experience no feeling more exultant than that of scoring a double on one rise.

Many gunners, particularly in America, feel inadequately equipped with any gun that doesn't hold at least three shells. If the first two shots miss, the bird will almost always be out of range or hidden by trees or other cover before the hunter can get off a well-directed third shot. On the other hand, even if one shot misses, the second may bring down a bird and the third may bring down another. Perhaps you needed the third shot, but you're still entitled to the satisfaction of having scored a double.

Does this mean a repeater—a pump gun or semiautomatic—is definitely the best choice for a game bird hunter? Not necessarily. In hunting ruffed grouse and woodcock, there's seldom an opportunity to get off a third well-directed shot. Such an opportunity almost never occurs in turkey hunting, even though most turkey hunters are partial to repeaters. With driven pheasants, I think my personal choice would be a repeater, but when I'm "walking them up" or shooting over a dog, there's much less chance of needing a third shot. For anyone who owns or can afford to buy two or more guns, there are excellent reasons to make at least one a repeater and at least one double-barreled—assuming that the shooter realizes each will handle differently and requires considerable practice for mastery.

The receiver of a repeater is necessarily longer than that of a double-barreled gun, because more space is needed for the mechanism itself and for the shells to be fed from the magazine (usually a tube under the barrel) rearward onto the shell carrier in the receiver, then upward and forward into the chamber. A repeater's overall length is therefore greater than that of a double gun, whether the latter is of the side-by-side or over/under configuration. The balance, feel, and appearance all differ.

The balance of a good double is usually better (meaning that it's pleasanter to carry and it mounts and swings more naturally). A double is often but not always lighter. Its relative shortness makes it easier to maneuver in dense cover—for instance, in a thick alder swale where woodcock may be all about. Most shooters find that a double swings faster, more fluidly and naturally, and most agree that it's invariably handsomer than a repeater as an example of gunmaking art.

For most of us, price is a major consideration. In the United States, doubles are higher-priced than repeaters partly because they're made or imported in smaller numbers—there's less demand for them. But there are other, unavoidable reasons. For one thing, the barrels must be "regulated" so that they'll fire their patterns of shot pellets to more or less the same point—or to overlap extensively—out where the target is flying. Also costly are the joining of the barrels and installation of the sighting rib on the upper barrel of an over/under or between those of a side-by-side.

At one time, all double-barreled guns employed two triggers—the forward trigger (slightly to the right of the rear trigger) firing the right barrel or lower barrel. Some, particularly side-by-sides, still have double triggers, and a few have non-selective single triggers (which fire the lower or right barrel on the first pull). Many have selective single triggers, with a sliding-button control to determine which barrel will be fired first. This can be an advantage because the lower or right barrel usually (not always) has a relatively open choke to spread the pellet pattern for a first, fast, close-range shot at flushed birds, while the other barrel has a tighter choke to produce an effective pellet pattern at longer range, as the birds fly away. On occasion, a gunner may want his first shot fired from the tight barrel because the birds are giving him nothing but long-range shots.

Regardless of which trigger mechanism the gun employs, it's more costly than that of a repeater—as are other details of the mechanisms governing cocking, firing, and ejecting. There are some reasonably priced field-grade double guns, but most of them cost considerably more than good-quality repeaters.

Apart from cost, the choice between a double and a repeater may be based in some instances on whether a particular kind of game bird hunting may be the owner's primary sport. Appearance may also be a factor, though not a very practical one. In other instances, the choice can be determined quite sensibly by which kind of gun feels most comfortable and swings and shoots best (most naturally, almost as an extension of the arms and upper body) for the individual who will be using it.

Without a doubt, a person who learns to shoot with one kind of gun and shoots that kind most often will perform better with it than with any other. Anyone new to the sport is well advised to visit a gun shop and handle the several types, mounting and swinging each (unloaded, of course) in order to get the feel and heft of each. It's even better, when possible, to do some shooting with each type before buying one. Perhaps a shooting coach or friend can help. There are also some public trap and skeet facilities where the management will provide a gun that can be tried for a round of clay-bird shooting. A small extra fee may be charged, or the shooter may have to pay only the normal fee for a round of trap or skeet plus the price of the ammunition. It's too bad there aren't more such ranges. Let's look now at the major features of each type of gun.

DOUBLE-BARRELED GUNS

As noted above, double-barreled guns tend to be shorter than repeaters—though there are some very long-barreled doubles—and most of them, both side-by-sides and over/unders, are well balanced and reasonably light. Some shooters vastly prefer a side-by-side (acknowledged by most gun fanciers to be the handsomest of all general classifications of firearms) while others are equally keen over/under advocates.

An argument sometimes cited in favor of the side-by-side is its trimness from top to bottom. An over/under is much deeper in profile owing to the position of its barrels. When opened ("broken open" in shotgunning parlance), the barrels must be tipped farther down than those of a side-by-side to expose the chamber, or rear, of the lower barrel and create an opening wide enough for that barrel's shell to be extracted and ejected, as well as for the insertion of a fresh shell into the lower barrel. This supposedly makes the over/under a little more cumbersome to load or unload when the gunner is in a cramped spot. I've never had a problem in that regard, and the argument strikes me as nonsense.

To load or eject shells, the action of a double-barreled gun is "broken"—opened fully. To fully expose the lower chamber of an over/under (bottom gun), it must be opened to a slightly deeper angle than a side-by-side, as shown here. Some hunters claim this is a disadvantage when shooting in tangled thickets, but the author has never found it to be a hindrance.

The forestock of an over/under is usually larger (deeper) than that of a side-by-side—again, owing to the configuration of the barrels. Indeed, the forestock, or "forearm," on some side-by-sides (especially older ones and some of those made primarily for the European market) is of the very slim, narrow "splinter" design—uncomfortably small for some shooters. On the other hand, a few side-by-sides have oversized "beavertail" forestocks, and so do quite a few over/unders. I like a fairly hand-filling forestock, but I don't believe an extra-large beavertail has any advantage unless the shooter has very large hands. The only way to find out whether a side-by-side or over/under is more comfortable for you to hold, point, and swing is to do just that with each type.

Some advocates of the over/under insist that its "single sighting plane" (along the rib that rides the upper barrel) is—like that on the single barrel of a repeater—an enormous help in tracking, lining up, and leading a target, whereas the top surfaces of a side-by-side supposedly provide a too-wide, imprecisely defined, hence confusing sighting plane. Personally, I find the opposite to be true, and I shoot better with a side-by-side. The modern ones have a raised rib between the barrels, and the barrels

Here (from top) are the author's SKB side-by-side, Ithaca Model 37 pump, and Winchester 101 over/under. Visible in the rear portion of the pump's trigger guard is the button (through-belt) safety, reversed in this instance for left-handed manipulation. The safety on the others—as on most doubles—is a thumb-operated ambidextrous slide on the top tang, behind the opening lever. For fire position, it's pushed forward. Both doubles have single selective triggers. The SKB's selector button is visible in the trigger. The 101's is in the safety slide, which can be "clicked" leftward to fire the upper rather than the lower barrel first.

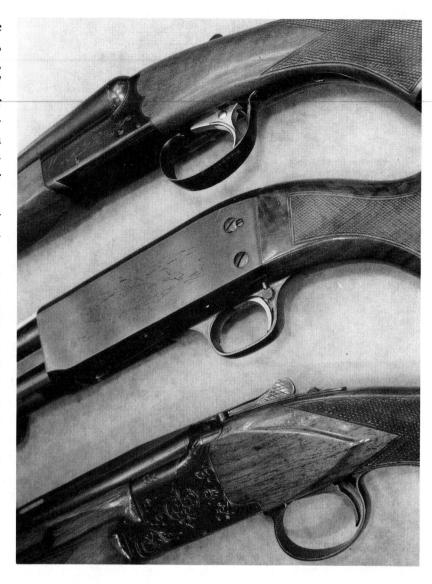

themselves, hemming the rib on each side, help direct my aim right along the center. Moreover, the width of the barrels helps me judge the margin of left or right "lead" (forward allowance) I need in order to make my shot pattern collide with a target flying to the left or right.

I can't believe either type of gun is intrinsically easier to aim; it depends merely on which type you've become accustomed to through practice. My own gun cabinet holds a favorite of each type.

Although I very seldom push the barrel-selector button on my gun when I'm out hunting, I don't like non-selective single triggers. Instant barrel selection is an obvious advantage, even if you make use of it only once in a season or two. I've done quite a bit of shooting with a two-trigger double, and speak from experience when I say it takes a little getting used to but is easily mastered. After a few practice sessions, the trigger finger moves from front to rear trigger automatically, without thinking about it, the instant the first trigger has been pulled. On many such guns, however, if the rear trigger is pulled first (to get off the first shot with the left or upper barrel), the recoil of the first shot slams the

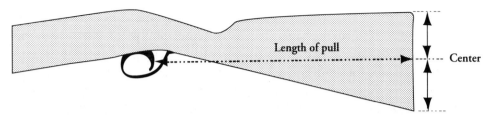

Gunstock length, commonly called length of pull, must be correct for your build (especially your arm length) if a gun is to shoot well for you. It's measured from the center of the trigger (front trigger if the gun has two) to the center of the butt. Among American shotguns, length of pull averages 14 inches, but standard, mass-produced models are available with a number of other lengths, from 13½ to 14½ inches. When shopping, try several and pick what feels comfortable and swings smoothly when mounted to your shoulder correctly (as described in Chapter 3, Tips on Wingshooting).

front trigger against the finger quite unpleasantly. Furthermore, it takes quite a bit of practice to move your finger forward instead of rearward after the first shot. For most gunners, a single selective trigger is the best choice.

Any good double-barreled hunting gun will have extractors (to push the shells rearward, partway out of the chambers when the gun is opened), and most will have ejectors (to knock the shells all the way out, clear of the gun when it's fully opened). Some shooters dislike ejectors because they don't want to search the ground for the empty shells that have been kicked out. A few people who handload their ammunition also insist that shells are occasionally damaged (stepped on) in this process. I've never personally had that happen, and I like ejectors—though I don't consider them essential since it's easy enough to pull an extracted shell from the gun and doesn't take enough time to matter even if the air is filled with birds. But if the gun does have ejectors, they should be selective; that is, when only one barrel has been fired, the spent shell should be ejected while the loaded one remains in place and doesn't have to be picked up and reinserted.

A few double guns have the trigger-selector button in the trigger or trigger guard, but most combine it with the safety slide on the top tang, just behind the opening lever at the top rear of the breech. I prefer it to be combined with the safety, but don't think it matters greatly. When it is combined, the safety slide moves forward for firing and right or left for barrel selection. What does matter in a field gun is that it should have an automatic safety which goes on every time the gun is closed and must be moved (slid forward by the thumb of the shooting hand) before the gun can be fired. Double guns designed primarily for clay-target shooting often have no safety at all or no automatic safety because they're not to be loaded until immediately before the shooter calls for a target and fires. Such guns are not safe for hunting.

The shape of the buttstock is very important. Its length, the height of its comb (top cheeking surface), width, drop at heel (upper corner of the rear end), drop at toe (bottom corner of the rear), and is some cases a slight angling to the left or right (called cast-on or cast-off, respectively) all affect the gun's fit and, therefore, how well you shoot it. Some expensive shotguns have custom-fitted stocks.

Most of the more or less mass-produced shotguns marketed in the United States and Canada have reasonably standardized stock shapes and dimensions that fit most shooters quite well enough for hunting, if not for competitive target shooting. There are, however, small differences in length, thickness, and height and drop. Bear in mind that a very narrow comb or excessive drop will accentuate recoil even if the stock feels comfortable. Before you buy a shotgun, mount and swing it to make sure the stock isn't too long or short for you and that when you bring the stock up to your cheek, your eye is naturally, automatically lined up with the bead or beads (a front one and often a smaller second one about halfway back along the rib) with only a little of the top rib surface itself showing. If it doesn't feel and look right, try another gun.

The "wrist" of the stock—the part your hand wraps around—is also important. It shouldn't be too large or small for comfort. On some double guns, it tends to be too slender either for comfort or durability. Most shotguns (whether double or not) have a pistol grip or semi-pistol grip—a downward curving of the wrist to help position your hand properly and firmly for trigger control. A few, however, have a straight wrist—no pistol grip at all. Many gunners seem to think the purpose of a straight-wristed stock is to achieve a classic and streamlined appearance. Its real purpose is to allow a very slight, easy shift of hand position from front to rear trigger. With a single-trigger gun it's an unnecessary affectation, and adversely affects some shooters with regard to consistent hand position and trigger control. I like it with a two-trigger gun and hate it with a single trigger. Whether the wrist is straight or pistol-gripped, it should have clean checkering, and so should the forestock. This feature, too, is practical rather than cosmetic; it helps prevent the hands from slipping forward or rearward.

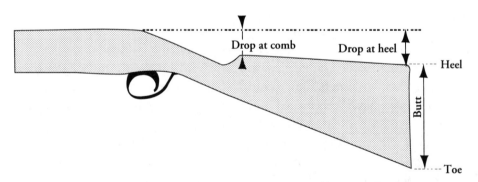

An average commercial shotgun stock has about a 1½-inch drop at comb, 2½-inch drop at heel, and a heel-to-toe butt length of about 5¼ inches. The butt should be long enough to protrude about an inch above and below its contact with the shoulder. Drop at comb and heel varies greatly today. The pronounced drop on some older guns accentuates recoil and muzzle rise, especially if the stock is thin. Some modern guns—trap models, for instance—have high, straight stocks with little drop (or have a raised comb portion known as a Monte Carlo). A stock with field or skeet contours is best for fast mounting, swinging, and shooting at game birds.

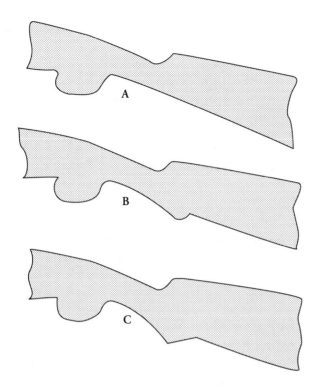

Shotguns are available with a surprising number of "wrist" (grip) designs, some of them exaggerated and impractical. The three best and most popular are the (A) straight grip, (B) half- or semi-pistol, and (C) full pistol. On single-trigger guns, the straight grip is an affectation that doesn't help in any way, but some shooters prefer its "classic" look. Its real purpose is to facilitate a slight rearward shift of the hand from front to rear trigger of a double-trigger gun. Even with a gun of that sort, many shooters prefer a half-pistol grip, which also permits good control with a shotgun of any other kind. Most popular on today's single-trigger shotguns (both repeaters and double-barreled models) is a full—but not excessive—pistol grip. Regardless of contours, it should be well checkered to prevent accidental sliding of the hand.

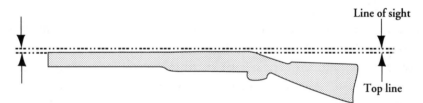

A shotgun's "top line" is simply the level of the barrel or rib. The "line of sight" is a straight line from the gunner's eye level (with the gun properly mounted to the shoulder) through the front bead, whose height is generally about ⅛ inch above the rib or barrel. For practical purposes, the shooter's eye should be about ¼ inch above the rear end of the action, so the line of sight is not quite parallel to the top line but nearly converges with it at the bead. If, when you mount and cheek your gun, you see a tiny bit of barrel or rib between action and bead, the gun fits, and your eye position is good.

You may have heard or read that the barrels of an over/under are easier to regulate than those of a side-by-side, so the former is apt to be more accurate than the latter. There's a grain of truth in the first part of that statement, a much smaller grain in the last part. With good-quality shotguns of either type, the difference in accuracy (when it exists at all) is too small to be meaningful. Such subtleties are of concern only to competitive gunners who shoot Olympic or universal (international-style) trap. They're irrelevant to hunting.

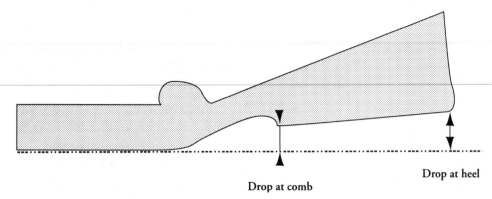

Drop at heel

Drop at comb

If you wish to check stock contours, an easy and accurate way to measure drop at comb and heel is to lay the gun upside down on a level surface, with the barrel or barrels held flat, and measure the space from surface to comb and heel.

REPEATERS

Most of the shotguns available today are made abroad, chiefly in Italy, Spain, Germany, and Japan, even when marketed by American manufacturers under familiar American brand names. (Notable exceptions are offered by Mossberg, Remington, Ruger, Savage, Winchester/U.S. Repeating Arms Company, and a few smaller makers.) Most of these guns are very good, regardless of origin. With regard to semiautomatics, or autoloaders, however, careful shopping is in order. Some of them will function fully and properly (fire, eject, cock, feed a fresh shell, and fire again) with all standard loads in a given gauge—for example, all 12-gauge shells from 2¾-inch field loads to 3- or even 3½-inch magnum loads. Others will function fully only with a limited variety of loads or must be taken down for some sort of adjustment (such as the repositioning of a piston ring) when switching from one load to another. Before buying an autoloader, be sure to read the specifications and owner's manual carefully.

Although there are semiautomatics with three-shot magazines, most autos and pumps hold five. They generally come with a removable plug (wood, metal, or plastic) in the tubular magazine beneath the barrel. This is because federal regulations restrict gun capacity to three shots for waterfowling—including a shell in the chamber and two in the magazine. In some places, capacity is legally restricted to three regardless of the game being hunted. I own three pump guns and a semiautomatic, and I've never removed the plugs from any of their magazines except for cleaning. Regardless of the kind of game birds I may be hunting, I can't imagine ever using more than three shots effectively before having time to reload.

Some of the older autoloaders occasionally failed to function properly under adverse conditions—especially in extremely cold weather or after a lot of shooting had left powder residue in the works. Once in a great while, such a gun might even malfunction with just a switch to a slightly heavier or lighter load or a switch in ammunition brands. I therefore grew up with a preference for pumps and double guns. However, most of the autos now being sold are far more "forgiving" and reliable. Extremely reliable autos with which I'm personally familiar include Brownings, Mossbergs, Remingtons, and Winchesters. I'm not advocating any particular brands; I've mentioned those I know from experience, and must add that there are surely

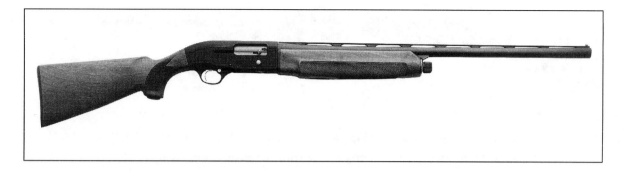

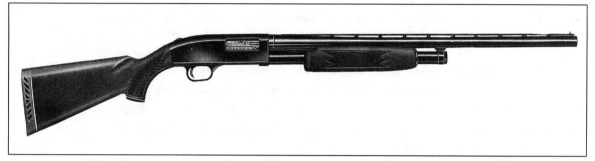

The Beretta autoloader (top) and Mossberg pump shown here, both with standard ventilated sighting ribs and single beads, are typical of today's hunting repeaters except that this pump-action's safety is a slide at the top rear of the receiver (like that on most doubles) instead of a through-bolt in the trigger guard.

others of equal dependability. Even among the few I've named, some models will handle a wider range of loads than others. The Remington 11-87 series is particularly versatile in this regard, but equally versatile guns may be introduced at any time, so the key, again, is to read the specifications.

Pump-action guns entail no problem with regard to lighter or heavier loads, since the shells are cycled manually—by sliding the forestock rearward and then forward again—rather than by the expanding gases produced by the propellant powder. However, some pumps (as well as some autos and double guns) are chambered to accommodate all shells in a given gauge while others will handle only the shorter shells and not the long magnums. Even if a gun won't be used for waterfowling, you may want the capability of shooting long magnums. They're the best (I'm tempted to say only) loads for turkeys,

and they're useful for pheasants in big, open fields where the shots may be very long.

For turkeys, 12-gauge magnums are needed, and some hunters go so far as to swear by the 10 gauge. All other upland birds can be hunted effectively with a 12, 16, 20, or even 28 gauge, but I see no sense in carrying a gun that won't handle the longest shells in its gauge. A 20 gauge with field loads is fine for woodcock, quail, doves, and grouse, but I'd like to use the same gun for pheasants, and for that purpose I prefer 20-gauge magnums. Whether I'm using a pump or auto (or, for that matter, a double) I want the option of using the long shells.

Since most of the newer autos are so reliable, what advantage does a pump have, if any? It's a simpler, manually operated mechanism and therefore even more reliable. A gunner who learned to shoot with an auto may be slowed down on the second shot by having to work the

Many of today's pump-action shotguns, like this Mossberg Model 835 Regal, will safely handle many loads, from 2¾- to 3½-inch shells (but be certain to read the manufacturer's specifications, as a wrong load can be extremely dangerous). Occasional innovations make such guns even more versatile. This one has a "Dual-Comb" stock. It can be used with the stock "naked" or with either of two interchangeable synthetic inserts, easily and quickly installed by the shooter. Shown here is the low-comb insert, best for all-around bird hunting and target shooting. With a higher, Monte Carlo insert, the same bird gun can be scoped and used effectively (with the appropriate interchangeable choke tube) for deer hunting.

pump handle, trombone-fashion, and this may even interfere with his swing until he becomes accustomed to it. Yet it's not true that an auto is inherently faster. Anyone who has learned to shoot a pump, and shoot it well, can get off a second shot as quickly as an auto shooter, working the pump without thinking about it and without impeding the gun swing or follow-through.

The choice between an auto and a pump is, therefore, largely a matter of personal preference and experience. Most pumps and autos have a crossbolt safety button, though a few have a sliding top-tang button like that on a double. It doesn't really matter, as long as it works positively and reliably.

GUN WEIGHT, BARREL LENGTH, AND CHOKE

The lighter a gun is, the heavier its recoil will be, but recoil is unnoticed or hardly noticed during a hunt. This is mostly explained by the hunter's excitement and concentration on the target. It's also because so few shots are taken by comparison with clay-target shooting. In most cases, recoil begins to bother a shotgunner only after he's fired quite a few shots. A long barrel and consequent extra weight—a muzzle-heavy feel—can help steady the gunner's stance, hold, and swing in trap shooting and in long-range pass-shooting at waterfowl. But the vast majority of shots at game birds must be made very quickly and at short to only moderately long range. Long, heavy barrels are of no help here.

On the contrary, a heavy gun becomes a burden when a hunter trudges uphill and down for hours. And too much weight will slow his reflexes and his swing. Ideally, a gun for game bird hunting should weigh between 6 pounds or a trifle less (in the smaller gauges) and 7½ pounds or a trifle more. A few of the better autos weigh 8 pounds or very close to it with a 28-inch barrel length. That's perfectly all right for a young hunter in fine physical condition but slightly heavier than I like. In the course of a long day, a few ounces can make a surprising difference. For woodcock, grouse, and quail, I like a very light, short gun. It isn't quite as important for dove shooting, which usually entails less walking than other bird hunting. For the rest of the game birds, I don't mind a slightly heavier gun.

The most common length for gun barrels is 28 inches, and that's a good, versatile length—sensible for most waterfowling as well as the uplands. Quite a few waterfowl guns have 30-inch barrels which, in my opinion, have very little advantage. If a gun is to be used in the uplands exclusively, or if it has an extra, interchangeable barrel or set of barrels, the ideal barrel length for game bird hunting is 26 inches. That's best for grouse and woodcock, and either best or very good for everything else except turkeys. (Midwestern pheasant hunters, who often shoot their birds at long range in giant fields, will perhaps disagree with me, preferring 28-inch barrels. I won't argue with them.)

Choke brings up stickier questions. Choke is nothing more than a bore constriction (a slight reduction of bore diameter, measured in thousandths of an inch) up near the muzzle. Its purpose, of course, is to control the size of the pattern—the spread of pellets—and keep that pattern fairly uniform and dense so that at least a few of the hundreds of pellets in the shot charge will strike the moving target. If the pattern spreads too much or too soon, it will have large gaps in it, so a relatively tight choke is used to produce a tight pattern for long-range shots. But that same pattern may be too tight—too small—

to hit swift targets consistently at short range. For that purpose, then, you want far less choke.

At least a couple of generations of shooting authorities have said that many (perhaps most) game bird hunters tend to use too much choke, thus firing over-tight patterns that wound or miss the game. Modern ammunition produces better patterns than ever before, so this is probably truer today than it was 20 or 30 years ago. There are many different chokes or choke settings, ranging from none at all—called cylinder or cylinder bore—to super-full. By far the two most useful constrictions for all game bird hunting are improved cylinder (very little choke) and modified (slightly more) but there are times when other constrictions are needed.

I dislike a single-barreled gun—in other words, a repeater—that has only the original, fixed choke cut into the barrel. I use and love several old double-barreled guns with fixed chokes, but each of them gives me an instant choice of two different chokes. Two are choked improved cylinder and modified (a very common combination); one is improved cylinder and improved modified (slightly tighter); and one has intermediate constrictions most easily described as slightly more open than modified and slightly more open than full.

Modern variable-choke devices are a great blessing to the hunter. Probably the oldest of these

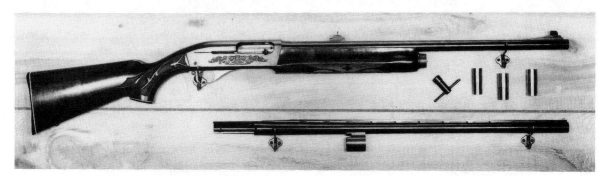

This is a Remington 1100 auto with interchangeable barrels (the one installed has rifle-type sights for deer hunting with slugs) and Hastings screw-in choke tubes. To the left of the small tubes is the wrench for quickly installing or removing them.

In this hunting scene, with a covey of quail erupting from cover in a characteristic flush, the woman at right is mounting a gun with a Cutts Compensator interchangeable choke— the oldest variable-choke device still manufactured. The close-up view shows the Poly-Choke, which is also still manufactured and is simply turned to the desired setting.

is the Cutts Compensator, now manufactured by Lyman Gunsight Corporation. It employs a rather long steel body that's installed at the muzzle and has a series of vents that allow gas to escape upward and downward. Since muzzle jump and muzzle flash aren't a problem in game bird hunt-ing, that's never struck me as an important fea-ture. What's really important is that it accommo-dates six interchangeable choke tubes, from a "Spreader" that actually enlarges the shot pattern to super-full and "Magnum Full." Along with its obvious advantages, it has two major disadvantages. First, it can be fitted only to a single barrel, not to double-barreled shotguns. Second, it takes a bit of time to switch from one choke tube to another, and one of the tubes might be lost.

Almost as old and somewhat smaller is the PolyChoke, made by Marble Arms Company. It's a shorter, slightly bulbous device with no tubes to switch. When it's installed, narrow slits are cut in the barrel's muzzle. This doesn't weaken the barrel at all, because the PolyChoke itself incorporates a reinforcing sleeve. It has a knurled or checkered ring around it that can be turned from one choke setting to another—nine in all on the currently produced version. Turning the ring tightens or loosens the sleeve slightly, constricting the bore or releasing it from constriction. Thus the choke can be changed instantly, without tubes or a tightening wrench, by a quick, short turn of the ring. I have this device on my old Ithaca pump gun, and it works wonderfully. Its disadvantages are that it detracts from the sleek appearance of the barrel (as does the Cutts) and (again like the Cutts) can't be used on a double-barreled shotgun.

Today's most popular variable-choke devices are interchangeable screw-in choke tubes. When in place, they're almost invisible. Most good-quality repeaters now come with them as a standard feature or option, and there are even quite a few double-barreled guns (the newer models) that come equipped with them. In addition, many fixed-choke guns (mostly repeaters) can be fitted with screw-in choke tubes by gunsmithing firms that specialize in such work.

It must be admitted that these universally lauded devices do have a couple of disadvantages. When one choke is switched for another, a tube must be loosened and removed, another put on and tightened with a small wrench. This takes a little time—not much, but you won't be switching to a tighter choke for a second shot—and it's possible the wrench or one of the tubes might be lost, necessitating replacement.

Usually, a set consists of three, four, or five tubes, fewer choices of constriction than with the older variable-choke devices. (Admittedly, the older devices had more settings than anyone needed.) Normally, you choose a tube—a given

When interchangeable choke tubes were first introduced, only single-barreled repeaters could accommodate them, but times have changed for the better. This is a side-by-side with Winchokes—one tube in place.

constriction that's likely to be best—before you start hunting. You stow the little packet of other tubes and wrench in a pocket of your hunting coat or vest, and if your first choice turns out to be wrong, you take a break from hunting and switch tubes. It takes but a minute. Let's say, for example, that you're hunting Hungarian partridges, and a stiff wind is making them "hawky." The coveys have started to "flush wild"—way out—so you switch from a modified tube to full choke. Result: You stop missing the 40- to 50-yard shots.

Specific suggestions about chokes or choke settings will be included in the discussion of each species of game bird.

GAUGE

If a shotgun is to be used for turkeys, or for waterfowling as well as upland hunting, I will state categorically that 12 gauge is the only bore size worth considering, and the gun should accommodate long magnum shells. For all other game bird hunting, the two best gauges are 12 and 20—meaning 20-gauge magnum. You certainly won't always want to use magnum loads, but you do want a gun that accommodates them when the situation demands a little extra shot velocity or a heavier shot charge. Probably the best *all-around* bore size for everything from pheasants down to such small birds as quail and doves is the 20, though a 12 is better for long-range shooting. The 16 gauge is enjoyable to shoot, but I think it has become a superfluous anachronism. Most authorities will agree that a gauge midway between 12 and 20 no longer has any advantages since a magnum 20 will do anything a 16 will do, and perhaps do it better. I don't like a 28 gauge for pheasants, although I have a friend who uses one very efficiently. For the smaller game birds it's fine, but in situations where a 28 will serve well, why not use light 20-gauge loads? Whereas 28-gauge guns and shells for them are becoming hard to find, 20-gauge guns and ammunition are universally available.

I've seen hunters kill grouse and woodcock with the puny .410—and I regarded every last shot as a stunt in rather bad taste. Even in expert hands the .410 is appropriate for nothing but clay targets or tin cans. It doesn't deliver enough pellets to assure clean kills even at modest range, and the pellets transmit insufficient energy. The best choice, then, is a 12 or 20, and whichever you select will elicit no criticism from any knowledgeable hunter.

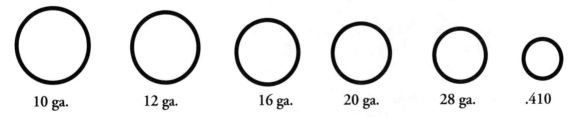

10 ga.   12 ga.   16 ga.   20 ga.   28 ga.   .410

Here are today's most common shotgun gauges, or bore sizes. Although a few hunters use the .410 for the smaller game birds, its pellet capacity is too small for consistently humane kills and it ought to be reserved for target shooting. The 10 gauge is too much gun for almost all game birds, although a few turkey hunters like its extra pellet capacity and power. The best and by far most popular gauges for all-around bird hunting are the 12 and 20.

2

Suitable Ammunition

In discussing specific game birds and hunting situations, I'll include some advice about loads and shot sizes. But first a few general comments are in order because their implications will be applicable in a wide variety of situations involving various game species in all North American locales.

Regardless of the game you're hunting or the bore size of your gun, using appropriate loads makes a bigger difference than some hunters seem to realize. Many of those who do realize it often choose their loads on the basis of seemingly logical but absolutely wrong assumptions—thereby ending up with worse rather than better ammunition for a given purpose. It's simply not true, for example, that high-velocity loads always bring birds down more efficiently than light field loads, or that "chilled" (hardened) shot is always better than cheap, soft, almost pure lead shot, or that magnum loads reach out to game with higher velocity and energy than standard loads, thus adding penetration (i.e., killing power). It isn't even true that high-velocity loads reduce the "stringing" of pellets—the elongation of the pellet swarm as it travels through air—and cause pellets to be fly-ing faster when they hit the target at long range.

It is important to understand the real effects of the enormous ammunition improvements that have come along in the last half-century. Before that, two of the most serious flaws in shotgun ammunition were: (1) substantial deformation of the pellets as they traveled through and rubbed against the steel surface of the gun's bore; (2) additional deformation as the forward pellets in the charge crunched back against the rear ones upon firing—a phenomenon known as setback, which is the same force that thrusts you back against your car seat when you step hard on the accelerator.

Soon after World War II, these faults were considerably reduced by the introduction of chilled shot—lead alloy pellets hardened by the inclusion of 2 to 3 percent antimony. Soon afterward, copper-plated pellets were introduced, and the plating further alleviated setback deformation. Chilled, copper-plated shot is often very useful (also relatively expensive)—but as you read on, bear in mind that pellet deformation is actually *desirable* for some kinds of hunting.

These ballistic-lab photos show an ideally balanced shot string delivered by a load using Remington's Power Piston—a one-piece shot collar and wad column. In the first picture, the string has traveled 18 inches from the muzzle and the wad column is beginning to fall behind; in the second, the pellets are 36 inches from the muzzle; in the third, they're 72 inches out and beginning to spread into a killing pattern. Too long a string critically reduces delivered energy and too short a string causes misses.

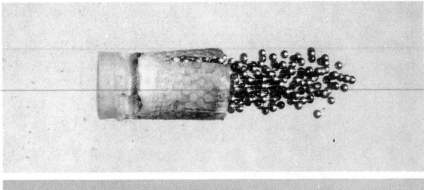

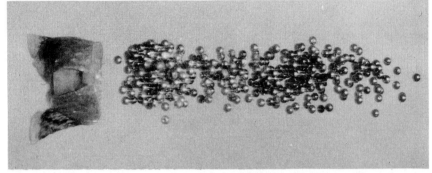

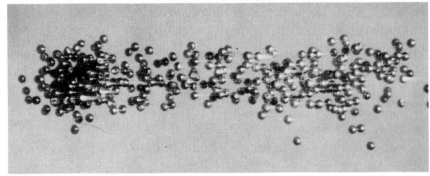

In the 1960s, deformation of shot against the bore was vastly reduced by the advent of plastic shot collars, which evolved into the present one-piece plastic wad columns. These wad columns not only collar the pellets but cushion them against setback by means of a wad-column base that functions rather like a recoil pad. (Also bear in mind as you read on that you can buy shotshells without these features.) The efforts at improvement didn't end in the '60s. Today, the very best, most expensive magnums have powdered plastic (called "Grex") mixed in with the pellets to cushion them upon ignition. Magnums without the Grex can be useful, but the extra cushioning is an excellent improvement for long-range shooting because magnums are very susceptible to deformation, owing to the inertia of their heavy shot charges.

Pellets, being round, are far less aerodynamically efficient than rifle bullets. Deformed pellets are still less efficient because their flattened, irregular surfaces encounter more air resistance than spherical pellets. Hence, they slow down sooner (elongating the shot string) and also begin flying erratically within a relatively short distance from the muzzle, flaring away from the main portion of the pattern.

Steel shot—not truly steel but an alloy far

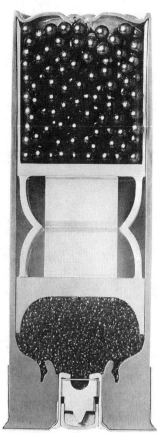

This cut-away view reveals typical construction and components of a shotshell. The thick, very strong base of the plastic casing would actually be sufficient (if built up slightly for proper chamber fit) without the brass head, but most manufacturers retain the brass—evidently for traditional appearance. At bottom center are the primer cup and primer, with an internal anvil to fire the priming mixture. Next comes the powder charge (which occupies less space than many shooters realize). Then comes the combination wad column and shot cup. Its "accordioned" middle structure allows for compression upon ignition, and its base fills and seals the bore efficiently so that energy isn't wasted by propellent gas escaping forward through the pellets. The pellets are encased in a protective cup to prevent or reduce deformation against the bore walls as the shot charge moves at incredible speed through the barrel. Upon exiting the barrel, the lightweight combination wad-cup begins to lag behind the shot charge and quickly falls away.

harder and also lighter than lead—is mandatory for waterfowling because ducks and geese in heavily hunted areas frequently swallow spent lead pellets along with the grit needed in their gizzards, and lead is lethally toxic. Waterfowlers have learned that although steel, being light, loses initial velocity much sooner than lead, it forms substantially tighter patterns at moderate ranges (out to 35 or 40 yards). Similarly, chilled shot, especially if plated, delivers tighter patterns than soft lead shot containing very little antimony.

ACHIEVING WIDE, DENSE PATTERNS

Both gunners and ammunition manufacturers have gone to great lengths to achieve tight patterns, but for some kinds of hunting, tight pat-

terns are precisely what you don't want. Skeet loads and skeet-choked guns (which have almost no choke at all) deliver wide rather than tight patterns, the purpose being to hit close, fast-crossing targets with at least some of the pellets in a wide-spraying pattern. "Spraying" is a key word here, because shot pellets don't travel in a short, tight swarm after emerging from the gun's muzzle; they spray, like water spraying from the nozzle of a garden hose. If they didn't spray—flare out, enlarging the pattern—but maintained the single tiny path of a rifle bullet, the chance of hitting a fast-flying target would be extremely slim. However, they're still concentrated while relatively close to the muzzle—they require some distance to flare out—so you want to enlarge the pattern as much as possible for close-range targets.

This being the case, some knowledgeable

Here are three of the many current, well-designed versions of the plastic shot collar and wad column. The loaded cut-away shell holds the one-piece Remington Power Piston. Above it is one of Winchester's versions (this one for inexpensive but effective field loads) using a plastic collar above fiber filler and base wads. Below it is Federal's all-plastic three-piece arrangement, which is also excellent.

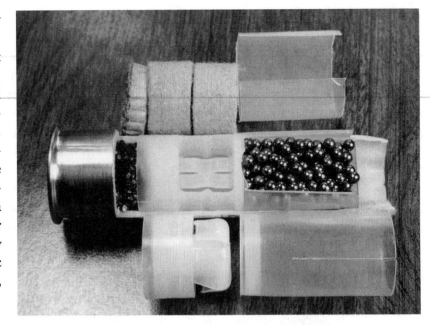

Some manufacturers prefer a multiple-piece wad column and shot cup. Shown here is the Federal Triple-Plus wad column. The cut-away shell at left reveals the components as loaded. The over-powder section has a pillar which is crushed back upon firing to cushion recoil. At center are the column components and shot charge, and to their right are the plastic parts recovered after firing.

hunters use skeet loads and a cylinder-bored gun—or a skeet or improved-cylinder barrel—for woodcock, quail, and even doves. (Those who do so for doves are the small minority who pass up all the long or even semi-long shots and therefore don't get a lot of shooting but bag more birds for the number of shells fired.) Some other knowledgeable hunters use a combination of fairly open choke with cheap field loads of soft lead shot for woodcock (but not if grouse

Practicing by the very enjoyable method of hunting live game on a preserve, the author folds a bird. Assuming the gunner is competent, this kind of game-bagging efficiency depends on a choke-and-ammunition combination that produces a proper shot string and dense, uniform pattern.

are present) and for close-rising quail over a good dog in thick cover.

Here, however, I must insert a caution. Not all loads, cheap or otherwise, are created equal. Not long ago I read an article by an esteemed colleague, Philip Bourjaily, who had done some pattern testing with various brands of shells containing the same pellet sizes and equal charges of powder and shot. The example he gave involved No. 6 shot—a good pellet size for pheasants in much Eastern and some Midwestern and Western cover. He did his patterning in the traditional way, by firing each load at a 30-inch circle at 40 yards. One brand of shell put an average of 80 pellets into the circle, whereas another put only 60 pellets into it, a difference equaling a full degree of choke.

It's important to note here that two guns nominally choked the same way usually will show some difference in patterning with the same load, just as two supposedly similar loads will pattern differently from the same gun. Some guns seem to have a "pet" brand of ammunition, and some will pattern better with shot of certain sizes. I have one that patterns better with 8s than with 7½s or 9s, so I use No. 8 in it (rather than 7½) for doves and No. 8 again (rather than 9) for woodcock. I get a wide but dense, uniform pattern that's very effective.

For even wider patterns, "scatter" or "spreader" loads are sometimes marketed, and some handloaders fashion their own. An old way of doing this was the compartmenting of the shot charge by careful insertion of a cardboard "X" in the shell, but this has a tendency to produce "blown" patterns with gaps in them. Spreader loads use soft shot and no plastic cup or collar. Some imported English spreader loads employ disc-shaped pellets—deformed in advance, you might say. This is all very useful if you also remember that for targets beyond about 30 yards deformation is the last thing you want because at that distance it can begin to blow patterns.

CHOKE AND PATTERN PERCENTAGES

The effect of choke is expressed as the percentage of the total number of pellets—that is, what percentage strikes within the 30-inch circle at 40 yards. Obviously, the larger the gauge, the more pellets a shell can hold, and magnums hold more pellets than standard shells. The total number of pellets isn't exact but average. A shell is charged with shot not by number but by weight, and manufacturers publish tables giving the average number of pellets in each size per ounce or fraction of an ounce. This is the number you use in determining the percentage. For example, one ounce of No. 7½ shot averages 350 pellets. If about 245 of them strike inside the circle, you have a full-choke pattern—a 70 percent pattern. If only about half of them strike inside the circle, you have an improved-cylinder pattern. As a general (far from ironclad) rule, you want at least four pellets to strike the bird—and penetrate—to achieve consistent one-shot kills. To find out whether a pattern will be effective for hunting, try sketching a life-size outline of a game bird such as a pheasant or quail or dove inside the 30-inch circle. Better yet, sketch several outlines here and there in the circle, because more often than not the center of the pattern won't be the part that strikes the moving bird.

The reason for using large shot sizes is to deliver more energy (penetration) per pellet for big, hardy, densely feathered game. Going up in size involves an inevitable trade-off between energy per pellet and the probable number of pellets that will connect. Whereas there are 350 pellets, on average, in an ounce of No. 7½, there are only 135 in an ounce of No. 4. A 70 percent pattern of 4's amounts to only about 94 pellets and far less chance that four or more will strike a flying bird at 40 yards. This is why, with the exception of turkeys, the smallest recommended size for the largest birds discussed in this book is No. 5. It's also why magnums are used in appropriate situations—they contain more shot. Here are the shot percentages that are generally accepted for the five most important choke designations:

Full	70%
Improved modified	65%
Modified	60%
Improved cylinder	50%
Cylinder or Skeet	35-40%

PRACTICAL PATTERN TESTING

That's fine as long as you understand that some full-choked guns will deliver patterns as dense as 80 percent or more with some loads, and others will deliver no more than 65 percent (or less with some cheap loads). That's why it's a good idea to pattern the loads you intend to hunt with. Sometimes it's also a good idea to forget about the standard 40-yard patterning distance

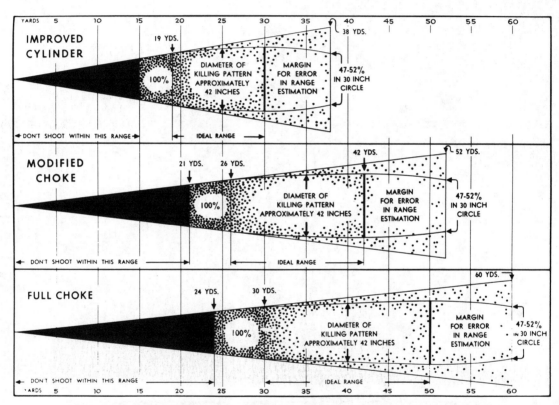

This diagram illustrates the average percentages of shot pellets striking within a 30-inch circle not merely at the conventional 40-yard patterning range but at several distances. Note that an improved-cylinder choke delivers up to 52% at 30 yards and not much less at 35 but becomes ineffective beyond that. A modified choke delivers the same percentage at 42 yards or a little beyond, and a full choke produces the equivalent at 50 yards or a little more. This chart was calculated on the basis of "traditional" ammunition. With the tighter-patterning loads now available, the ideal improved-cylinder shooting range is stretched to nearly 40 yards, modified to 45 or 50, and full to 55 or possible 60. (Courtesy of Winchester Ammunition)

Because individual guns pattern somewhat differently at a given range with various loads containing the same shot size, it's wise to do your own pattern testing at a range duplicating the average expected target distance for a given type of game bird. Here a hunter examines a turkey-load pattern, which must cluster densely on the head and neck area rather than the body.

and test your patterns at some other distance—say 20 yards for woodcock or 30 for quail. Again, sketch the bird outlines inside the 30-inch circle, and don't worry much about precise percentages. What you're seeking is a sufficiently wide, reasonably uniform pattern of hits at the expected game-shooting distance.

Deformation, advantageous as it may be at short range, is a calamity at medium to long range for two reasons. First, deformed pellets fly through the air slowly, stretching the shot string to as much as 12 feet in length. By the time most of the deformed pellets arrive at their theoretical destination, the bird will be somewhere else unless in swinging your gun you led the target (gave it forward allowance) by a far greater space than most shooters can judge, much less master. Second, deformed pellets don't penetrate nearly as well as round ones. For medium to long range, you want hard, deformation-resistant pellets to reduce stringing and penetrate better.

HIGH-VELOCITY AND TRAP LOADS

This long-range performance isn't generally achieved by high-velocity loads, which achieve their best performance at short to medium range—out to 40 yards or so. The more velocity is imparted to a sphere, the sooner it slows down, so the magnificent initial velocity just isn't there at long range. Beyond about 40 yards, therefore, the number of pellets striking the target is more important than any extra velocity. It's at moderate ranges that high-velocity shotgun loads have advantages—two of them. At such ranges they do hit the target harder, and at those ranges they also arrive a little sooner, requiring less forward allowance by the shooter. The difference won't be much, maybe six or eight inches, in terms of how far you lead the bird, but I'll take all the help I can get. Six inches may well be the difference between my bringing a pheasant down by hitting

its body and merely giving it reason to preen its long tail after it lands.

Having mentioned skeet loads, I must now call your attention to trap loads. Generally speaking, the trap loads marketed by the well-known manufacturers are of very high quality and not very expensive. Trapshooters use so much ammo that it's produced in large quantity, and every maker wants its brand to be used by the top guns at the big regional and national competitions. For medium range and even a bit beyond, trap loads are excellent for hunting certain game. As with skeet loads, they're limited to small shot—No. 7½, 8, or 9—but those are the sizes you want for most of the smaller game birds. Trap loads, combining hard shot and excellent components, will often deliver more pellets to the target than high-velocity hunting loads.

There's also a fairly widespread misconception that high velocity reduces pellet drop (downward deviation because of gravity) at long range. On the contrary, high velocity increases the severity of setback and deformation, thus increasing the number of pellets that stray from the pattern in all directions, including downward. Besides, pellet drop is insignificant under most circumstances—perhaps 1½ inches at 30 yards and double that at 40.

PELLET SIZE AND MAGNUM LOADS

In overcoming drop as well as sideward wind drift, pellet size is more important than increased velocity. Big pellets retain velocity better than small ones, reaching the target in less time and therefore subject to gravitational pull for less time. Moreover, big pellets aren't deflected by wind as much as small ones, and they cluster more tightly than the small sizes, giving better results at long range. That's why No. 5 shot is recommended for pheasant hunting in big fields where the range is often well over 40 yards.

That—and not more power or velocity—is

the real advantage of magnum loads. Even in the large shot sizes, they contain more pellets than standard loads, so you have an extra number of big, velocity-retaining pellets reaching the target. Some magnums actually have a trifle less velocity than other loads, but tend to retain their speed better.

THE EFFECT OF BARREL LENGTH

Still another popular misconception concerns barrel length. The increased sight radius of a long barrel can be of help in the relatively slow, deliberate swinging and sustained leading that typifies pass-shooting at long-range targets, but it does not add any useful velocity. In the era of black powder, which was very slow-burning, a long barrel was needed to utilize the full powder charge and achieve maximum acceleration before the shot left the muzzle. With modern ammunition, however, it just isn't so.

If a shot charge leaving a 26-inch barrel has a muzzle velocity of 1,150 feet per second, firing the same charge in a 28-inch barrel will increase that velocity by a mere 14 feet per second—not enough to make any practical difference. The choice of barrel length should be based on intended hunting uses—short for fast swinging in thick cover at close targets, longer for more deliberate swinging in open terrain. The most common length in America—28 inches—is a good compromise and excellent for most pheasant and dove shooting, but 26 inches is better for most grouse, woodcock, and quail hunting.

THE ENERGY TO BAG BIRDS

Since velocity affects the amount of energy transmitted to the target, it's the *retained* velocity that I've been emphasizing which makes ammunition efficient. As an example, let's take a big, velocity-retaining shot size, a No. 4 pellet, in a high-velocity load that leaves the muzzle at a speed of approximately 1,330 feet per second. At 40 yards, it has a speed of about 815 feet per second, and its energy has dropped from 12.7 foot-pounds (per individual pellet) to about 7.3 foot-pounds. But that's enough. It's excellent for turkeys in relatively open timber or comparable terrain, where shots are apt to be made at 40 yards or more. For pheasants, you need pellet

COMMON SHOT SIZES FOR GAME BIRDS

	•	•	•	•	•	•	•
NUMBER	9	8	7½	6	5	4	2
DIAM. (INCHES)	.08	.09	.095	.11	.12	.13	.15
APPROX. PELLETS IN 1 OZ.	585	410	350	225	170	135	90

This chart shows lead-pellet sizes for upland game birds only—the subject of this book—not steel-shot sizes for waterfowl. The most common and useful sizes range from No. 9 (for small game birds at close range) up to No. 5 (for larger birds at long range.) Turkey hunters occasionally use larger shot, but pellets as small as No. 6 perform very well for those who can call their birds in close, and they should check their state regulations because many states prohibit turkey hunting with shot larger than a stipulated size.

energy of only 2.5 foot-pounds (assuming four pellets strike the target) and still less for smaller birds. All else being equal, the smaller the game bird is, the smaller the pellets should be. Specific recommendations will be made in the discussions of the various species.

An accompanying chart shows the actual diameter of shot sizes commonly used in hunting game birds—from No. 4 down to the smallest widely available shot, No. 9. For those who may be wondering how to figure out for themselves the actual sizes indicated by these absurdly arbitrary but traditional numbers (as I wondered for years), here's a simple formula that works. To find the diameter of birdshot in hundredths of an inch, subtract its numerical designation from 17. Subtract 9 from 17 and you get 8, so No. 9 pellets have a diameter of .08 inch. Subtract 6 from 17 and you'll find that No. 6 shot is .11 inch in diameter. That seems absurdly small, yet it's quite big enough for its purpose. Just four pellets of that size will kill a big cock pheasant more than 40 yards from the muzzle of your gun.

3

Tips on Wingshooting

It's probably a safe assumption that a great many readers of this book are adept wingshooters. It's probably an equally safe assumption that some are not; that even those who are rather skillful will welcome and benefit from a few reminders and tips; and that almost all of us can use an occasional refresher course. For the tips in this chapter to work effectively, they must be put into practice repeatedly—which is to say, repeated practice is the key.

Generally speaking, the least efficient way to learn or improve wingshooting techniques is from a book. In part, this is because thorough memorization of motion is almost impossible by reading alone. To transform what's read into a series of actions and motor responses requires physical repetition, pretty much like piano practice. Of course, the practice itself is fun, but there's always a danger of repeatedly practicing mistakes (or misinterpretations of printed instructions) until they become ingrained habits—bad shooting habits that cause misses.

I've found fault with most of the instructional books I've read, including some by eminent shooting authorities. One exception was Larry Koller's *How to Shoot,* originally published in 1964. Years later I had the privilege of updating and revising *How to Shoot* (Doubleday, 1976), and much of the following advice will be based on the excellent tips Larry offered in that book.

But even though I have complete confidence in these tips, I must caution you that the best way to become an accomplished wingshooter is to take lessons from a shooting instructor. The second best way is to practice what you read here under the guidance of a coach. A friend who happens to be a wingshooter will serve nicely. Even if he or she isn't a masterful shotgunner, this can be extremely helpful. While you shoot, the friend watches closely (often from behind your shoulder) and points out any mistakes he or she sees so you can correct them immediately as you go through the informal drill again. Then you can switch places and you coach your friend. Keep this book handy during the practice sessions for quick reference. Inevitably, you'll find a cordial shooting rivalry quickly developing between you and your

Art Scheck, a skilled shotgunner, takes his turn with a hand-trap, lobbing clay birds for a partner during a practice session. This is recommended not only for novices but for experienced wingshooters who want to cure a slump or merely keep their gun mounting and swinging in good form.

friend, which is all to the good. It adds an incentive to concentrate on every target (concentration being vital to good shooting) and to increase the number of practice sessions.

Besides all that, there's a very practical need for a practice companion. You should not try to toss up your own moving targets, as that just imposes total interference with your stance, hold, swing—everything your body is supposed to be doing—and spoils your concentration, too. The best (I'm almost tempted to say the only) way to master flying targets is to have someone fling clay targets for you with a hand-

trap or, better yet, an anchored, lanyard-operated trap. As soon as you're hitting the easy ones with fair consistency, the trap operator (standing to one side and slightly behind you) should start varying their elevations and angles, and occasionally fling a double—two clays simultaneously. The idea, after all, is to mimic the unpredictable flushes and flight paths of live birds.

Even the speed of the target can be varied. With a hand-trap, this is governed by the power of your friend's throwing arm, and to some degree by the design of the hand-held tossing device. With a lanyard-operated trap, it's easily accomplished by a spring that can be tightened or relaxed, usually by turning a wing nut.

Bearing all of this in mind, let's begin by looking at how the shotgun is operated. Probably the most common early mistake is to aim it like a rifle, with a rigid hold and an attempt at precise alignment with the target. There are times when a shotgun is, indeed, aimed pretty much like a rifle—for example, when a turkey is moving slowly (relatively speaking) on the ground. And it's aimed exactly like a rifle when hunting deer with rifled or saboted slugs and a slug barrel. In fact, slug barrels are equipped with rifle-type front and rear sights, and a telescopic sight is often installed on a shotgun for this kind of shooting. But wingshooting is an entirely different art, requiring *fluid motion which does not stop as the trigger is pulled.*

This being the case, guns intended for wingshooting don't have true sights. There's a small bead atop the barrel or sighting rib near the muzzle. Very often, there's a slightly smaller bead about midway back on the rib. Originally, the smaller bead was intended to assist in aligning the barrel (without inadvertent right or left angling) on clay targets in trapshooting, which theoretically demands a slightly more deliberate swing or point than wingshooting. Contrary to the opinion of some hunters who have never used a shotgun with the second bead, it does not slow you down. After shooting such a gun a few times, you align it instantly, without even being conscious of it, as the stock comes to your cheek and your master eye is directed along the barrel to the front bead and target.

I own and use guns with and without the second bead. I'm convinced that its presence helps me a little—just a little—with flying game. And I'm also convinced that it's not really important since you can become deadly with or without it. What's far more important is the rib, about which more in a moment.

The front bead may be a dull brass or bronze color, white, silver, or gold—rarely black, which shows up poorly against dark backgrounds— and the rear bead, if present, may be the same or another color (theoretically for contrast). Personally, I like both white and brass. There are also mildly fluorescent front beads. I have a side-by-side SKB double and a PolyChoked Ithaca pump, each equipped with a fluorescent bead in a more or less pink color, somewhere between orange and rose. They're marvelous in dim light or against dark backgrounds but look about as elegant as mismatched shoes. Fortunately, they have standard-sized screw-in stems, so they can be interchanged with a more traditional bead.

I learned to shoot with an ancient Winchester pump gun that had a single bead directly atop the ribless barrel. I think my boyhood gunning would have improved faster had that old Model 97 been equipped with a raised, flat sighting rib. There's no question at all that a rib helps in alignment, the judgment of target lead, or forward allowance, and the prevention of canting (tilting the gun to left or right). Even today, some ribless shotguns are marketed, but I don't like them.

Some models (including almost all side-by-side doubles) have relatively low, solid-ribs, but the majority have slightly higher, ventilated ribs. The "vent" rib originally was intended for clay-target guns. Although venting reduces weight very slightly, its primary purpose is to leave air spaces along the top of the barrel to help dissipate the heat generated by repeated firing. This is unimportant with a hunting gun, so either type of rib is fine.

However, some models have extra-high ventilated ribs, recognizable at a glance, and these are a hindrance in wingshooting. They're supposed to be used in combination with a high, very straight-combed stock on a trap gun, and they help with relatively deliberate swinging or pointing as a receding target is tracked. With live game, they'll merely slow you down. Remember, you must mount the gun, point, swing, pull the trigger, and continue the swing slightly in follow-through, all in one fluid motion, and the gun must help you do it.

SHOTGUNNING STANCE

It's hard for most people to accept that what's right with a rifle is wrong with a shotgun. They tend to stand sideways or almost sideways to the target, with the left foot (if they're right-handed) downrange—that is, closer to the target. Larry Koller used to tell his shotgunning students to forget about their feet—that they could shoot just as well with their feet crossed. It was only a slight exaggeration.

Beginning with an unloaded gun (because stance and hold should be mastered before any shooting is done), pick an object, any object, 25 or 30 yards away as an imaginary target. Don't raise the gun yet. Just hold it comfortably with your non-shooting hand cradling the forestock, your shooting hand grasping the stock's pistol grip, or wrist, with the trigger finger resting alongside or against the trigger guard—not on the trigger itself.

Now face the target, with your feet planted comfortably. For good balance and comfort, your feet should be spread slightly, the distance between them depending on your build. Most people find about 14 or 15 inches to be about right, but the distance isn't at all critical. Just be comfortable and relaxed. Now move your left

As if walking in to flush game over a bird dog's point, the gunner prepares for a clay target by planting his feet comfortably and holding the gun in port position, ready to mount it quickly.

foot (if you're right-handed) slightly forward, maybe half a step.

Theoretically, that's it—you're in position. But in hunting it seldom works quite that way. In the driven-bird shoots popular in England and Europe and on some American shooting preserves, it would be fine because you stand still and wait for birds to fly within range. However, most of our hunting consists of walking and seeking game (called rough shooting by the English) with or without a dog. Without one, a bird or birds will likely go up as you walk or pause. With one, the dog may flush the bird, or with a pointing dog you may walk in and flush it while the dog remains on point. Regardless of all the variations on this critical moment, you'll probably have to stop in midstride to mount the gun, swing, and shoot. So practice doing just that.

Remember, you began by facing an imaginary target, with one foot slightly ahead of the other. Now, as if you were walking, take two steps forward, stop—and you're in position in reality as well as theory. I've seen experienced skeet and trap gunners mess up a shot at live game because, out of habit, they paid too much attention to their feet, stopping and trying to assume a solid target stance while a winged target decided not to wait.

There are some shotgunners who stand quite straight while swinging the gun (and some instructors who teach this straight posture). For most of us, however, it's both more comfortable and more effective to lean slightly forward from the waist—to "lean into the gun," as shooting instructors say. During the swing of the gun, your body from the waist to the top of your head must follow the barrel toward and "through" the target, demanding a forward movement of the upper body. This movement must be relaxed or the swing will be jerky. If you find your stomach muscles tensing—a very common fault—stop, relax, and get into position again. Many hunting shots will require you to pivot, and that pivot must be smooth, relaxed.

To achieve the essential freedom of movement, your arms and upper body should form a bent "Y" while your legs and feet provide a stable but relaxed shooting platform. If the gun begins to feel heavy during practice, lower it, rest, then start again. Never tense your muscles. *Rigidity destroys swing and accuracy* while also magnifying recoil.

Let me interject here that the recoil of a 12-gauge shotgun is no more severe than that of most hunting rifles, and milder than the kick of some. All the same, it does bother some inexperienced shotgunners. It won't if you have the gun snug against your shoulder and cheek—as I'll explain shortly—and if you're relaxed so that your upper body rides back with the recoil. I learned to shoot with a 12 gauge and started both of my sons with a 20 gauge (which is probably ideal).

I don't believe in starting anyone with a .410 or a 28 gauge because hitting a moving target is too difficult with the very light shot charge that goes with such small bores. Needlessly consistent misses discourage any shooter. They can make you think you're just not cut out to be a game bird hunter. The fact is, shotgunning requires no significant athletic ability and no particular talent.

In an actual hunting situation, gunners seldom even realize that the gun has recoiled (and sometimes they don't consciously hear their own shots) because they're excited by the sudden sight of game and concentrating totally on hitting it. It's a mistake to avoid recoil by using too little gun. Instead, practice a relaxed stance and the proper hold and gun position, thereby taming the recoil.

MOUNTING THE GUN

"Mounting the gun" is the common expression for bringing the gun to shoulder and cheek. Having assumed a good, relaxed stance, hold the gun in the position called port or high port in military parlance. This means it's held across your body, with the muzzle considerably higher than the buttstock. Now modify this—a very important modification for safety—by bringing your non-shooting hand (cradling the fore-stock) slightly forward so that the muzzle is not only pointing upward but out in front of you. When you expect, or hope, to see game at any moment, this is how you'll carry the gun as you walk. In other words, you'll switch to this port hold from a normal "field carry" employed for comfort and safety (and discussed in Chapter 5) when a flushing dog acts intensely "birdy" or a pointing dog points.

Even if no companion or dog is moving along to your left or right, you want the gun to be pointing ahead if a shot is expected, and always under complete control. Other people or animals may be somewhere near, whether you know it or not, and besides, you can mount the gun fast and smoothly from this port position.

Now, as you bring the gun up, thrust it slightly forward in the direction of the target and then back against your shoulder and cheek. If you bring it straight up, without the arc of a slight forward thrust, the butt will sometimes snag on your clothing. Most shooters, whether they do it intentionally or without realizing it, begin the little "lean into the gun" before it reaches the shoulder, making the slight forward thrust all the more important.

As you raise the gun, your forward hand

The gun is brought up in a slight arc, thrusting it (or "throwing" it, as gunners often say) forward just enough so it won't snag clothing on its way to the shoulder. At the same time, the gunner begins to lean forward slightly.

As the gun begins to come up, the index finger of the shooting hand rests on the trigger guard (or on the safety if it's located on the guard). With an over/under like this or a side-by-side, the thumb will push the safety off an instant before the butt snugs against the shooter's shoulder. The index finger of the forward hand can be cupped around the forestock or extended under it as if pointing.

merely cradles the forestock. Your rear (shooting) hand releases the safety as it comes up, when it's almost to your shoulder. Until then, the safety should always be on. Some guns have a through-bolt safety in the rear portion of the trigger guard. It's released by pushing it with your trigger finger—which is an excellent occupation for your trigger finger since it shouldn't be on the trigger until the gun is in position to shoot. Double-barreled guns (as well as a few repeaters) have a sliding safety on the top tang connecting the action to the stock. With this type, the thumb of your shooting hand pushes the safety forward—off—as the gun is mounted.

As the stock reaches your shoulder, you move your head forward a little to make the stock's comb reach your cheek. You'll probably move your head downward a little at the same time, but try not to overdo this. Too great a downward nod of the head will put your eyes too low with relation to the top of the barrel, so practice making the stock come up to meet your cheek with as little downward nod as possible. Leaning into the gun is a great help here. The butt should contact your shoulder at the same moment the comb contacts your cheek. With your shooting arm crooked comfortably so that your hand is on the pistol grip and your finger within easy reach of the trigger, a "pocket" is formed by your shoulder joint. The butt comes to rest in this pocket. It must be snug and firm there and at your cheek.

The gun is now mounted firmly against the shoulder and the swing has begun. Note the slight forward lean. In hunting, the swing often begins before the butt touches the shoulder. For speed and accuracy, mount-and-swing must blend into one fluid movement.

If the gun is loosely held against your shoulder, recoil will slam it into you, whereas if it's snug it merely shoves your shoulder rearward a bit. A gun in recoil moves both rearward and upward—that is, the muzzle rises—so if the comb isn't likewise firm against your cheek it will punch your face (and maybe the side of your nose as well). Here, too, snugness is the preventive.

Now practice the whole procedure to make it swift and *fluid*. What's supposed to happen is this: the gun comes up in a slight arc to the shoulder, the safety is released as it comes up, the shooting finger moves to the trigger as the stock meets shoulder and cheek, and as the gun swings to or past the target (depending on whether the target must be led), the trigger is pulled.

All of this should happen in one *uninterrupted, smooth movement*. After practicing it a few times, it becomes natural and easy. It's easier still when a real rather than imaginary target is out in front, because the target seems to draw you into the swing. In effect, your body and arms point to the moving target, and the gun becomes an extension of the human pointer.

HAND POSITIONS

The forward hand, cradling the forestock, guides the gun as it swings with the target.

There are differences of opinion about how far forward that hand should be. Many of the finest wingshooters extend it all the way to the front end or almost the end of the forestock, and this seems to help them point and swing more precisely. But that much stretch is uncomfortable for some shooters and seems to reduce their control. For them, it's easier and perhaps better to place the hand about midway or two-thirds of the way along the forestock. That's where I put my right hand (being a left-handed shooter). Instructors have told me more than once that I'd shoot better if I extended my hand farther, but that feels slightly awkward to me.

Whichever way you've been doing it, my advice is to try it the other way and find out which position gives you a more controlled swing. What you don't want to do is place your hand as far back—that is, as close to your body—as you would in aiming a rifle. Doing so will make you too rigid, and you'll have to straighten your arm a bit if the barrel is to swing properly.

The forearm lies in the cup of your forward hand, braced (but not so tightly as to be rigid) between thumb and fingers. When using a side-by-side double with a slim forestock, some shooters wrap the thumb and fingers almost around the barrels. Many instructors in this country—though not in some others—view this as a serious fault. What worries them is that the thumb and fingers tend to come up around the barrels far enough to interfere with the sight plane. But it can be done correctly, with the thumb and fin-

The forward hand must be cupped around the bottom of the forestock firmly but not rigidly, and the cheek must be firmly down against the stock. The trigger is pulled (some gunners say "slapped") rather than squeezed as with a rifle, so the first joint of the shooting finger curls over it.

gers merely riding the sides of the barrels. In fact, some gun shops sell short, black elastic sleeves (imported from England, I believe) that fit around the barrels and tip of the forestock, so that the shooter's forward hand can cup the non-slip sleeve rather than wood and metal.

With any other type of gun, the hand should not wrap around the barrel or barrels. It merely holds the forestock, and some forestocks have grooves or a thinned portion (in cross-section) to help position the finger tips.

But here, too, there's a difference of opinion. Some very skillful shooters cup only three fingers around the forestock while extending the index finger straight along its bottom, in line with the barrel or barrels, as if pointing at the target. I've tried it (on the advice of one shooting instructor) and found that it helped a little if I experienced a slump in my shooting—missing two or three birds in a row. The theory is that the pointing finger helps guide the barrel and the shooter's eye. I'm skeptical.

I admit it helped me cure a slump, but I suspect it did so by giving me something extra to think about and taking my mind off trying too hard to correct my target lead or eye alignment. Wingshooters have a tendency, after missing a couple of birds, to decide they're giving their targets too much or too little forward allowance or else mounting the gun improperly. Most often, what they've really done wrong is to stop the swing or lift the cheek from the comb. Trying to correct themselves, they overcorrect or change something that needs no changing. Remembering to point that index finger may just require a tiny bit of mental attention that prevents them from thinking too much about where the gun should point—thereby overcorrecting—instead of pointing and swinging naturally, instinctively.

I used to shoot skeet with a pump gun (as quite a few skeet gunners do). I never became an outstanding competitor, but I generally hit my doubles—crossing targets thrown simulta-neously from the high house and low house—because the need to pull the pump rearward and push it forward again after the first shot didn't give me time to think too much about where the muzzle should be in relation to the fast second target. Perhaps pointing the index finger under the forestock functions in about the same way as working the pump. In any case, my advice is to hold your forward hand in a position that's comfortable for you and helps you swing freely but in a totally controlled manner.

The position of the rear, shooting hand isn't as critical as in rifle shooting. Some gunners wrap the thumb over the pistol grip, or wrist of the stock. Others rest the thumb on the upper side, roughly parallel to the barrel. Whichever way feels comfortable is fine. The index finger extends forward to operate the trigger, of course, so the stock is gripped firmly with the thumb and other three fingers.

Slowly, deliberately squeezing the trigger, as with a rifle, will just about guarantee that you'll stop your swing or deflect it, or perhaps just slow it down. You'll then shoot behind the bird. Instead of squeezing, you simply pull or slap the trigger. If the gun has a single trigger, the index finger curls over it. If it has two, the ball of the finger normally touches the front trigger so that you can quickly and easily move the finger rearward for the second trigger. (If you elect to fire the rear trigger first for a particular shot, the ball of the finger is still the contact portion so that you can move it forward quickly for a second shot.)

For safety's sake, the trigger shouldn't be touched until the butt is at or nearly at your shoulder. Your finger can ride the outside of the trigger guard or the receiver just above it while the gun is held at port, before you mount it.

EYE ALIGNMENT

Probably the most common mistake in cheeking a shotgun is to tilt the head. A very, very slight tilt is almost unavoidable, but try to keep your head as perpendicular as possible (or comfortably possible) so that your eyes are pretty nearly horizontal. If you're right-handed, your right eye will be directly behind the breech, in line with the barrel, when you cheek your gun. That's as it should be, because the right eye is usually the "master eye," the stronger one, if you're right-handed, and it will perform most of the job of aligning the barrel and tracking the target. All the same, it's best to keep both eyes open. Doing so will vastly improve your peripheral vision, which is important with crossing targets, and will also give you better depth perception, making your instinctive judgment of target distance and speed more accurate.

Many hunters, especially riflemen, close one eye when shooting because doing so helps the master eye attain a fast, sharp sight picture. But even some riflemen train themselves to shoot with both eyes open, and it's a definite help. I find it difficult, so I often find myself squinting with my right eye. (As I'm left-handed, my left eye is behind the barrel and is my master eye.) I suppose the squint is a less than ideal compromise, but it works for me. I still retain fairly good peripheral vision and depth perception. If you have difficulty lining up your master eye instantly and keeping it aligned with your other eye fully opened, I suggest trying my compromise.

Eye position is obviously critical. Make sure it's right by mounting the gun as described above and then aiming—yes, *aiming* in this

To expand peripheral vision and maintain optimal depth perception, try to keep both eyes open—even though the master eye governs the tracking of the target. The head should be held as nearly vertical as possible. Head-lifting may be the commonest cause of misses.

instance—at any small, stationary target 20 to 30 yards away. If you have a custom-fitted gun, what you now see should be correct unless you're cheeking or shouldering your gun improperly. But I'll assume that, like me, you shoot a mass-produced gun with more or less standard or "average" stock dimensions. Now let's get back to aiming (but still with both eyes open, if possible).

If you're right-handed and you can see part of the barrel's left side, the stock is too thick or you don't have your cheek firmly against it. It's unlikely that you'll see the sighting plane (rib or top of barrel) from an angle slightly to the right rather than left. If you do, however, the comb may be much too thin and/or you may be tilting your head over the stock. Your master eye should be in line with—directly behind—the barrel.

If you're looking directly over the barrel but seeing its full length, the comb has the right thickness for you but is too high, which means you'll still miss birds. If you see only the breech and none of the barrel, the stock is too low or has too much drop (downward angle from front of comb to top of butt).

A stock is easily made thicker or higher with a pad available at gun shops. If it must be lowered or slimmed, you'll need stockwork by a competent gunsmith unless you're very adept at woodworking and refinishing. A proper sight picture is worth the expense or effort. What you *should* see is just a little bit of barrel or rib and the bead. If the gun has two beads, the rear, smaller one, should be directly behind the front one, and you may notice it now, with the gun held stationary, but you probably won't even see it when you swing on a game bird.

Just before I began to write this chapter, I came across an item in a widely respected sporting magazine stating that a shotgun bead is intended only for aiming at deer or turkeys. If this were true, there would be no bead on any

In both of these drawings, the gunner's eye is aligned correctly, with only a tiny bit of the barrel visible under the front bead. In the drawing at left, however, the gunner isn't yet ready to pull the trigger. He has brought the gun up and started his swing with the barrel behind the bird. He must quickly and smoothly swing through the target, firing when the barrel is ahead of the bird, as in the drawing at right, maintaining his swing (follow-through) as he pulls the trigger. When this is done, the gunner automatically and unconsciously accelerates his barrel swing in order to pass the target. This swing-through method is best for most gunners because it reduces the forward allowance—consciously perceived lead—needed to hit the target.

shotgun designed for small flying game or clay targets. The bead is a tremendous help as long as, paradoxically, you don't concentrate on it. Aim again at that stationary target, lining the gun up so the target "sits" on the bead. That's how it ought to look when a bird is coming straight at you and perhaps descending slightly, or flying straight away from you but not rising at all.

When swinging the gun to hit a moving target, however, you'll lose all your instantaneous pointing ability and fluidity of swing if you consciously line the bead up with the target. Don't try to. Your eye will do it automatically, without even registering its image in your brain. All you should be conscious of at the moment of firing is the barrel tracking your target, not the bead sight.

LEAD, OR FORWARD ALLOWANCE

If you fire at a stationary target, it may seem as if the shot charge hits that target at the instant you fire, but of course it doesn't. A tiny bit of time elapses while the charge reaches the point of aim. Therefore, if that target were moving to the left, the charge would miss it, passing on the right; if moving to the right, the charge would pass on the left. Leading a target means firing far enough ahead of it for the target and the shot charge to arrive in the same space at the same instant, thus colliding.

Because speed and distance are extremely hard to judge, especially while quickly swinging a gun and tracking a bird that may fly erratically, and because one person's perceptions never match another person's, it's impossible to tell anyone how far to lead a given target—how much forward allowance to give it. Add to this the fact that shot velocities differ from load to load and from gun to gun, plus the likelihood that one pheasant or sharptail grouse may be crossing 40 yards away at 35 miles an hour while the next may be crossing 38 yards away at

30 miles an hour, and you can appreciate the impossibility.

Nevertheless, some gunners arrive at their own rules of lead, such as the following: a lead of two body lengths for a pheasant-sized bird crossing at 40 yards, three body lengths for the same bird crossing at nearly 60 (too long a range for most of us), and a reduction of lead length by half if the bird is flying at a quartering angle. This works for some shotgunners who have somehow established a mental picture of bird sizes, distances, speeds, and imaginary bird lengths. I tried it as an experiment several times, on clay targets and doves. Even though the target for each shot was right there, crossing in front of me, I couldn't instantly visualize the amount of space, or distance in target lengths, between gun barrel and target. The result was an indecisive, spasmodic swing. That sort of thing is self-defeating.

You'll master your own correct "sight picture," or lead distance that works for you, by simple shooting practice, without thinking about or consciously knowing that distance for a given target, speed, and distance. The ability comes quickly if you have a coach standing behind you as you fire at flying clay targets. You miss the first, and he says, "You shot behind it a little." "You were under it," he says on the next shot, or "You were just a bit over it." After a few shots, you hit one, and somehow, subconsciously, you remember how you did it. Soon you're hitting three out of five, then four of five....

Some gunners learn to do this by maintaining what's called a "sustained lead." They're able to get on target very quickly, swing out in front of the bird, and then smoothly maintain that exact speed of swing—and thus the margin of forward allowance—as they pull the trigger and follow through. Most of us never master that, and despite claims to the contrary, it isn't necessary. Instead, we naturally, almost automatically, learn the "swing-through" approach, in which the gun swing accelerates to make the muzzle pass the bird and, as it continues beyond the bird the trigger is pulled at the instant the forward allowance becomes sufficient. It's natural and easier than it may sound.

That leaves the question of when forward allowance is needed and what direction it must take. This list of basic barrel positions will enable you to bag birds:

- Target flying straight away: shoot dead on, with the bird "sitting" on the barrel.
- Target flying straight away and rising: hold over it, "blotting it out" with the barrel.
- Target flying straight away and descending: hold under it, with a little space between bird and barrel.
- Target flying to the left and rising: shoot high and to the left.
- Target flying to the right and rising: shoot high and to the right.

- Target flying away and descending to the left: shoot below and to the left.
- Target flying away and descending to the right: shoot below and to the right.
- Target crossing: swing ahead of it in the appropriate direction, left or right.
- Target flying toward you ("incoming"): hold ahead of it, blotting it out, or hold slightly below if it's descending sharply.

After trying these basic leads a few times with flying clay targets, you'll use them naturally, without having to memorize them.

PRACTICE WITH CLAY TARGETS

The summer before last, after suffering an injury in an auto accident, I did no shooting at clay targets. When the game season opened, I did a lot of missing until I canceled a day's out-

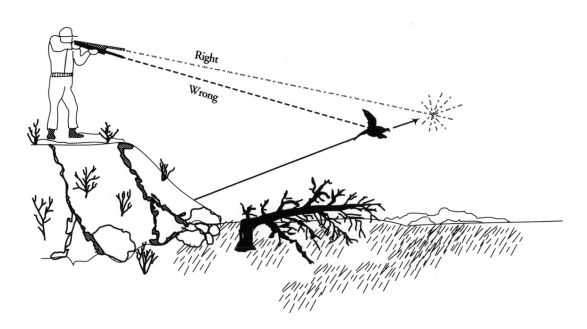

Most upland guns are built to shoot a trifle high, thereby forgiving minor errors with the most frequent targets—rising birds. All the same, the greatest cause of misses is shooting behind or below the moving target. A bird flushed from below the gunner may look like a straight-away shot, but it seldom is. This drawing shows the wrong and right of the situation.

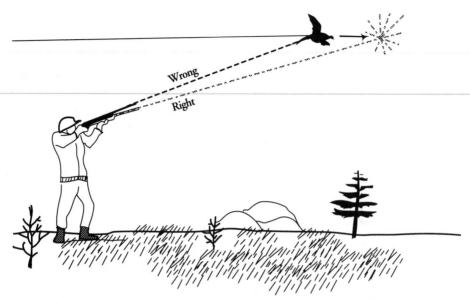

Here, the bird has come from behind the gunner but is departing fast. Again, it looks like a straight-away shot, but a "dead-on" hold will be behind—and this time above—the target. If the shot pattern and bird are to collide, the gunner must swing ahead of the target.

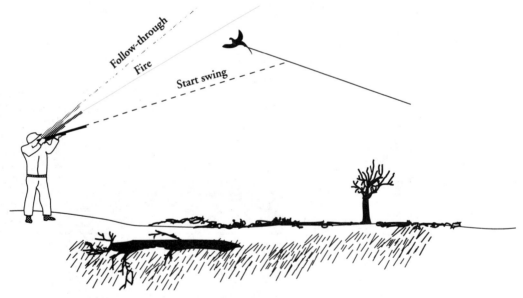

To get on your target, you must initially see it—generally above or to one side of your barrel. The problem is the natural urge to continue seeing it as you fire, which is possible with a crossing bird but not always with a rising one. This drawing shows a good shot. The swing begins behind the bird, with the target clearly visible. The gunner accelerates his swing, through and ahead of the bird, firing quickly after passing it. Even then, if he stops his swing he'll shoot behind it because the bird is still moving. He must therefore follow through.

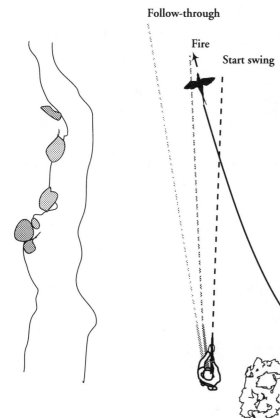

Follow-through

Fire

Start swing

With a slightly angling bird, as with a rising or fully crossing one, the swing begins behind the target, pulls ahead, and continues a bit after firing. This is an easy shot, but is frequently missed because it looks so nearly straightaway.

This hunter has brought the gun up perfectly. He's leaning into the gun, with his hands in comfortable position for a fluid swing, his head erect, his cheek against the stock, and his eyes at the correct level. He's far behind and below the sharptail grouse because he's just beginning his swing, which will bring the bead and rib up and to the left—ahead of the bird.

When coaching a novice, start him on stationary targets such as this clay bird propped on a stick. This will give him a quick grasp of the sight picture, with the target seeming to rest atop the bead, and will instill target-breaking confidence. Note that the shooter is wearing "earmuff" hearing protectors.

ing to put in some time breaking clays. Whatever I was doing wrong, that cured it. No matter how good you are, practice with clay targets will either make you better or keep you as good as you are.

If you're a novice, begin your practice with stationary clay targets, hanging them from upright sticks in front of a safe backstop about 20 yards away. Slowly mount the gun, mentally check that you have the correct sight picture described above, and fire. You'll probably hit the very first one. Try it once or twice more to make sure. The next step is to begin with the gun at the port position while facing just slightly away from a stationary target—to one side or the other so that

you'll have to pivot a bit. Now mount and swing the gun quickly, as smoothly as you can, firing as the barrel passes the target. Break a few that way, and you'll have the hang of it well enough to proceed to flying clays.

Have a companion lob the clays, gently at first and as straight away as possible, with a hand-trap or lanyard-operated trap. When you begin hitting them consistently, have him increase the speed and toss them at varying angles, to the right or left. Every time you miss, he should tell you what mistakes he thinks you made or where your barrel was—left, right, under, over—and then he should try to duplicate the target angle and speed on his next throw.

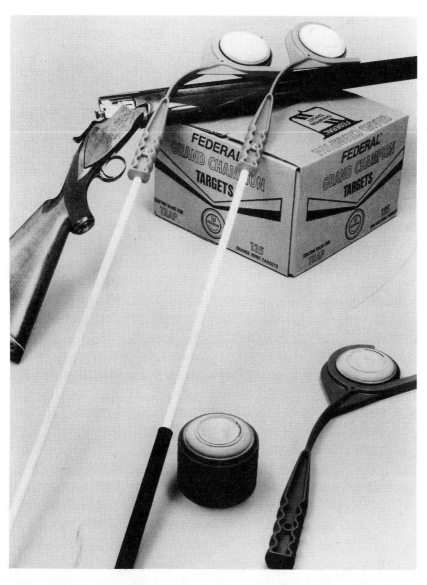

Many kinds of hand-traps are available for throwing practice targets, and clay birds aren't very expensive. The shooters can take turns, with the one throwing the clays coaching the one who shoots—and pointing out where the misses went. The two long-handled target throwers will fling clays harder and farther than the short one but require a faster, more powerful swing of the arm.

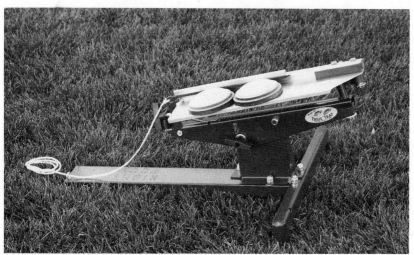

Some hand-traps can throw doubles (two targets that fly on divergent courses) but a spring-powered, lanyard-release trap does it much more easily, throwing faster targets to greater distances. Height and direction are altered at will, and target speed can be varied by quick adjustments of the spring tension.

Your main fault will probably be a tendency to stop the follow-through as the trigger is pulled or to swing erratically—speeding up, slowing down, changing direction, or hesitating because you think you're making a mistake. Repetition of speed and angle will soon correct these mistakes and you'll feel the glowing satisfaction of breaking five or ten straight.

If there's a public trap or skeet range near enough to your home—or a range operated by a club you can join—you'll find that it takes only one session to learn the basic rules of trap or skeet, and such practice blends great fun with fast improvement in wingshooting. If you're fairly adept, try to seek out facilities that provide the game of Sporting Clays. The speeds and angles in this game vary much more than in trap or skeet, and there are multiple clay targets—sometimes thrown simultaneously or almost simultaneously—at a given shooting station. The surprise "flushes" and varying, unpredictable speeds and angles duplicate hunting situations far more closely than the more conventional clay-target sports. Such practice will make anyone a better wingshooter and hunter.

4

With or Without a Dog

From sportsmen fortunate enough never to have lacked a fine gun dog come statements like these: "Without a good dog, you'll walk right over more woodcock than you'll ever see." "I wouldn't even bother to hunt quail if I didn't have a good pointing dog." "The pheasants around here are hunted so hard they wise up after the first couple of days of the season. You won't find one, much less put one up without a dog." And so on.

Yes, you surely will walk right over more woodcock than you'll see if you hunt without a dog, and you'll have to hunt harder—or more skillfully—to get shots at quail or ringnecks. There's a grain of truth in such statements, but I think a hunter who stays home for lack of a dog is a fool. There are effective ways to flush woodcock for yourself, for example. The simplest is merely go-and-stop, go-and-stop movement through likely cover. Often, when you stop walking, the cessation of movement and sound makes a bird fear that some predator has detected it and stopped prowling to plan a stalk and lunge. The sudden alarm prompts the bird to flush. The dogless hunting of quail or ring-

necks involves that technique plus others, and becomes a whole lot more practical if you hunt with at least one companion, preferably more. I'll offer tips on effective dogless methods for these and other species in the chapters devoted to them. Here I'll content myself with the declaration that you can have marvelous game bird hunting without a canine assistant—if necessity compels you to.

Having said that, I must emphasize that a talented, well-trained gun dog vastly enhances the enjoyment and the chance of success in hunting all game birds except the noble turkey during the spring season and the lowly (but astonishingly shrewd) crow. A dog also furthers the objectives of conservation. Like a great many wingshooters, I've hunted doves without a dog, and very successfully. After all, no pointing or flushing is involved in traditional and conventional dove shoots. But I've also spent a good half-hour searching for a dove felled amid soybeans. Eventually I spotted a little patch of gray under the leaves and put that bird in the bag, but a retrieving dog would have found it in a minute or two. How many such birds are never found?

You may expect me to talk now of the warm rewards of canine companionship and the delights of watching a good dog hunt difficult cover with uncanny knowledge, push through the most daunting brambles, point or flush exquisitely, and make seemingly impossible retrieves. Well, I'm not going to talk about that because I'm sure you already know about it as well as I do—and come to think of it, there are times when nothing like that happens. I'd much rather hunt without a dog than with a poorly trained or untalented one. So let's skip the accolades and get to practical considerations, such as the various types of dogs and which of them might suit you.

THE POINTING BREEDS

There are a great many breeds whose primary job is to locate game and approach it—not so closely as to panic it into flight, although that occasionally happens even with a well-trained dog, but closely enough so that the birds will sit still, hoping to escape detection by the predator they perceive looming close—and then to indicate the direction and proximity of the game by "pointing it." Occasionally, a pointing dog will lift one foreleg as if actually pointing it at the bird or birds, but that's not at all what's meant by pointing and it doesn't happen very often with most dogs. A dog points by suddenly stopping in its tracks, tensing, usually with tail held stylishly high, and gazing intently toward the game it has located, which is often invisible in brush or undergrowth. It recognizes game by the scent, of course, and perceives the location and distance of the game by the strength of the scent.

Most American pointing dogs are trained to hold a point staunchly while the hunter or hunters walk past it to flush the game from hiding and then shoot at the bird or birds in flight. Some dogs, however, are trained to hold a point only until given a command to flush, thereupon lunging forward and flushing the game for the hunter or hunters. Which way it's done depends not on breed but on training.

The reason why the majority of hunters prefer to flush the birds for themselves while the dog remains "steady to wing and shot" is that they don't want the dog rushing forward after low-flying birds. If that happens, the hunter must pass up his shot or he'll endanger the dog. After the shot is made—assuming it connects—the hunter gives a command such as "Fetch!" or "Dead bird!" A good gun dog will have watched the bird rise—and fall—and having "marked it down," can run forward and retrieve it. A bird that comes down wounded can't outrun or outmaneuver a competent gun dog, though it may take the dog a few minutes to find one that falls at a considerable distance, hits the ground running, and finds a good hiding place.

The pointing breeds include the English setter, English pointer, German shorthaired pointer, Brittany spaniel (the only spaniel that normally points instead of flushing without a point), and Weimaraner. The Weimaraner is unquestionably a talented pointer, but isn't as common or popular in America as the others listed.

Several additional pointing breeds occasionally show up in the hunting fields, but they're used by only a small minority of American hunters. They include the German wirehaired pointer, wirehaired pointing griffon, Vizsla, Irish setter, and Gordon setter. It's sometimes hard to find (and relatively expensive to acquire) a good hunting dog of one of these breeds because most strains have long been bred for show rather than field work.

Any hunter who tells you one pointing breed or another has the "best nose" or the greatest innate ability to recognize bird-holding cover and quarter it effectively—well, that hunter is biased. But there are differences among the breeds. I'll have to indulge in some generalizations here, first cautioning you that an individual dog may be an exception to any statement I make as I describe the most widely used breeds. From coast to coast in the Northern states and Canada, the three most popular are almost certainly the English setter, Brittany spaniel, and German shorthaired pointer.

English Setter

The setter tends to be a fast, intense, very stylish hunter and—if allowed to—will "range wide" in big, open fields, a characteristic that can be useful in the Midwest and West, and some parts of the South as well. A wide-ranging dog will cover much ground in such country, an asset as long as the dog can be seen or heard and will hold its point until the hunters arrive for the flush. Fortunately, setters can also be trained, quite easily, to hunt close in the woodlots, brush, and patchwork fields of the Northeast.

There's so much white in the coat of a typical setter or Brit that the hunter has a relatively easy time keeping track of the dog in dense cover.

The author walks in over a staunch point exhibited by a champion English setter.

Attached to this setter's orange collar is a fairly loud but lightweight bell that helps his owner keep track of him in thick cover. When it stops tinkling for more than a short interval, the owner approaches with gun ready even before he can see what's going on, because the dog is probably pointing.

But even the whitest setter sometimes vanishes in a thicket. This is why so many hunters bell their dogs. When the bell stops tinkling for more than a few seconds, the hunter walks toward the silence, expecting the dog either to be on point or responding to another variety of nature's calls. If the bell's tinkling resumes again, the hunter follows the sound. Some hunters use an electronic beeping collar for this purpose, but I like the old-fashioned bell.

With or without a bell, a blaze-orange nylon collar is an extremely popular item of equipment—an easily visible marker on the dog even in thick brush. It's especially valuable on darker gun dogs such as the German short-haired pointer and Labrador retriever, but I

think it's also a great help even on the whitest setter. For hunters who may still have trouble keeping track of their dogs, blaze-orange canine vests are available from hunting-dog supply companies.

German Shorthair

The German shorthaired pointer has so much brown in its coat that it can quickly become invisible in thick cover, but the bell and/or a bright collar or vest will more or less solve that problem. The shorthair, as it's commonly called, tends to hunt close and—at least in my experience—not quite as fast as the setter or Brit. Moreover, it's very "biddable." That is, it's eas-

Head high and body rigid, a German shorthaired pointer lets the gunner know there's a covey hidden ahead in the grass.

ily trained, very obedient, and often willing to hunt for anyone who knows the voice commands and hand or whistle signals with which it's been trained. For these reasons it may well be the most popular breed among owners of shooting preserves.

All three of these breeds are fine family dogs and make excellent house pets. You can hardly have a better, happier companion than a shorthair if it's to be kept indoors. But if the bird dog is to be kenneled outdoors in a region of cold climate, one of the longer-haired breeds—a setter or Brit—might be a better choice.

Brittany Spaniel

The Brittany spaniel is a bit smaller than the setter or shorthair and is a long-haired dog with a naturally short tail—an unusual combination in a pointing breed. Being smaller than the other pointing breeds, this one is the easiest to transport, kennel, or house, and a typical white

A Brittany spaniel points a covey while her bracemate, a German shorthair, freezes in midstride to "back her," or honor her point.

and orange Brit is also lovely to look at and a quietly affectionate pet. The average well-trained Brit tends to work about as close as a German shorthair but in a somewhat faster, livelier manner, perhaps best described as midway between shorthair and setter. Easily trained if the person in charge takes a gentle, patient approach, this is a dog with a very keen nose and great perseverance in hunting. Moreover, like other spaniels, the Brit is usually an exceptionally good retriever.

English Pointer

The English pointer, like the setter, is a fast, intense, stylish hunter, the sort of dog sometimes described as a bird-finding machine. In fact, most pointers are apt to move faster and range wider, as the field trialers say. Being mostly white, the pointer shares the setter's advantage of high visibility in screening brush, but the pointer's short coat and ranginess make the breed exceptionally suitable for hunting the sprawling fields still to be found in many parts of the warm South. And although such fields have been traditionally associated with plantation country, they're also found in much of the upper and lower Midwest. In this kind of habitat, a pointer is a wonderful dog for hunting quail or pheasant.

Moreover, like the German shorthair, the English pointer is usually so eager to hunt that it won't be at all fussy about who's handling it—the dog is likely to hunt well for anyone who knows the voice, hand, and whistle commands that were used in its training. With regard to "hunting up" birds, the pointer merely tends to be speedier and rangier. Generally speaking,

The English pointer, at right, has locked onto game during a Florida quail hunt, and an English setter has stopped short to honor the point.

however, the pointer isn't as eager a retriever as the other pointing breeds. In finding birds, pointing, and remaining steady to wing and shot, the pointer learns early, easily, and fast, but retrieving can require quite a bit of training.

One other criticism is sometimes heard concerning this breed—a cold personality. Pointers are friendly but not given to shows of emotion. If a few display great affection for their humans, most are so aloof that this trait, too, may contribute to their reputation as "hunting machines."

Weimaraner

The Weimaraner breed originated near Weimar, Germany, in the early 19th century, but was almost unknown in America until the 1940s. For some years, the Weimaraner was highly touted (and evidently exploited by some breeders) as a do-everything utility dog that could handle all sorts of game from grouse to foxes and raccoons and was also a great water retriever for duck hunters. No single breed is truly ideal for every job, and to some extent the Weimaraner inevitably fell from grace. All the same, those Weimaraners specifically bred and trained for hunting game birds have sufficient range, speed, "nose," and the other requisite talents. Today, a lot more Weimaraners are prized as house pets than as gun dogs, but it's quite possible that interest in their field abilities will rise again sooner or later.

Weimaraners, characteristically silver-gray and sleekly handsome, point a pheasant concealed beneath a clumped canopy of weeds in a fallow field.

THE FLUSHING AND RETRIEVING BREEDS

Most hunters will agree that any good bird dog should retrieve, and do so eagerly and skillfully. However, the breeds designated as retrievers or retrieving dogs are those originally bred to retrieve ducks and geese from water. Often called water dogs, they include, most notably, the Labrador retriever, golden retriever, and Chesa-peake Bay retriever. Although the "Chessy" is a magnificent water dog, the breed doesn't gener-ally show the verve or efficiency displayed on land by the others. The golden and, most espe-cially, the Lab make extremely fine flushing dogs for upland birds. In addition, like the other flush-ing breeds, they make wonderful pets whether housed indoors or kenneled outside.

A flushing dog, by customary and logical def-inition, is one that doesn't stop and point but

This springer spaniel isn't being unsteady to wing and shot. He simply hasn't had time to "hup" (sit and stay) after flushing an unexpected bird. The gunner, having seen his dog suddenly act "birdy," was alert enough to get his gun up fast.

instead rushes in and forces a bird or birds to take flight. Occasionally, one of these dogs shows an inclination to point, and a few hunters go out of their way to find and train such dogs, but I'll never understand why. It seems to me that he who wants a pointing dog should choose a pointing breed, whereas a flushing dog ought to flush. I may be biased, but a great many hunters on this continent and in all parts of the world will agree with me that the finest flushing breed ever developed is the springer spaniel.

The springer, like the Lab, comes surprisingly close to the impossible ideal of the all-around utility dog. In England, where the springer spaniel originated, the breed is expected to hunt—and be adept at hunting—whatever game presents itself. That generally means rabbits as well as pheasants, grouse, woodcock, and other game birds. The breed is also expected to make water retrieves as skillfully as land retrieves. Since springers are smaller than Labs, they can't as easily pick up a big Canada goose and carry it back over a sprawling field to the waterfowler's blind. They do it well and eagerly, but most of the goose is apt to drag on the ground.

Many American hunters (and hunters everywhere who use pointing dogs) exert considerable effort to train their dogs, or have them professionally trained, to ignore all quarry except game birds. A setter that points rabbits is likely to be called off point by the owner or trainer and "cast" again to look for birds.

A puppy of any breed, flushing or pointing, often goes after grasshoppers, field mice, sparrows, or almost anything alive, but training discourages that and rewards only the quest for game birds. A pointing dog that continues to run rabbits incorrigibly will probably be demoted to the status of house pet.

This selectivity isn't entirely a matter of snobbery. For one thing, the habit of pointing rabbits (or squirrels or whatever) can distract the dog from hunting game birds. For another, it usually produces uncertain, unsteady points because a rabbit neither smells nor behaves like a bird in ground cover. The rabbit will either bolt as the dog approaches or freeze until the dog is close and then bolt. Either way, the dog's natural inclination is to run after it, defeating the whole purpose of the pointing method. A flushing dog, on the other hand, is supposed to chase its quarry, crowding a bird into flight or panicking a rabbit from its hiding place into relatively open spaces where the hunter can get a shot at it.

This presents a major potential problem—the possibility that the dog may move into the line of fire. Just as a pointing dog is taught to remain (more or less) steady to wing and shot, a flushing dog is (at least theoretically) taught to sit instantly upon hearing the command, "Hup!"—which is given when a bird flushes. The same command is also used to call the dog off game, and even a very enthusiastic dog will obey it if the training has been thorough, with the lesson repeated many times.

Those who use flushing dogs tend to be somewhat more lenient than pointing-dog owners about instilling steadiness. Typically, if not taught to sit for the bird's rise, a dog will rear up or even leap as the quarry explodes into the air. Assuming that the hunter himself is reasonably well trained, the dog isn't endangered because the hunter doesn't shoot until the bird is high over the dog's head. I trained my springer, Rocky, without the aid (or expense) of a professional trainer, and I must confess that because I didn't have the leisure time for all the recommended polishing, he never learned to "hup." But in all the years I hunted him, that never presented a hazard.

You can tell when a dog gets "birdy" by his behavior, and if you know your dog, you can also tell what kind of game is causing the excitement. When Rocky was on a bird, his stubby tail whirled like an egg beater, his head went down close to the ground, he lowered his forequarters slightly in the expectation of wriggling through or under brush or ground tangles, and he plunged forward with a certain start-and-stop-and-start-again jerkiness of movement. When he sniffed a rabbit, his tail didn't whir quite as fast and he broke into an immediate straightforward run after the quarry. In either event, I wouldn't have fired until the game was well above or ahead of him.

Far from discouraging him from running rabbits, I encouraged him to. I enjoy both rabbit hunting and rabbit dinners. The decision whether to restrict a flushing breed exclusively to game birds is simply a personal choice. Rocky never mastered water retrieves because he became overeager one day when he was just a puppy and was nearly drowned. After that, water intimidated him. But he did everything else a hunter could wish.

Springer Spaniels

These dogs love to hunt and are almost invariably very affectionate and eager to please their masters. Thus they learn very quickly, and because they have an almost uncanny ability to retain what

A champion springer promptly and gently delivers a cock pheasant to the hunter's hand.

they've learned, they seldom need much if any pre-season refresher training. In my admittedly biased opinion, they have a slight edge over Labs and goldens in the uplands because—evidently as a result of keener scenting ability—they move faster as they search the covers. Of course, if a dog moves too far from the gun and flushes a bird at 50 or 60 yards, the hunter may never see that bird, much less get a reasonable shot at it. But since a springer is easily trained to hunt close to the gun, ranging too wide or far is usually a fault of the trainer or master.

Springer spaniels were so named because they sprang after the game. Cocker spaniels were so named because they were originally favored for flushing woodcock. Smaller than springers, they're perhaps the most energetic of all the sporting breeds. Those bred for field work may weigh as much as 30 pounds, but their small size does somewhat limit their uses. More importantly, in recent generations most of them have been bred for show rather than field. Like show springers, they tend to be underequipped with scenting ability and overequipped with long fur—especially on the legs—that not only mats but catches and holds every burr encountered. Worse still, those bred for show tend to lack hunting temperament. If you locate a cocker bred from a hunting strain, however, it can probably be trained as an excellent bird dog, and its small size is a great advantage if it's to live indoors with the family.

Springers are almost always white and liver (reddish brown) or white and black—easy to see in the woods. Field cockers—unlike those bred for show—usually have one of those same color combinations, although variations such as solid tan, gold, or black are not uncommon.

Labrador Retrievers

Labs come in a choice of three colors—black, chocolate, or yellow (blond). In the case of the Lab, those hard-to-see colors are no detriment

A chocolate Lab trots back to the hunter with a firmly but gently gripped sharptailed grouse. Game meat is undamaged when fetched by a good, soft-mouthed retriever.

in the uplands, because the breed is large and very easily taught to work close to the gun. Besides, you can always bell your dog and put an orange collar or vest on him. Outstanding intelligence, quick trainability, obedience, versatility, loyalty, gentleness, and a quietly affectionate nature have made the Lab one of the most popular hunting breeds in the United States and Canada.

A Lab isn't as fast or maneuverable as a springer in the uplands, and doesn't usually have quite as keen a nose, but certainly has at least as many adherents. Labs seem to be almost literally tireless, almost impervious to weather, exceptionally adroit at learning and following hand or whistle signals, and they're superlative water dogs. Like springers, they seem to have an innate bird sense (or maybe it's intelligence) that helps them outmaneuver a bird that's running or sneaking through ground cover. I've seen a Lab circle a skulking cock pheasant and "herd" it back toward the gunner so that the bird was alarmed into flight, and I've seen one crowd a ringneck toward water to make it take off.

Come to think of it, I've seen one of my friend John Falk's fine English setters pin down a nervous covey of Hungarian partridges by circling through a stubble field to point them from the far side. All the popular breeds of bird dogs are intelligent, so the selection should take additional factors into account—the climate, terrain, and types of birds in your region; your preferred hunting style; whether the animal will be a kennel dog or dwell in your home; and any fondness you may have for one breed or another.

Golden Retriever

Like the Lab, the golden retriever is a big dog (averaging 60 or 70 pounds or sometimes a bit more) and a very handsome one in disposition and personality as well as appearance. The breed's name describes its color. The coat is silkier and somewhat longer than the Lab's, but either breed is undaunted by cold air or water temperatures. I suspect that the typical golden has a slightly keener nose than the typical Lab, and no breed is better at searching undergrowth and finding crippled birds even under poor scenting conditions—but I doubt that anyone will ever prove which breed has the best nose. The golden quickly and easily learns whatever is taught, retains the lessons well, and has a strong urge to please. In style, intelligence, and personality, then, the golden and Lab are much alike and, in fact, they'll usually work well together. All hunting dogs will gaze after a flushed bird and mark its fall if it's hit, but the golden and the Lab (perhaps because of all those generations of breeding for water retrieves) seem to be especially adept at marking the fall of game.

Since two dogs can't occupy precisely the same space at the same instant, when they're worked as a brace one of them usually locates a given bird or birds ahead of the other one. With pointing dogs, the first dog locks into a point and the second, if well trained, halts behind the first or to one side, "backing" or "honoring" the point. Otherwise, the birds might either run or flush before the gunner arrives within shooting range. Such honoring is less important with dogs that are supposed to rush in and flush the game, but something very like it happens with a brace of well-trained flushing dogs. The first one lunges in; the second either hangs back a little or rushes around the quarry to get on the far side, forcing the birds to fly instead of run. That's by no means always the way it happens, but when it does it's beautiful to remember, and when it doesn't it's nice to dream about.

ACQUIRING AND TRAINING A DOG

The purpose of this book is to make you a better game bird hunter, not to teach you dog training. The latter subject would require a whole separate book, and indeed, there are

A silky-coated golden retriever brings in a hen pheasant.

many such books. If you plan to train a bird dog and haven't had any previous experience, I strongly advise you to follow closely the instructions in one of the books by an acknowledged expert such as John R. Falk or Dick Wolters.

If you own a full-grown but untrained dog of an appropriate breed, you might try training it yourself or sending it to a professional trainer—the dog will almost undoubtedly have the requisite instincts, scenting ability, and hunting desire. But bear in mind that training a dog late is much, much harder than training one early, and the results are rarely as good.

If you wish to purchase a bird dog, it's best either to shop for a pup or choose a trained, fully grown, but young dog. A young animal usually will adapt well to a new master and new surroundings, and will give you many years of companionship and hunting. Whether you get

a pup or an adult dog, don't buy just any dog of the breed you choose. Breed alone doesn't make a good hunting dog. A dog that comes from a hunting breed but not from hunting stock—including both remote and immediate ancestors—may not turn out well at all in the field.

Find a breeder (preferably someone who breeds *and* trains) specializing in the breed you've decided on. About the only exception to that rule of advice is when a friend's outstanding hunting bitch has a litter of pups, some or all of which need a home. You'll surely know about it before she whelps, and you can begin planning. That planning may include a decision as to whether you want a male or female, but don't believe anyone who tells you one gender or the other makes a better hunter.

Some reputable, even famous, kennels sell pups by mail order, shipping them on an approval basis, with a return possible within a given maximum period of time. If you're familiar with the kennel or have a friend who's familiar with it, or if you're sufficiently impressed by the breeder's reputation, credentials, assurances, references, and the pup's pedigree, there's nothing wrong with acquiring a pup that way. Before the pup's shipped, you'll know what shots have been administered, how old it is, its sex and appearance, its size now and potential size when grown, what boosters and other shots are still to be given, its diet, and even a little about its personality—in short, just about everything you need to know. Although no reputable breeder will ship a pup that isn't healthy, I believe the first thing to do upon receiving a pup (regardless of whether it's shipped or you bring it home in your car) is to have it examined by a veterinarian.

Unless mail-order purchase is unavoidable, the best way to shop for a dog—especially a pup—is to visit the kennel and get acquainted with the animal before buying. Watch the way a pup acts with its mother and litter mates. You want one that's friendly, active, inquisitive, and not easily intimidated. You don't necessarily want one that bullies all its litter mates, but you don't want one that's easily intimidated or acts subordinate to all the others, either.

If a pup acts unhappy, that's a bad sign. If a pup occasionally leaves off playing with its siblings to explore every corner and shadowy nook of the kennel, that's probably a good sign. If all the pups are asleep when you arrive, wait around to see what they do when they wake up. Another advantage of visiting a breeder's kennel is the opportunity to see the adult dogs that have been bred—and perhaps even trained—

Ellen Elman, the author's wife, uses a retrieving dummy during the puppy stage of training the Elman springer, Rocky. All pups love to play tug of war but can be quickly taught that a soft delivery is rewarded.

The author fires a blank in a starter's gun while teaching Lennie Rue's springer, Freckles, steadiness to wing and shot. His friend John Falk controls a long check cord, used in training dogs to work close enough to the gun.

there. That will give you some indication of what to expect when your pup is grown.

There are a number of ways to find the names and addresses of reputable breeders, both in your home region and throughout the nation. The nearest veterinarian may be able to help you. Magazines devoted to the field sports often carry advertisements for breeders. Classified phone directories contain listings and ads. When contacting a breeder located in this way, ask for any promotional literature or other relevant information he can furnish, plus the names, addresses, and phone numbers of references—people who have purchased dogs there and/or had dogs trained there.

I should emphasize here that the word "pup"

in this context doesn't always mean an animal that has just been weaned, although it can mean that. It may also mean a six-month-old dog that's been "started" or a dog from about eight months to more than a year old that's been "well started" or even partly trained. Such a dog will cost more than a very young pup, and will still need training—but considerably less of it. The trainer himself will give you extremely useful tips and instructions about further training, and in a few cases little more than a first season of closely controlled hunting is needed.

Some gunners pick a very young pup and leave it at the kennel or at some other kennel that has the services of a professional trainer, bringing it home later, when the animal has been partly or fully trained. Some bring the pup home and send it to a professional trainer a bit later. Either route costs money, of course. Suppose you're buying a fully trained dog; well, you're not unless the animal is at least two years old. This also means that if you send the dog to a trainer you'll have to do so more than once before training is truly complete and you have a fully polished bird dog.

The costs, the periods of absence, and the admission, if only to yourself, that your dog is good because someone else trained it—those are the drawbacks of having a dog professionally trained. The advantage is that the dog is apt to be trained to the full extent of its natural potential. Training a dog yourself, on the other hand, is enormously satisfying, lots of fun during every stage, and the best way to build an exceptionally close bond with the animal. It's also somewhat time-consuming, and although there's nothing mysterious or difficult about it, some people are naturally good at it while others just can't seem to get the hang of it.

If you've had a dog before, housebroken it, and simply given it basic obedience training, you should be able to judge for yourself whether you understand animals well enough to train a bird dog. For a great many hunters, perhaps most, the best compromise is to have a dog well started or partly trained and finish the schooling themselves.

Regardless of which route you choose, I can't resist offering one tip I haven't found in the books. Some dogs dislike wearing a bell unless they've been accustomed to it from the time they were young pups. If you train your dog yourself, don't wait until the well-started stage to put the bell on the pup's collar. Small dog bells (which look like miniature cow bells) are available inexpensively from hunting-dog supply outlets.

Most dogs don't mind the bell and will soon ignore it, but I waited too long to discover that Rocky was one of the exceptions. When I put the bell on him—the first time was during the "partly trained" stage after I temporarily lost track of him one day in the woods—he regarded it as some sort of restraint or punishment, and refused to hunt. If he had worn a bell since his puppy days, there would have been no problem.

Maybe this proves I should have let a professional trainer start the best dog I ever owned. Or maybe it proves no bird dog—not even a Rocky—is absolutely perfect.

5

Safety and Comfort

The so-called Ten Commandments of Gun Safety have been published in many books, magazines, and pamphlets, and every one of those commandments is a matter of simple common sense. At one time, I thought they were so obvious I might not have bothered to include them here. Two recent incidents have changed my mind.

The first occurred during a quail hunt with several friends in Tennessee. The names will be changed to protect the guilty from embarrassment. My friend Hubert was carrying a fine Spanish double-barreled gun, and an acquaintance whom I shall call Boeotian expressed his admiration for it. Upon returning to our host's house that evening, we racked our empty guns and went into the living room for cocktails. Boeotian asked if he might examine the Spanish gun, and naturally Hubert told him to go ahead—whereupon Boeotian returned to the gun room, set his drink atop the rack, picked up the gun, mounted and swung it to feel its weight and balance, and pulled the trigger on an imaginary bobwhite.

Yes, of course the gun was unloaded; of course Boeotian was perfectly sober; and of course nothing happened but a harmless click. In my opinion, none of that excuses his action. He should have examined the gun before even thinking about having an alcoholic drink, and even though he knew the gun was unloaded he should have opened it immediately—before doing anything else—just to make sure. Here was an experienced shooter who had broken the first and tenth of the Ten Commandments.

Incidentally, some guns—particularly old ones and many doubles, new or old—should be dry-fired seldom if ever because doing so can eventually weaken or damage a firing pin. For this reason, some shooters insert snap caps in their guns after cleaning them and before putting them away. A snap cap is a short, shell-shaped device—essentially a dummy shell—with a rubber cushion where the primer of a loaded shell would be. When you pull the trigger, the snap cap cushions the head of the firing pin as it's driven forward.

Snap caps seem to be available only in some of the better gun shops, and they tend to be expensive, but you can make your own by prying the spent primer from the base of a fired shell and then jamming a carefully shaped piece of rubber pencil eraser into the empty primer cup to serve as the cushion. (There was no real danger of damaging that Spanish gun by pulling the trigger—my point in relating the incident involves safety, not gun maintenance—but since Boeotian did dry fire it, this is an appropriate place to mention the usefulness of snap caps, whether commercial or homemade.)

The second incident that comes to mind involved a shooter at a skeet field who was carrying a box of 12-gauge shells in a belt holder (a handy accessory for clay-target shooting) and also had several 20-gauge shells, left over from a morning of hunting, in a pocket of his shooting jacket. He absent-mindedly loaded a 20-gauge shell into the 12-gauge gun he was using. Very fortunately for himself as well as the gun, nothing happened when he pulled the trigger because the undersized shell had slid forward in the chamber just far enough so that the firing pin failed to indent and thus ignite the primer.

If the shell hadn't stuck in a forward position, the shooter's carelessness might have produced catastrophic results for himself as well as the gun. He, too, was an experienced shooter, yet he had broken the Third Commandment. Per-

The gun at left holds 20-gauge metal snap caps with rubber plungers in their heads, where a shell's primer would be. The gun at right holds 20-gauge snap caps—empty shells with cylinders of rubber pencil eraser tightly inserted in the vacated primer pockets. In the foreground are 12-gauge metal snap caps with plastic plungers and a 12-gauge "snap shell"—plastic encased in synthetic fleece, like a cleaning jag, to absorb any excess oil in the chamber.

This shooting instructor displays a demonstration gun (which can't be fired), with a cutaway chamber, forcing cone, and barrel to show what can happen when familiarity breeds carelessness and a gunner leaves shells of more than one gauge in his pockets. A 20-gauge shell, loaded into a 12-gauge gun, has slid forward into the barrel. If a correct shell were then chambered and fired, the gun would explode.

haps the rules aren't as obvious as I supposed. All that can be done here is to print them below; they should be engraved in your mind.

THE TEN COMMANDMENTS OF GUN SAFETY

1. Treat every gun with the respect due to a loaded gun. (And that means every gun is always assumed to be loaded until you check both chamber and magazine.)

2. Guns carried into camp or home, or when otherwise not in use, must always be unloaded and either taken down or have their actions open; guns should be carried in cases to the hunting or shooting area. (And bear in mind that in some states it's illegal to have an uncased firearm in a vehicle; if it can be and is legally transported in a vehicle rack, it must be unloaded and open.)

3. Always be sure barrel and action are clear of obstructions and that you have only ammunition of the proper size for the gun you're carrying. Remove oil or grease from the chamber before firing.

4. Always carry your gun so that you can con-

trol the direction of the muzzle even if you stumble; keep the safety on until you're ready to shoot.

5. Be sure of your target before you pull the trigger; know the identifying features of the game you're after.

6. Never point a gun at anything you don't intend to shoot; avoid all horseplay while handling a gun.

7. Unattended guns should be unloaded; guns and ammunition should be stored separately and beyond reach of children—or careless adults.

8. Never climb a tree or fence or jump a ditch with a loaded gun; never pull a gun toward you by the muzzle.

9. Never shoot a bullet at a flat, hard surface or the surface of water, as it may ricochet dangerously; when at target practice, be sure your backstop is adequate. (The caution regarding water is chiefly applicable to rifles and handguns. Occasionally, if you have no dog to retrieve an injured bird that has fallen into water, it's necessary to fire your shotgun at it again, delivering a coup de grace in order to prevent its escape. Pellets fired at an angle toward the water won't ricochet as unpredictably and dangerously as a bullet—most often they'll penetrate the water harmlessly or ricochet only a very short distance—but caution is essential all the same. Be certain no person or animal is present beyond the bird or in any position where there's even a remote possibility of a ricochet, and deliver your shot from a safe distance.)

10. Avoid alcoholic drinks before and during shooting or hunting.

To these basic rules, I feel compelled to add a few cautionary words with regard to the maintenance of guns and the acceptable methods of carrying them while hunting. It's rare for a shotgun to malfunction in any dangerous way merely because it's been improperly cleaned or poorly maintained, but it's likely that poor maintenance will blow your patterns, spoil the gun's accuracy, and possibly cause a failure to function. Autoloading actions are most critical in this regard, but it can happen with any shotgun. Besides, there is that slim chance that poor maintenance will cause an accident. Anyone who takes any chance whatever with a gun is a fool, and I don't want him anywhere near me in the field.

GUN MAINTENANCE

An essential aspect of maintenance, and one that does have a direct bearing on safety, is to make sure the barrel and action are clean, dry, and free of obstructions. (A trace of leftover oil in the barrel will have no real effect, though it may somewhat undermine the pattern of your first shot.) Oil or grease in the chamber or action can attract and hold dirt, dust, debris such as tiny leaf particles, and powder and metal residue that's produced with every shot. Some greases and oils can also thicken enough to slow or stop functioning in very cold weather. It's easy enough before you go hunting to run dry, clean patches through the chamber and bore, and to wipe the action dry and clean.

Some shooters make the terrible mistake of plugging or capping a gun's muzzle after cleaning it and before storing it in a locked cabinet, gun safe, closet, or other storage place. The idea—a very foolish one—is to keep dust or dirt out. But no matter how dry you think the storage area is, the air has some degree of humidity; sooner or later, moisture will condense in the bore and rust will result. The bore may even become pitted. There's absolutely no benefit in capping the muzzle of a stored gun.

Presumably, most readers of this book know how to clean a gun, and anyone who doesn't can read the instructions that come with some cleaning kits or the guidelines included in the instructions or owner's manuals that come with some guns—to say nothing of the magazine articles and whole books devoted to gunnery rather than hunting. However, a few tips may be in order here.

The first thing to do is field strip your gun; that is, remove the barrel from the action, but disassemble the gun only to the extent specified in the manufacturer's instructions or owner's manual. Further disassembly is unnecessary and can void a manufacturer's warranty. Moreover, if you aren't a truly competent amateur gunsmith, disassembly of the action or trigger mechanism can cause damage, and incorrect reassembly may even produce a dangerous condition. Some guns have removable trigger assemblies that are easily taken out for thorough cleaning. If your gun has such a trigger assembly, you'll know it because you will have paid a premium price for the gun and you will have read the illustrated instructions packaged with it. In the event that you bought the gun secondhand and the instructions were missing, I must assume that you accepted the gun only after a qualified gunsmith tested it and showed you how all the features worked.

Some double-barreled guns (whether or not they have removable trigger assemblies) have removable sideplates that allow access for cleaning certain parts of the action. In this case, too, you'll know it for the same reasons that apply to trigger assemblies. With most shotguns, however, field stripping goes only far enough to allow easy access to the entire barrel (with the forestock removed), the magazine if there is one, the exposed portions of the action, and all external surfaces.

I prefer to run a couple of solvent-soaked patches through the bore and then set the barrel aside to let the solvent loosen dirt and residue while I clean the other parts. Using a clean rag dampened with solvent, followed by a dry rag, I clean all the exposed metal surfaces, and with a repeater I also uncap and clean the tubular magazine. Then I go back to the bore and run dry patches through it.

If the gun has been fired more than a couple of times, that generally doesn't suffice. Powder residue and even metal residue from the pellets will still adhere, so I let some more solvent soak in, then wipe the bore semi-dry, and then run a cleaning brush through it a few times. After that, one more application of solvent, followed by a final drying with clean patches. Then, before reassembling and storing the gun, I run a couple of patches through it to apply an extremely light, thin, protective film of oil. (I'm convinced some of the modern synthetic-based solvents and oils work better than the old-fashioned ones, but I'm also convinced that any name brand of gun solvent or gun oil does just about everything the maker claims.)

For cleaning some gun actions, one of those small, long-handled, angled mirrors used by dentists will give you a better view of barely exposed parts and recesses, and will also reflect light onto whatever you're inspecting. Gun shops also sell small, battery-operated lights with flexible stems or handles, and they, too, work very well. If some part of an action looks grimy to me, I go over it with a small, angled toothbrush. Once the action is clean and dry, I apply a very light coating of gun oil, reassemble the gun, wipe all external surfaces, and apply a very light coating of oil to those as well.

A problem in storage is that when a gun is racked more or less vertically, with the butt down, oil can run downward from the bore into the action—and excess oil in the action is far worse than none at all. Some racks hold guns almost horizontally but with the muzzle slightly lower than the action, thus solving the problem. I think an even better way is to store guns as I do, more or less vertically but muzzle down. The reason most racks aren't built to do this is possible damage to the muzzle or bead (or to a rifle's front sight) if a firearm is rested on its muzzle. However, this is easily solved by placing a soft mat of rubber or felt under the muzzle and making certain the gun is securely propped, held, or racked so that it can't slip or topple. I realize that almost no one does it this way, but I've had an "upside-down" rack built into one of my gun cabinets to hold both shotguns and rifles muzzle down. I don't know about current fashions, but at one time some European racks were made in this manner.

SAFE FIELD CARRIES

How you hold your gun as you walk along hunting—your field carry—is crucial to your safety and that of any companions. Only three carries can be recommended.

Probably the most useful is with the gun cradled over the crook of one arm (the bend of the elbow) and the hand of that arm grasping the stock. The other hand can either swing freely or rest comfortably on the gun. If you're hunting alone and you're right-handed, most of the time you'll want to cradle the gun over your left arm. If you expect to get a shot in the next few seconds—as when a dog points—you can shift the gun to the port position, ready to mount it.

Even when you don't have time to do that (because a bird rises suddenly and unexpectedly), this carry permits fast and fluid action. Begin with the gun over your left arm and visualize a sudden flush. Quickly move the gun to the right while your shooting hand slides up the

A safe and practical field carry is with the gun cradled over the crook of the left elbow (for a right-handed hunter) and the left hand grasping the stock. In this photo, the hunter is preparing to mount the gun fast by sliding his left hand forward toward the forestock and bringing his right (shooting) hand up to the stock's pistol grip.

stock, grasps the pistol grip, and begins mounting the gun to your shoulder as your left hand slides forward to support the forestock. In this manner, both of your hands and arms work together to mount and swing the gun.

You'll find that you can cradle the gun over either arm and still mount it with almost equal ease and speed. When you're working a field or piece of cover with a companion on your left, you don't want to cradle the gun over your left arm because the muzzle should point away from him. Switch, and practice mounting the gun from the cradle of your right arm.

Admittedly, cradling the gun over the "wrong" arm and mounting it from that position is awkward for some shooters. If you find it difficult, the over-the-shoulder carry will be comfortable and safe when you're hunting alone or have a companion moving along to your left. With this second carry, you rest the gun over your right shoulder with the muzzle pointing upward somewhat and the gun upside-down. In other words, the top of the barrel or barrels will be resting on your shoulder, and the trigger guard will be up. Your right hand will be grasping the pistol grip with your trigger finger resting both safely and conveniently on the bottom of the guard. When a bird rises suddenly, you can instantly swing the gun in a forward arc, bringing the butt down into the pocket formed by your shoulder, with the muzzle pointing forward. The mount and the swing blend into a single movement.

The third carry results in somewhat slower mounting, but can be a restful temporary alternative when you're tired after hours of walking and gun toting. You cradle the gun in the crook of your right arm with its balance point on your forearm and the muzzle pointed slightly toward the ground. If you trip or stumble while carrying the gun this way, you'll find you can swing the muzzle upward very quickly to keep it clear. But if it ever does strike the ground—or anything else—do not continue hunting until

Another safe, practical field carry is with the gun upside-down over the shoulder, its muzzle pointing to the rear and slightly up. The shooting hand grasps the pistol grip, with the index finger outside of the trigger guard.

The author, holding up a brace of ringneck roosters with his free hand, demonstrates the third of the three safe field carries. The gun is cradled over the crook of the arm with the muzzle pointing forward and slightly down.

you've opened it and carefully inspected the bore. Even a partial or light obstruction can blow up a barrel upon firing.

With the gun over your right arm in the position just described, you can still mount it fairly fast, thrusting your left arm forward to grasp the forestock. (Left-handed shooters will naturally reverse all the directions I've given.) This carry is very comfortable with many guns, but not with some pumps and semiautomatics. The balance point on most guns is at the rear of the forestock or under the receiver. With a repeater, you may find that the loading port rests directly on your forearm and soon begins to dig in, turning a restful carry into a very uncomfortable one.

No matter how you carry your gun, don't hold onto it while climbing through or over a fence. Open it, leave no shell in the chamber or chambers, lay it on the ground within reach from the other side—or lay it on the far side if that's easier—and then negotiate the fence, retrieve your gun, and reload. If absolutely necessary, you can prop your unloaded gun against the fence, but take care that it won't fall over and be scratched or dented.

Quick-detachable (slip-on) carrying slings are available, and they're useful for turkey hunting as well as waterfowling. I've also used one to tote my dove gun when I was carrying a cooler, collapsible seat, and decoys to the field. But I don't use a sling when I'm hunting other game birds unless I have to make a long hike to the hunting area. If you don't have your hands full, you should be using them to hold your gun, ready for a flush.

BLAZE ORANGE

Upland hunters are almost universally required to wear a certain expanse (number of square inches) of bright blaze orange—also aptly known as safety orange. State regulations vary, but you'll probably be within the law (and safe) if you wear an orange hat and/or jacket or vest with large orange front and back patches. Of course, your vest or jacket can be all orange, though in some states you'll be legal if you merely wear an orange backpack of the type sometimes used as a game bag.

For certain types of hunting, camouflage clothing or at least drab clothing that blends with the cover is an enormous advantage. This being the case, your state may not require blaze orange for spring turkey hunting, or perhaps for crow hunting—and maybe not even for dove hunting. Some hunting apparel is printed with a camouflage pattern on an orange background, and this isn't a bad compromise. The orange remains glaringly visible to other hunters in timber or brush, but is so broken up by the print pattern that if you stay very still your quarry probably won't detect it. And when you're hunting turkeys or crows (or even doves under certain circumstances) you do stay very still, preferably hidden by natural cover or a blind.

Until a few years ago, I would have scoffed at anyone wearing orange—even "camo orange"—during a spring turkey hunt. But today there are a few regions where I'd be afraid to hunt without

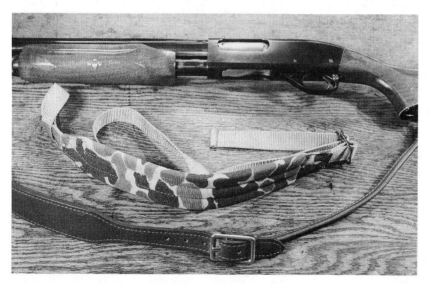

A slip-on sling, widening along the shoulder section, is a great help when carrying decoys or other gear. Look for padded ones, made of fabric or good leather.

Camouflage clothing is a big advantage when hunting doves, crows, and especially turkeys, but in some situations it causes a potential safety problem. The hunter standing against the tree is wearing the Trebark camo pattern in conventional colors. The other hunter is wearing Blaze Camo, which has foliage-colored splotches on a safety-orange background. It's highly visible to any gunners in the woods but doesn't seem to spook game if the wearer remains still.

it because there are so many hunters in the woods. Incidentally, in states that have a fall turkey season as well as a spring season, you may be able to dispense with orange only for spring hunting and will have to wear it in the fall—the normal season for other game birds.

It's true that birds perceive colors, but this is no disadvantage in most game bird hunting. There's relatively little pass-shooting (except for doves, wild pigeons, and crows). For the most part, your dog or you will flush the birds—"kick them up." Until you do, the birds will try for safety by remaining very still in the undergrowth or moving through it, away from you. In either case, they know perfectly well you're approaching, and how you're colored matters not at all. I have stopped my gun in midswing as a covey of quail flushed and sped toward trees

ahead of me and I glimpsed a flicker of blaze orange amid those trees. Statistics gathered and analyzed by many states prove beyond any doubt that blaze orange has drastically reduced the incidence of hunting accidents.

I almost always wear a hat—blaze-orange, of course. In warm weather I use the baseball-cap type, and preferably one that's mostly mesh. It keeps the sun off, allows air to flow through, and keeps my head cool. I also have a lightweight, fully brimmed hat of the "crusher" type. It's easily stuffed into a pocket, doesn't seem to get knocked off my head by twigs or branches as easily as a billed cap, and helps a little in keeping the sun—or rain—off the back of my neck. For really cold weather, an insulated hat or a knitted wool or synthetic yarn cap can be a comfort. There are also insulated billed caps with a second, rear bill or a neck-and-ear flap that can be turned down to ward off cold wind and snow. All of these are available in safety-orange and all serve their purpose admirably. For the kind of late-season weather that daunts birds, dogs, and sensible people but not all hunters, ski masks can be helpful.

EYE AND EAR PROTECTION

Shatterproof spectacles are another valuable item for safety. My regular, all-purpose prescription glasses are shatter-proof, so I use them as my shooting glasses. I have two pairs—sunglasses for very bright days or when shooting over snow glare, and ordinary, colorless glasses for all other weather. I'm not at all worried about burning propellant gasses or particles flashing back into my face when I shoot modern, safe shotguns with proper ammunition. The reason for my "industrial strength" shatterproof lenses is that they may get knocked off by a branch some day and trampled underfoot. I'd wear glasses for most of my game bird hunting even if I didn't need corrective lenses. A friend of mine once had his

The author, holding a ruffed grouse, models some of his favorite cold-day hunting attire. The boots are lug-soled water-proof leather with speed-lacing; the brush pants have reinforced facings and are lined for warmth; the reversible jacket has black and red wool on one side, blaze orange synthetic fabric on the other, insulation between, oversized pockets on both sides, and a big slit-entry game pouch at the rear; the hat is a soft blaze-orange "crusher" that can be stuffed into a pants pocket.

eye scratched by a thorn. After that, he didn't leave home without his glasses.

For target shooting, pattern testing, and practice, ear protection is strongly recommended. Repeated gunfire can damage your hearing. There are some very effective ear plugs, but in general I think the earmuff type of protector is better. If you attend a dove shoot where there's apt to be a great deal of firing, perhaps it's a good idea to wear plugs (the muffs being too cumbersome for use afield), but there's no need for ear protection in ordinary hunting because there just isn't that much gunfire.

HANDS AND FEET

Early in the season, I prefer to hunt barehanded. A little later, when the cold winds rise and a drizzle feels like burning needles stabbing my reddened skin, I like shooting gloves or golf gloves. Today's shooting gloves, even the expensive ones, rarely seem to be as thin and snug as those made when I was a youngster. If they're bulky enough to interfere with your trigger pull or even muffle your feel of the trigger, they can cause misses. I happen to have one pair that I really like, but sometimes I use golf gloves. Not

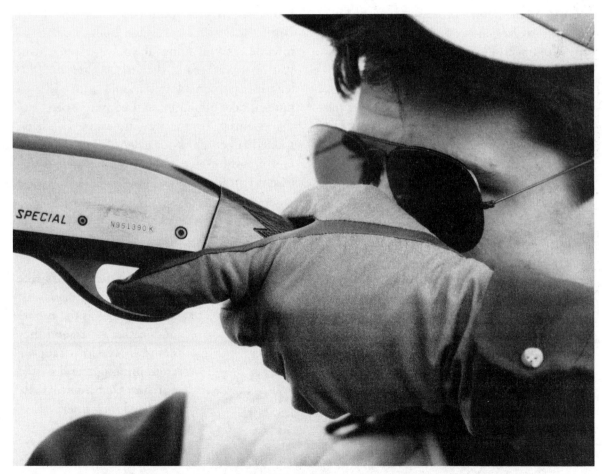

This gunner is wearing shooting glasses—a recommended protection from twigs and thorns—and Remington Upland Gloves, a type of shooting glove that's lined at the palm for a firm grip and close-fitting enough for finger dexterity.

being an avid golfer, I was surprised to discover that golf gloves don't always come in pairs. They are, however, made for both right- and left-handed golfers, so it's no problem to buy the same kind for each hand in order to have a matching pair. Some golf gloves are wonderfully thin and snug. Most have a lot of perforations, air vents, but they're sufficiently protective and don't make your hands sweat.

While buying a saddle last year, I discovered that some tack shops have equally good riding gloves, and I've noticed that people who drive sports cars in rallies often wear comparable driving gloves. For very cold weather, there are hunting gloves that feature a slit through which you can momentarily expose your trigger finger for good trigger control, and there are even mittens with finger slits.

Footwear is enormously more comfortable—not to mention dry—than it was a couple of decades ago. For early-season hunting in relatively dry terrain, modern hiking boots are wonderful. I refer here to the lightweight type with fabric sections and vents that allow plenty of air flow. They're ideal for early dove shoots and, in some regions, for hunting the various prairie grouse, wild pigeons, chukars, Huns,

woodcock, all kinds of quail, and even crows.

Throughout most of the game bird seasons in most regions, I don't think anything new outdoes the venerable rubber-bottomed, leather-topped boots made famous generations ago by L.L. Bean and still offered by that firm and by Eddie Bauer and many others. Wearing them, I walk through shallow seeps and creeks without having to resort to stone-hopping. But where the going is slippery or jagged, Vibram-soled boots with deep treads may be the best prescription.

I'm astonished by how much has been written about the "proper" height for hunting boots—a teapot tempest reminiscent of all the treatises about the need for left-handed garden tools. (Being left-handed, I can say that.) Until the 1940s, knee-high boots were fashionable, as you know if you've tripped over your grandfather's in the attic. Ankle- or shin-length is fashionable today, and a lot easier to put on, take off, and lace. I consider speed lacing essential, by the way, now that I've been spoiled. The right boot height for you is whatever is comfortable, ankle-supporting, and sufficiently protective. But low boots should have scree-proof rims or tops.

Knee-high boots (or alternatively, knee-high

Fabric-shelled boots like these include models just as waterproof as the rubber and leather types, and they come in versions ranging from ultra-light and vented for hot weather to fully insulated for winter.

leggings), usually made of tough leather, are a good precaution where rattlers or other venomous snakes are abundant, particularly in the Southwest and parts of the South. Snake-proof boots are a comforting insurance against fang penetration. In snake-infested desert country, some hunters even outfit their dogs with booties and leg wrappings to provide at least some protection against snakes as well as thorns and other such menaces.

For late-season (winter) hunting in cold regions, modern insulated boots with high-traction soles are recommended. Those with removable felt liners are excellent for warding off frostbite when you freeze your—well, the rest of you—in a duck blind or while sitting on a stump waiting for a deer to appear before you succumb to hypothermia, but they're awful for long-distance walking. Boots suitable for most game bird hunting are those with thin, built-in liners containing thin but very effective synthetic insulation.

I used to buy winter boots a size too large, for wear with two pairs of socks (wool over cotton). Some very cold-sensitive hunters still buy oversized insulated boots for this purpose and wear

This Browning Upland Vest is typical of warm-weather vests with securely closed but easily opened pockets, a roomy game pouch at the rear, and lightly padded shoulder sections for shooting comfort.

This hunter is wearing a camouflage jacket and pants, carrying a camouflaged gun, and toting a backpack blaze-orange game bag that can be pocketed until needed but is large enough to hold a gobbler.

This is a traditional Continental ammunition and sundries bag made of high-quality leather. The dangling thongs with terminal metal rings are game slings which can be looped to hold the legs of birds securely. The adjustable carrying strap is slung over the shoulder and across the chest in the manner of a Sam Browne belt.

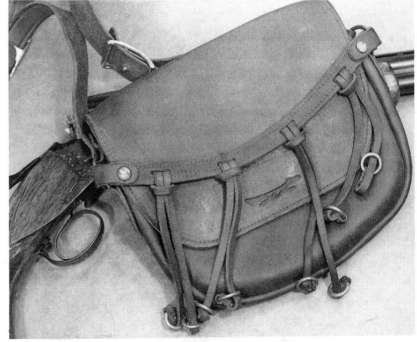

thick, cushiony socks over very thin thermal socks. I seldom find that necessary, a single pair of warm, cushiony socks being sufficient since walking maintains a person's circulation and keeps the feet warm enough.

Some of my boots are a half-size larger than my everyday shoes to accommodate these thick socks and because cramped boots are a torment. But boots that are too loose are equally tormenting and raise blisters. Because boot sizes aren't precisely standard (regardless of manufacturers' claims), I don't buy mine by mail order. I try them on in the store, over the kind of socks I'll be wearing with them. A size 9 boot of one brand or model may equal a size 9½ of another brand or model.

Some hunters prefer all-rubber boots (which are popular in England and Europe). Those with a sure tread are fine for extremely wet going, but they make my legs and feet feel a little clammy after a couple of hours. This doesn't happen (or is less noticeable, at least) with the truly waterproof boots made today of leather or various combinations of leather, rubber, and synthetics. If they're all-leather, the waterproofing will eventually begin to leak slightly, especially at the seams. This can be prevented or postponed with periodic applications of waterproofing solutions or pastes, some natural, some synthetic, all about equally effective in my experience.

CLOTHING

In very hot weather, you may be hunting in your shirtsleeves, which presents the problems of how to dampen recoil against your shoulder if you're particularly sensitive to it, and where to stow the birds you shoot. Manufacturers of hunting apparel offer a reasonably wide array of lightweight shooting shirts (some with short sleeves) featuring shoulder pads on the right side, left side, or both. There are also strap-on shoulder pads and Velcro-attachment pads, but they may interfere slightly with natural gun mounting and very few shooters need them. Some guns, particularly those chambered for heavy magnum shells, have rubber recoil pads on their butts, and there are also recoil-reducing stocks (with internal shock absorbers). For the kinds of hunting under discussion here, I consider them superfluous.

The problem of game stowage (and shell stowage) is easily solved. One approach is the old-fashioned leather or fabric game bag, which can be hitched to your belt or hung over your shoulder (with the strap across your chest like that of a Sam Browne belt to prevent slipping). Another is a light, preferably orange, backpack-style game bag. And still another is a game sling that hitches to your belt. It consists of thongs with metal rings or sewn loops at the ends, and it works very well with small birds. When a thong is looped through the ring or sewn-in end loop, it securely holds a bird by the legs or neck.

Personally, I prefer the built-in game pouch in the rear panel of a light hunting vest. Virtually all hunting vests and jackets have a pouch with a wide access slit at each side, and its interior should be rubberized or otherwise moisture-proofed. On one of my jackets, the pouch unzips at the top so it can be dropped to form a rubberized rear flap that keeps my bottom dry if I sit down on a wet rock or stump.

Any good vest or jacket also has roomy pockets for ammunition, sandwiches, and so on. Often there are elastic shell-holder bands inside the lower pockets—an excellent feature. The vest or jacket should either be safety-orange or have large orange panels. In cool weather, I wear a light hunting jacket, and in winter I switch to an insulated jacket. (Some are called coats and tend to be slightly longer.) I particularly like the kind with a zip-out insulated liner. Depending on the weather, I can wear the total unit or just the outer shell or just the liner.

Brush pants are more durable than jeans and their reinforced facing shield your legs from thorns and burs. There are light ones for mild weather, heavier ones for colder days, and even insulated ones for winter.

6

Pheasant: Our Universal Game Bird

To hunters in the United States, the ringnecked pheasant seems as American as the right to vote, yet the bird is an Asian species, virtually unknown on this continent a century ago. For many hundreds of years, pheasants were hunted in Asia and then in Europe with hawks and with nets (sometimes aided by dogs to flush them into the air for hawking or to move them toward the entrapping nets). By the 18th century, ringneck hunting with shotguns was a popular sport in Europe, while in America the birds were imported and stocked by such eminent wingshooters as George Washington, Governor James Montgomery of New York, and Benjamin Franklin's son-in-law, Richard Bache. However, early attempts to breed and establish them on this continent were unsuccessful.

Finally, in 1881, the U.S. Consul-General at Shanghai, Owen H. Denny, shipped 21 Chinese ringnecked pheasants to his brother's farm near Corvallis, Oregon, and there they thrived. Within a decade, descendants of those birds had spread through the Willamette Valley, and during the next few decades pheasants were released in a growing number of states from coast to coast.

Their introduction remained controversial for many years. Well after the turn of the century, for example, New York farmers expressed a fear that ringnecks might devastate their crops. Still more recently in some regions, sportsmen charged that these alien birds—being large, strong, and aggressive—were driving quail out. Actually, bobwhites were being diminished by changing agricultural practices, not by the introduction of pheasants, which (like the chukar and the Hungarian partridge) turned out to fill a vacant or partially vacant ecological niche and did not compete adversely with native wildlife.

A mature cock pheasant is apt to measure about 30 to 36 inches long—a full yard—from beak to the tip of its pointed tail, but at least half of its length consists of those smoothly tapering, buff-brown, black-barred tail plumes. An adult male usually weighs less than three pounds. On a close rise or truly straightaway shot, the entire (often blurred) bird is the target, but for longer shots and angling flight, a hunter should force himself not to perceive the whole form or its center as the focal area in swinging the gun to pro-

Here are a typical ringneck cock and hen. The much gaudier cock has a longer tail and is usually larger than the hen at maturity, but doesn't always look larger in flight.

Many hunters are sure the tail alone is sufficient to distinguish a cock pheasant from a hen in flight, but that isn't always true. The highest bird in this picture is a cock with a much shorter tail than that of either hen. It may have been lost to a predator but more likely was shot away by a hunter. But even when the birds look almost like black silhouettes, the male's white neck ring and contrasting color patterns usually show.

vide forward allowance, or lead. Instead, concentrate on and swing beyond the forward third, or even just the head when possible.

Failing to do so accounts for the almost tailless or half-tailed roosters occasionally seen. Where hens are fully protected, they're sometimes hard to tell from male tail-amputees on the wing. The gaudy male colors are usually conspicuous, but not always. In dim light or with the sun behind a bird, it may momentarily appear as an almost black silhouette. In this situation, rushing your shot is more than usually unwise.

The spectacularly handsome Americanized ringneck cock normally has an iridescent blackish-green head with glints of violet and low "ear" tufts. Around the yellow eye and on the cheek, naked red skin combines comb and wattle. A bright white collar usually circles the lower neck but may be broken or absent. The body is a blend of brown, copper, and russet, scaled with black and a little white. A vague, light blue wash often saddles the lower back near the rump, and the wings are a paler brown with pale barring. The bloodlines of American pheasants blend Chinese, Korean, and Manchurian strains, with a small infusion of Japanese green and Caucasian blackneck genes. Largely as a result of this ancestral mixture, black or almost black roosters are seen now and then. Albinos are quite rare, but once in a while Midwestern hunters bag pheasants mottled with white.

Though subdued in form and coloration, hens are no less beautiful. An average hen, uniformly light sandy brown with darker mottling, weighs a pound or less and has an overall length

This is the kind of farmland—broken into habitat pockets by brushy or weedy patches, fencerows, occasional shrubs or trees, and shelterbelt lines of trees—that will hold good populations of ringnecks.

of perhaps 20 or 21 inches. All the same, a close-rising female (and she's likely to flush closer than a male) may look quite large. Her tail is shorter than the male's and may seem wider at the rump because its taper is more abrupt—her central tail feathers being the ones that are relatively abbreviated. Despite her smaller size, a hen on the wing is often easier to hit than a male because her contours are less deceptive to the human eye.

Traditional farming practices, especially in the Midwest, benefitted pheasants until shortly after World War II, when the birds became enormously abundant, achieving the status of America's most popular feathered game. Then, with the reduction in diversified family farms and the trend toward huge single-crop agribusiness corporations, there began a long, steady decline in ringneck numbers.

The fields of corn and other grains were bigger than ever, but no longer interspersed with the other necessities of the pheasant's life cycle—windbreaks, groves, brush-rimmed ponds and potholes to provide watering places as well as nesting and escape cover. For many years, the decline was aggravated by governmental policies subsidizing the practice of retiring fields and leaving them plowed and bare.

During the last 20 years, pheasant populations have experienced ups and downs, but we now seem to be enjoying an early phase of what promises to be a long period of abundance, thanks to several factors. Wildlife management has been of major importance. A number of experiments in propagation have been conducted with various subspecies of pheasants from Korea, China, and elsewhere in order to produce hardier, wilder, fast-flying (but nonetheless tender and tasty) birds. Wild, hardy birds are more adept than others at escaping such predators as foxes, coyotes, hawks, owls, raccoons, and cats (as well as human hunters). And the stronger they are, the less vulnerable they are to winter-kill or to an excessively wet or dry spring that may ruin nesting attempts or kill off chicks.

In addition, both on state-managed lands and many farms, provisions have been made for watering and for nesting and escape cover. Some years ago, I came upon several winter-killed ringneck roosters in a shallow ditch. Pheasants withstand snowfall rather well, but these had succumbed to rain followed by cold wind. Unable to find an effective windbreak, they had huddled there and died as ice formed among their feathers and in their nostrils. They'd have been saved by nothing more than a thick hedgerow or deeper, brush-lined ditch. In recent years, state agencies, landowners, and conservation groups have been combating such decimation by improving and maintaining habitat, often involving food and cover plantings. There's even a national organization of conservationist sportsmen called Pheasants Forever, devoted to the welfare of the species (see Appendix III).

State game departments have been greatly assisted in their efforts by a federal program that encourages farmers to maintain habitat for pheasants, quail, and other upland wildlife, as well as waterfowl. One of the most successful upland conservation initiatives in our history, the Conservation Reserve Program (CRP), is at least partly responsible for the resurgence of good bird hunting—for pheasants, especially—throughout the Midwestern and Great Plains states. Originally incorporated into the 1985 Federal Farm Bill, it provides funds to pay farmers for removing highly erodible and certain environmentally sensitive croplands from production for 10 to 15 years to protect and improve soil and water resources.

At the time of this writing, the five states with the most farmland signed into the program are, in order of acreage, Texas, North Dakota, Kansas, Montana, and Iowa. The quilted pattern of crop fields interspersed with grass, brush, and so on which results from set-

The author bags a pheasant flushed from stripline crops on an Illinois farm operated by Winchester/Olin to achieve a combination of good agricultural yield and wildlife conservation.

aside CRP patches has increased nesting and survival rates for upland birds, upland-nesting waterfowl, and many non-game species. By 1992, more than 34 million acres were enrolled. Although pressure to bring CRP acreage back into crop production is expected to mount, the original goal of 45 million acres may ultimately be met or nearly met.

Currently, the northern limit of pheasant distribution on this continent lies across lower Canada—as far north as about 400 miles above the border in Alberta and Saskatchewan, where the hunting is excellent on the prairie farms. Far to the south, ringneck range has been expanding. Until the 1970s, the lower limit of distribution in the East (apart from preserve stock) was an indistinct line from Chesapeake Bay to central Illinois. In the Midwest, this line dipped through upper Missouri into Kansas and west-

ward through southern Colorado, then roughly straight across to central California. Historically, pheasants have fared poorly in the Southern realm of quail, and small scattered populations in that region failed to grow or spread. In the 1920s, the great conservationist and game manager Aldo Leopold first advanced a widely accepted theory that calcium requirements were the limiting factor. For laying success, hen pheasants seem to need more calcium than is needed by birds that evolved on this continent, and they have thrived historically only as far south as glaciers carried heavy lime deposits—or in unglaciated pockets of habitat rich in the proper type of lime. In addition, game biologists have found that hatching success is reduced by high ground temperatures.

Despite these obstacles, ringneck distribution has spread dramatically, thanks to such factors as hybridization, habitat management, and heavy annual stocking by various game departments. Pheasants can now be hunted in quite a few parts of the South. I was pleasantly surprised recently to discover that there's a short open season even in Louisiana.

This once exotic bird is now America's most nearly universal upland species, hunted in most states and probably the most popular with the greatest number of hunters. Daily limits, depending on current abundance, generally run from one to four, and many states have a cocks-only law to assure the survival of plenty of hens for the production of next year's brood. Fortunately, the gaudy male ringneck—unlike many other upland birds—is usually easy to distinguish from the female even in flight.

The Midwest still boasts the greatest annual ringneck harvests, with the very best hunting usually in Iowa, both of the Dakotas, and Illinois. But in spite of yearly fluctuations, the hunting is usually fine in most Midwestern and Plains states, in California, and in a large number of Eastern states that maintain extensive stocking programs.

HUNTING ACCESS

The resurgence of pheasant populations notwithstanding, successful hunting has

Although many states have copious public lands, including game-rich Wildlife Management Areas, some of the best hunting is apt to be on private land. Gaining access is a problem that can often be overcome by advance planning, diligent exploration and inquiry, and old-fashioned courtesy.

become more complicated than it used to be because of modern farming methods and the posting of many private lands. In my own state of New Jersey, pheasant hunting on many public Wildlife Management Areas is excellent, especially in the early days of the season, and I know from personal experience that this also holds true in Pennsylvania. I recall that when I lived in Oklahoma, a state far better known for turkeys, doves, and quail, there were at least a couple of Wildlife Management Areas teeming with pheasants, especially in the Panhandle region, and most states have similar hunting opportunities.

But it's also true that in the states I've mentioned and most others, much of the very best hunting is on private farmland. Some of the farmers lease hunting rights to local or regional clubs, and club membership is the only way to gain access. Still others allow "trespass" for a fee, or serve as paid guides, or lease hunting rights to guides, so you can have a good hunt by paying for it. And still others simply post their property against hunting—but surprisingly often you can obtain permission to hunt such property by having a friendly chat with the owner, convincing him that you and perhaps a friend or two will hunt safely, in specified areas only and away from buildings or livestock, will leave no litter whatever—not even an empty plastic shotshell—and will close gates after you and otherwise respect his property.

It pays to do some scouting and asking around in advance of the season, perhaps make a few phone calls, and maybe pay a visit to a farmer or two at a time when you won't interfere with work hours. Sometimes it may help to bring a small gift such as a cake or pie, or ask the owner if he'd like a couple of birds for his table. If you're familiar with farm work, you might even offer to help with some chores. Chances are, the farmer won't want your help but will be pleased by the offer. You have to sound out each individual.

One time a farmer had to hide a chuckle when I offered to do chores, but then he said, "Tell you what. If you can see your way clear to making a $10 contribution to our volunteer emergency squad, you and your buddy can come on my place and hunt the CRP patch down by the river."

Bear in mind that in some states you must have written permission. Several years ago in Pennsylvania, my brother-in-law obtained a note of permission from an acquaintance, and I went out with him and two of his friends for a morning of excellent ringneck hunting. Among us, we bagged seven roosters. We were about ready to call it a day when the local Game Protector (Pennsylvania warden) stopped us. If we hadn't been able to produce our written permission, all four of us would have been in trouble.

HUNTING METHODS

Since food and cover are invariable keys to the whereabouts of game birds, it pays to know the kinds of foods that attract ringnecks. Surveys in the East show that favorites include corn (which tops the list in all regions where it's grown), ragweed, wild grape, oats, oak mast, elderberry, wild cherry, wheat and buckwheat, bristlegrass, nightshade, sumac, burdock, soybeans, and even dogwood. Surveys in the Midwest and West reveal the same preferred foods where available, plus barley, wild oats, snowberry, various beans, sunflower, wild lettuce, dandelion, sorghum, alfalfa, sweet clover, and Russian thistle. My personal experience in various regions leads me to add goldenrod, foxtail, blackberry, and assorted orchard fruits and seeds.

Pheasants also like skunk cabbage, which is about gone by the time the season opens, but it tells you something that many hunters don't seem to realize: ringnecks like moist, lush areas near water if the weather isn't too cold, not only for drinking but for food and cover. Now and then on windy days or late in the season, after

Situated between a cornfield and a woodlot, this uncultivated plot of goldenrod, lespedeza, and other food and cover vegetation is perfect for ringnecks. Absent for years from big, single-crop farming operations, such habitat is being partially restored in the form of Conservation Reserve Program (CRP) patches.

fruitlessly hunting "classic" stubblefield cover, I've flushed them out of cattails.

As a general rule, in fact, hunting today is somewhat more productive in relatively permanent cover—woodlots, sloughs, ditches, fencerows, weedy field terraces, and the like—than in standing corn or other such crops, which tend to scatter the birds over large areas. Anyone who has hunted pheasants has learned

the hard and frustrating way that pheasants amid standing corn and other row crops are especially inclined to run rather than fly. This tendency to run helps ringnecks get clean away far more often than flying, even when a hunter isn't a particularly deft wingshooter. Another cornfield disadvantage is the lack of ground cover to hold scent for a pointing or flushing dog. For all of these reasons, hunting the edges of the fields and the rushy or bushy clumps and patches will often produce the most birds—with or without a dog. Abandoned railroad beds and weedy powerline rights-of-way are also very productive in some areas, as they provide both weed seeds and cover.

Pretty much the same kind of tactics that work in grouse hunting will also work in putting up pheasants; that is, two or three gunners will do well with a dog working patches of cover at a relatively slow pace. Move through the woods or brush toward open ground when possible, because the birds will sneak or run far out ahead of the dog and the guns until the end of screening cover is reached. When the bird approaches clear ground, it will most likely hesitate and then, when pressed by dog or human, fly.

"Quartering" a field or a patch or strip of cover is a common old term for the general manner in which a dog works, zigzagging to sniff out all likely hiding places. But the term is somewhat misleading. A good pointing or flushing dog—especially an experienced one—seldom investigates all parts of a given piece of cover thoroughly. Rather, the dog will recognize and primarily concentrate on those parts of the cover most likely to hide a bird, such as overgrown edges, thickets of undergrowth, brushy hollows, or any area that may be holding scent.

Sometimes the dog will return again and again to one little area, searching it futilely until called off. Usually this means a bird was there quite recently but flew off before the dog arrived. It's a mistake to call off a dog too soon, however. A smart hunter trusts his dog's nose and the powerful canine instinct about where to search for prey.

Since pheasants (and most game birds) do a lot of feeding in the morning, that's a good time to hunt overgrown fields or move through fields of standing crops out toward the edges in the hope that at least one or two ringnecks may flush rather than run while others will fly when finally pushed to an edge. Bear in mind that as the season progresses, a great many pheasants will move into corn or other standing crops and will stay around until it's harvested, after which they head for thicker cover, including woodlots and tall marsh grasses.

Around midday, try the fencerows, swales, field edges, and grassy hillsides. The resting birds often sun themselves on hillsides—the lee slopes if there's a wind. In fact, a strong wind can move them into valleys or weedy bottomlands, the same type of cover they seek throughout most of the day later in the season. But midday is also a good time to hunt dusting and grit-pecking spots such as overgrown gravel pits and even the edges of farm roads, paths, ditches, or other open places providing grit and dust.

In the afternoon, the birds are likely to drift back into standing crops, meadow edges, hedgerows, or whatever food is most abundant. Occasionally, a pheasant will perch in a bush or on a low tree limb, but they're ground-roosting birds. Toward dusk they head for roosting cover such as high clover, hay, or stubble.

With the coming of winter, ringnecks begin to take shelter in clumps of willow, Russian olive, sumac and wild-plum thickets, weedy ditches, windbreaks, cattails, or high brush along sloughs and marsh edges. Sometimes they form flocks, often segregated by sex, in confined shelter areas. Flocks of hens are usually larger than rooster flocks, but I've seen a couple of dozen cock birds flushed from a willow-choked ditch.

A windy day will make game birds skittish, and constantly changing wind direction can frustrate both dog and hunter. But a breeze is advantageous if you can hunt into it. The sound of approaching intruders, which birds can hear at a considerable distance, is what prompts ringnecks to skulk or run away before you come within range. Wind coming toward you can muffle your sound while also carrying bird scent to your dog. A drizzle can help, too. On gently rainy days, the birds seem to "hold tighter," staying put until you've come fairly close and then

As the season progresses, solitary pheasants tend to start gathering into sexually segregated flocks. Sometimes a single gathering of roosters offers the hunter an opportunity to take his limit.

flushing; and the moisture seems to carry scent well, improving conditions for the dog. A downpour, on the other hand, will drown scent and usually make for poor hunting.

Regardless of conditions, a hunter or hunting party with one fast, wide-ranging dog and one slower, close-working dog is often blessed, particularly when combing fields where pheasants tend to run. The wide-ranging dog can be cast far ahead to work in a roughly circular pattern while the close-working dog moves cautiously and within easy shooting range. The birds are apt to run back toward the close worker and the hunters in order to put distance between themselves and the wide ranger. This pins them between two approaching dogs, and often they'll flush toward the hunter or hunters.

I've even seen a single fast dog perform this stunt effectively without benefit of a slower, close-in dog. The animal in this instance was a very canny pointing dog that had learned to run toward the end of a narrow field or strip of cover and work back through it toward his master.

With winter, thinning cover and snow increase visibility, making the birds nervous and inclined to flush beyond gunshot. But a thin blanket of fresh snow enables a hunter to track the birds. The prints show three thin, long, widely separated toes and a little nub at the rear juncture. Often more than three inches long, the prints of roosters are larger than those of hens. The birds tend to move rather directly through fields, along furrows or between rows of stubble, before eventually milling about to seek food or snuggle for shelter on the lee sides of hummocks, clods, stalks, or exposed roots. Sometimes a whole flock can be trailed a short distance before the tracks become a maze. Where they begin to mill about, be ready for your dog to point or flush one.

It isn't only severe weather but also prolonged hunting pressure that influences the movements of pheasants as the season progresses. Those that aren't bagged learn to avoid dogs and hunters by seeking thick cover—usually, but not invariably, the thicker the better. Among their favored haunts are any high, dry patches in the interior of marshes. Some of these can be reached by a hunter wearing waterproof boots or insulated hip boots, though the walking is apt to be difficult. And after a severe cold snap, marsh ice may be hard and thick enough for you to walk where you ordinarily couldn't go—that is, if you're careful enough and willing to expend the effort.

If you don't find roosters in thick cover toward the end of the season, it's sometimes worthwhile to try the opposite kind of habitat—cover so sparse that you think no birds will be there. Try, for example, little patches of weedy cover surrounded by plowed fields, or sparse but grassy hedgerows. If the weather hasn't been very severe, pheasants will sometimes gather in such places for the obvious reason that they prefer to be where no hunters disturb them—and the hunters at that time of year are following the advice of writers like me by concentrating on thicker cover.

METHODS WITHOUT A DOG

Dogless hunters always fare best on opening day, before the ringnecks have learned to run from the sound of approaching feet—but then, so do hunters who do have dogs. An important tactic for a lone dogless hunter or a party of two or three is to move slowly and sporadically—go and stop, go and stop. All ground-feeding birds instinctively interpret approaching footsteps as the sound of a hunting or stalking predator. When the sound abruptly ceases, what it means to them is that the predator has come close enough to pounce or

A dogless hunter can sometimes prod ringnecks to flush from a stubble field by walking slowly and frequently stopping. The stops are what generally panic the birds into flight.

begin a final brief stalk. Often they sit tight or move slowly and quietly away while the sound continues, hoping to escape detection. Then, when the sound stops, they feel they've been detected, after all, and they're sufficiently alarmed to take flight. You may flush a pheasant as you move along, but you're likely to flush one more often when you stop.

In fact, there's a better than even chance that you've walked right past a hiding pheasant. Whenever you stop, be sure to look behind you. A rooster may be clattering into the air very close to where you were walking moments ago. For the same reason, it's also wise to double back for a short distance occasionally, and to move in a roughly zigzag pattern when hunting alone and without a dog.

This tactic becomes somewhat less effective after the first days of the season, because ringnecks quickly learn to retreat from footsteps and keep on retreating. Often, however, you can still walk up birds by moving through cover toward an open edge where there's nothing left to hide them, or toward a bluff or water—an obstacle that eliminates the walking option and forces them into the air.

The go-and-stop tactic again works well when the wind is up and snow is on the ground, or during a light snowfall. You can then trail the birds through stubblefields or low ground cover to the areas where they're sheltering in the lee of little tussocks, ditches, or other windbreaks—sometimes merely huddling in a furrow. Now and then you may actually see a bird quite far ahead and try to jump it by sneaking within gunshot before it flies. More often, you'll walk right past ringnecks, but if you stop and turn frequently, sooner or later one of them is likely to catapult itself into the air in a panicky flurry.

Without a dog, it's also possible for two or three hunters to conduct a drive through small woodlots or along a hedgerow, a thin line of trees, or some other narrow strip of windbreak cover. When two hunters work such a strip, they move along its sides, occasionally trudging across and out again in the hope—often fulfilled—that a bird will feel hemmed in and fly in panic or will move ahead to the end of the strip and then flush. If a third hunter is present, it's wise to station one person at the end of the strip. Somewhat wider but tapering cover can be worked in a similar manner. The hunters in this case should move from the wider to the smaller end of the tapering cover, so that any pheasants are likely to flush from one small area rather than anywhere along a wide line.

Field drives involving more hunters are traditional in many Midwestern and Western regions. Morning is generally the best time for such a drive, as the pheasants will probably be scattered through the fields to feed on grain. Depending on the chosen field's size, up to a dozen drivers may work through it while pretty much the same number of standers or "blockers" will be stationed at the far end. As a rule, it's best to drive toward a hedgerow, fence, corner, slough, or even a farm road, so the birds will rise as they approach the end of cover.

The drivers should be in position and ready to start moving before the blockers take their stations or the birds may become prematurely aware of the blocking line and skulk away to the sides of the field. Also to forestall escape to the sides as the drivers move forward, the driving line should be somewhat cupped, with those at each end ahead of those in the middle.

The blockers should take up their positions quietly and remain quiet or the pheasants will go up or out to the sides long before they're within range. Where possible, if the cover is dry and noisy, the drive should be made against the wind. The birds will tend to rise away, into the wind, but some will fly close enough to give the drivers occasional shots or will circle and fly back over them, while many of the others will furnish pass-shooting for the blockers.

The two most common mistakes in this type

In big fields known to hold pheasants, an organized drive can be very productive. Here the drivers move toward their start positions at one end of a field (behind the trees). The blockers will then take their stations at the far end of the field.

of hunt are to space the drivers too far apart and to move too quickly and directly. A space of 20 yards is wide enough for a pheasant to slip through unseen, between two drivers, and even when the line is that tight the participants should move in a slightly wavering or zigzag manner as they advance.

Obviously, with so many people in a field— even a big field—and with the drivers and blockers facing one another, safety is of paramount concern. During most of the drive, only high shots may be taken. And after the line of drivers reaches a certain point, the blockers may take only overhead shots or shots at birds that have already passed them so that they're firing away from their comrades in the driving line. The drivers, of course, are under the same obligation not to fire in any direction that might endanger another hunter. Usually one

person is in charge of the drive and gives careful, explicit instructions. An agreed-upon ceasefire signal can be used to tell everyone when the drive is over.

GUNS AND LOADS

The 12 gauge is by far the most popular pheasant gun and the best choice if a single gun is to be used for all types of pheasant hunting. Probably the best all-around shot size is No. 5, though it's hard to find in some regions. But optimum choices are dictated by type of habitat and hunting method.

In thick cover where few birds are shot at more than 40 yards and most are within 30, a 20-gauge magnum with an improved-cylinder or modified choke (or both in the case of a double-barreled gun) is an excellent selection. And the same gun will be a fine choice for other game birds such as quail, ruffed grouse, woodcock, doves, Huns, and chukars. What's wanted is a relatively wide but dense shot pattern produced by the combination of relatively open choke and relatively small pellets. For this kind of pheasant hunting, No. 6 is the recommended pellet size and (depending on cover) the loads don't always have to be magnums.

For hunting in big, open fields and pastures, especially in the Midwest and West, the 12 gauge is far more efficient. Larger shot is needed, the preferred size generally being No. 5 and sometimes even 4. I personally feel that the best single choke for this is modified, but I certainly wouldn't argue with an Iowa marksman who can consistently bring down pheasants at 50 yards and wants the tight pattern of a full choke for the purpose. Improved-modified isn't a bad compromise, and some hunters use double-barreled guns choked improved and full, with high-brass loads of 4s or 5s.

7

Bobwhite Quail:
Yesterday's Tradition, Today's New Wave

More than 20 subspecies of bobwhite are indigenous to the eastern half of the United States and adjacent southwestern regions down through Mexico and Central America. These rotund little birds are New World relatives of the even smaller common quail of Europe and the Asian quails, including the Japanese quail, or coturnix, which has been established on the Hawaiian Islands.

The prototype, or at least the race familiar to the largest number of American hunters, is the Eastern bobwhite (*Colinus virginianus*). Extremely similar in appearance, habits, and general type of habitat is the plains bobwhite (*C.v. taylori*) which is most abundant in the Midwest and in Oklahoma and Texas and has been successfully introduced throughout much of the Far West.

A great many of our states now have wild bobwhite populations. Since the bobwhite is also a very popular bird on shooting preserves, is easier to propagate than some other American game birds, and is inclined to retain fairly wild characteristics even when pen-raised, it can be bagged in many additional regions outside of its native range and the regions where it's been introduced in the wild.

Typically, the bobwhite is a mottled brown bird—usually ruddy or chestnut but sometimes grayish-brown—with a short, dark bill and a rounded tail that fans out wide in flight. Its stubby, rounded body and rounded wings make it look heavier and shorter-winged than it really is. Like the woodcock, it looks as if it shouldn't be able to fly very fast, but it has a rapid, strong wingbeat and can fly considerably faster than a woodcock, especially on take-off. A quail bursting into the air in a blur is a difficult target. It's a small target, too, seldom longer than ten inches or so and weighing only six or seven ounces.

The cock has a white chin and throat and a white stripe from the bill up through the eye and usually arcing down again to the base of the neck. The hen has buff or creamy yellow markings instead of white, and the surrounding feathers are browner than the male's, with less blackish contrast. Once in a while, a hunter will spot bobwhites amid the ground cover, before they fly. More typically, they bounce from hid-

This is a typical specimen of the Eastern race bobwhite quail. Its white chin and throat and the white stripe from the bill through the eye, continuing in a thinning arc to the base of the neck, distinguish it as a male. The female has buff or creamy yellow facial markings rather than white, and the surrounding feathers are browner than the male's, with less blackish contrast.

ing upon being flushed and fly away from the hunter, so it's rarely possible to distinguish the sexes in flight—nor is it necessary, since both sexes are legal game. Nevertheless, almost every hunter takes a deep interest in wildlife and, upon taking the warm little bird from his dog, is likely to notice whether it's a male or female.

A few subspecies differ somewhat in size or markings. The Florida bobwhite, for example, is rather small and dark, while some of the arid-country birds such as the Texas bobwhite are relatively pale. These adaptations to habitat make them all the harder for predators—or human hunters—to spot until they take wing.

A separate but closely related species found in southeastern Arizona, parts of New Mexico, and much of Mexico is the Mearns quail, also known as the harlequin quail, painted quail, crazy quail, massena quail, or Montezuma quail. It's the size of a Florida bobwhite (seldom more than about 9½ inches long) and the female looks very much like a female bobwhite except that she has a small buffy crest and a darker head, with less distinct facial markings. The male, on the other hand, is rather spectacular. He has a white and black or bluish-black facial pattern and a brown crest, more pronounced than the female's, curving back and down over his nape. His upper parts are dark, mottled brown, with a grayish or olive cast. The breast and belly are dark brown at the center, but toward the sides they become a dark slate-gray, almost black, with a great many round spots of white plus less conspicuous spots of buff and cinnamon.

This bird isn't very abundant above the Mexican border but is legal game in Arizona. I had difficulty deciding whether to mention it here or describe it in the next chapter, with the scaled quail—another crested species—and the three plumed quails of the Southwest and Far West. Despite its geographic range and appear-ance, I believe it merits brief comment here because it tends to behave as if it were a bob-white transplanted to semi-arid, grassy high-lands bordering desert regions.

Often flushed from live-oak stands and from hills blessed with tall grass, it has the bobwhite's reluctance to run or fly at the approach of an intruder, counting instead on escaping detec-tion by remaining hidden and stationary until the last moment and then exploding into the air. It "lies close," as hunters say, and "holds for a dog" as well as any bobwhite. The same meth-

These birds are Mearns quail; their markings clearly indicate why they're also known as harlequin quail. Although they inhabit relatively arid parts of the Southwest, they're closely related to bobwhites and are hunted by the same methods.

ods are therefore used in hunting it, with or without a dog.

For the Mearns quail, conditions have remained relatively stable for a great many years, but the bobwhite has needed and received substantial help following a degradation of its habitat. Beginning in the 1960s or perhaps even earlier, bobwhite populations experienced increasingly hard times, especially in the East and Midwest, as a result of giant single-crop farms and the substitution of vast manicured fields for the old patchwork family farm. These birds are even more dependent than pheasants on interspersed areas of feed and cover. They need grasses or weeds for nesting cover and, to some extent, for spring and summer feeding and roosting. In any area where wild foods no longer abound, they need croplands for summer and fall feeding (and for midday dusting and resting). They also need surface water or plenty of dew, which is why arid-country bobwhites are almost invariably bagged along river valleys, near springs or cattle tanks, or on irrigated lands. And they need woods in winter for feeding and the year around for escape cover.

Although they eat insects and assorted types of vegetable matter, seeds account for more than 90 percent of their fall diet. Ragweed and lespedeza almost invariably attract bobwhites. Other preferred foods, both cultivated and wild, include soybeans, sorghum, corn, partridgepea, cowpea, trailing wild bean, wheat, sunflower, smartweed, and beggarweed.

They can perch in trees but they roost on the ground, usually in tangled grass, brush, or a woodland edge, and very often on an unshaded south slope where the ground retains warmth in late afternoon. A patch of weedy herbs no higher than a hunter's knee or thigh will often hide a roost, and even wheat stubble sometimes suffices. Quail watch for predators and retain body heat by roosting with their bodies touching in a circular or disk formation, sometimes called a "roosting ring" or "pie." A hunter—

with or without a dog—will do well to remember that quail use the same roosts repeatedly and move from their roosting cover only far enough to feed. This is why coveys that aren't starved out, hunted out, or otherwise dispersed or destroyed often inhabit one small area for so many years that they come to be identified by place names such as the Schoolhouse Covey.

For a good many years, quail in many states were increasingly deprived of suitable home-range habitat that would support coveys year after year. In recent times, however, many state game departments have worked assiduously to develop and maintain proper habitat on state-managed lands and to redevelop privately owned habitat with the cooperation of farmers and other landowners. I recall reading a couple of years ago that Missouri—to cite just one exemplary state—had achieved a very considerable resurgence of its quail populations. In addition, a nonprofit organization, Quail Unlimited (see Appendix III), has done excellent work in many states, and the federal Conservation Reserve Program, described in the previous chapter, has substantially benefitted quail as well as pheasants and other wildlife.

HUNTING METHODS

Quail leave their roosting grounds to head for nearby fields and seed-rich weedy areas early in the morning, but on raw, windy days or in wet weather they often postpone feeding and remain roosted until late in the morning. If the vegetation is very wet, hunting may be better in a roosting area at almost any time of day than in foraging fields, and in states where the season extends much beyond Christmas, field hunting is likely to be better at noon than in early morning.

This isn't meant to imply that quail never roost within a cultivated field or open fallow field. Any patch of seemingly low cover, even in the middle of a field, may serve as an amply protected night roost and therefore bears investigation in the morning. The productive field edges that hold so much wildlife are by no means confined to outer edges.

The composition of a covey changes through the year. During hunting season, the group usually contains mixed families and mixed ages. The average home range for a covey of 10 or even 20 birds is only about 24 acres, a great advantage to a hunter who has scouted or informed himself of the whereabouts of local coveys. He can move from roosting area to feeding area as the day progresses, and in late afternoon or toward dusk, head again for roosting brush and thickets near field edges.

Because bobwhites (unlike some other quail species) tend to lie tight until a dog comes quite close, these birds can be hunted pretty successfully with flushing dogs. However, doing so can't compare with the delights of classic quail hunting over good pointing dogs. Much of the pleasure lies in watching the dogs work: quartering fields thoroughly, combing the edges, checking little brush piles or patches that might easily have escaped your notice—and then freezing into a stylish point, sometimes quivering with intensity.

Some gunners prefer close-working dogs for this purpose, particularly in regions of dense or very mixed cover, but nothing can rival a hunt with a fast, wide-ranging setter, pointer, or Brit that holds a point staunchly while the hunter comes up. Bragging jokes are told about champion pointers that were lost—owing to the lack of a bell or blaze-orange collar—because they froze on point somewhere in the brush, and neither dog nor quail moved again. The typical story claims that the skeleton of such a dog was found, still on point, the following spring—standing over the skeletons of a covey still holding tight. Quail do occasionally run if they're close to heavy escape cover, but they generally lie tighter than most other game birds, and all the tighter if they've been hunted.

As a general rule, with exceptions frequent enough to keep it interesting, quail are most active on sunny, somewhat chilly days, neither so dry that scenting is difficult nor so wet that they stay roosted and fail to lay scent trails on the ground and through the vegetation. And on such cool, sunny days a dog will perform best, catching scent frequently, strongly, and in plenty of time to avoid "bumping" birds—overrunning and accidentally flushing them before the hunter can come within range.

The birds in a flushed covey may seem to spray out in all directions, but observe them closely and you'll see a definite tendency to head in one general direction—away from you and toward woods, brush, or any other escape cover, however meager it may be. Thus you'll have a fair idea of which way most of the birds will fly after erupting from the ground cover. They'll be still more likely to fly in that direction if the covey is between the dog or dogs and the nearest tangles or thickets. Your tactic is simply to walk in over the dog so that the birds perceive danger concentrated at one point and will fly toward the escape cover—their curtain of safety—in the opposite direction.

In this situation, at least a couple of targets should offer more or less straightaway shots, and there's seldom time for more than a couple even with a semiautomatic. Yet there is time for a reasonably deliberate gun swing, and you must convince yourself of that. A common error is shooting too fast, doubting that the birds will straighten out. Many veteran quail hunters can snap-shoot so expertly that they often bring down doubles as the birds spray into the air, but most of us will do better if we don't hurry our shots.

By prodding the birds into roughly straightaway flight, you'll also be encouraging them to come down again in a relatively small area where the dog can most easily find the scattered singles. When a fleeing bobwhite lands after being separated from the covey, it remains very still for a little while, instinctively reluctant to

Bobwhites, whether flushed in coveys or singly, will usually fly toward woods or other escape cover. Knowing which way the quarry will probably fly, hunters can sometimes get more or less straight-away shots by approaching from the opposite direction to flush them.

move and thereby spread body scent while some unknown predator seems to be hunting it. Unless "marked down" precisely by hunter or dog, a single can be hard to find at first. But if the unmarked singles are left alone for a little while (often no more than 15 minutes or so), they'll start whistling to one another and will move about to regather.

They'll be "coveyed up" again in an hour or

so, but there's no need to wait that long. My partners and I try to mark down as many singles as possible after shooting. Unless we've performed disgracefully, a few minutes will pass while the dogs retrieve the birds we've downed. Then we cast the dogs toward the marked singles, one at a time. If, after working those birds, we still need more in the bag, enough time has elapsed so that the dogs can comb the area

An English setter, well trained and "soft-mouthed," brings a New England bobwhite to hand. These quail seldom weigh more than 6 or 7 ounces, yet their scent is sufficiently strong and distinctive to lead a good dog to scattered, hidden singles or to birds that fall in thick, high ground cover.

effectively for unmarked singles, which are now calling and on the move again.

There are still scattered plantations in the South (some for the owners' use only, some for the membership of hunting clubs, and some operated commercially for fee-paying hunters) where quail shoots are conducted in traditional 19th-century style—partly for the sake of classic, nostalgic appeal and partly because the plantations are large and the coveys may be in widely scattered locations. Mule-drawn wagons are used to reach the hunting sites. Often the dogs are conveyed in these wagons, and sometimes the hunters as well. In other cases the hunters ride separately, on horses, with guns either scabbarded or aboard the wagons. The dogs are released where a covey is expected to be found, and the hunters then dismount or climb down from the wagons to load their guns and walk in over the points.

For those who can afford such luxury, there's much to be said for the pleasure and comfort of riding to the birds and later riding back to the big house. It surely isn't as tiring as a day of walking.

But, like most hunters, I enjoy walking and feel more at home trudging after my dog over farms where I've obtained hunting permission and through the many wildlife management areas open to the public. I've done it that way in a number of places from New Jersey to Tennessee and, thanks to modern wildlife management, I've put up my share of birds without benefit of horse or wagon. On the other hand, there are parts of the West where walking rather than hunting would occupy much of the day if no means of transportation were available. Hunters in those regions often use today's equivalent of the mule-drawn wagon—a four-wheel-drive vehicle that accommodates both the gunners and their dogs.

Without a Dog

I've known a couple of hunters who used hawk calls and one who used an owl-hooter (normally

There are still some traditional quail-shooting plantations in the South where the dogs are conveyed to the hunting areas in mule-drawn wagons and the hunters arrive on horseback or in other wagons. The plantation pictured here is in Tennessee. In some regions, wagons, mules, and horses have been replaced by four-wheel-drive motor vehicles.

reserved for turkey hunting) to make quail hold tight in low cover. I doubt that such stratagems are often necessary, but I myself have used a commercial quail whistle that imitates bobwhites better than most of us can by unaided whistling. It didn't draw scattered birds, but it did bring a couple of answering calls that made the singles easier for me to find without a dog. I'm not very good at whistling, with or without a mechanical aid, but most people have little trouble imitating the bobwhite's mellow, far-carrying, whistling calls. The one advantage of a metal quail whistle is that it projects sound much farther than human lips and breath alone.

Using a call to locate quail isn't a widespread practice but is certainly worth trying if you know the quail's vocabulary. Once in a while—not often—you may hear the feeding call: *tu-tu-tu-tu-tu*. If you do and you can tell the direction of the sound (which tends to be ventriloquial),

To locate scattered singles, some hunters mimic the bobwhite's call—with or without the aid of a mechanical whistle. The birds don't normally come to the sound but they'll often answer it, revealing their locations. Commercial calls for such additional species as California (valley) quail, dove, pheasant, and chukar are also offered by Burnham Brothers, Olt, Haydel's, and other manufacturers.

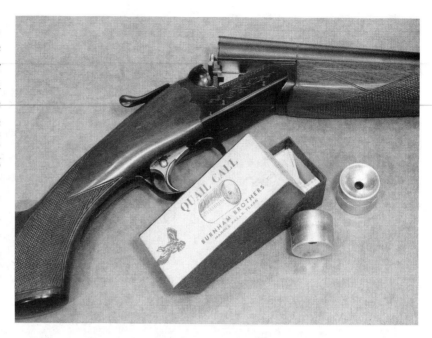

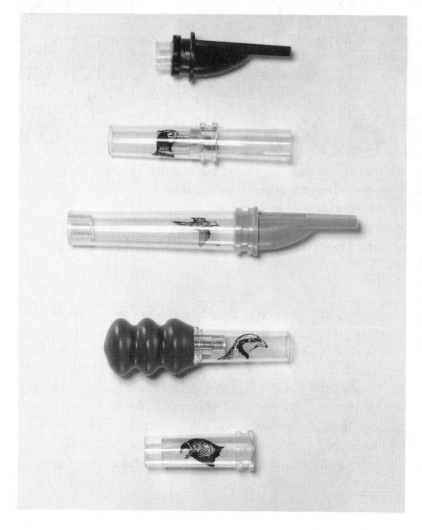

Upland bird calls seem to be more popular among hunters than they used to be—perhaps because some of them have been improved. These (from top) are a bobwhite whistle, pheasant call, dove whistle, chukar call, and hawk "screamer." The author has effectively used a bobwhite whistle to draw answers from scattered singles and thus locate them. Some hunters use hawk calls to hold quail or other game-birds tight in low cover—deterring them from running or flushing too far out.

you've located a covey and have no need to imitate the feeding call; the birds probably won't respond anyway. The relatively piercing double- and triple-noted calls for which the birds are named—*bob-white, bob-bob-white*—are most often heard (at least in my experience) late in the day. Sometimes quail will answer that sound. More helpful to the hunter trying to walk up singles is the somewhat shrill rallying call, which sounds to me like a whistled *hoy, hoy-ee!* It may give you direction but is intermittent until the repeated calls eventually become a louder series. It can't hurt to whistle back in order to encourage more calling.

More important is your general manner of hunting without a dog. Keep in mind the kinds of roosting and feeding areas I've described, and move through them slowly and very quietly. Wildlife biologists have observed that quail don't immediately stop moving and sit statue-still when they hear someone approach. Upon hearing a hunter move close, they start milling around or retreating along the ground. A dog can trail them by scent, and when the birds realize they haven't eluded the supposed predator, they freeze. But a hunter can't trail them by scent, so he doesn't want to make them nervous prematurely.

Sometimes the go-and-stop tactic works, as in pheasant hunting. More often, in my experience, just moving along steadily but slowly and as silently as possible is at least as productive. Keep at it and, assuming there's a covey to be found where you're hunting, sooner or later you're likely to put up a few nervous birds or the whole covey—often within good shotgun range.

Toward noon, hunt cool-looking retreats if the weather is warm; if it's cool, the birds may be sunning and dusting on lee rises or in thin brush. Also try any hedgerows or timber strips that border feeding fields. Later in the afternoon, try the edges of row-crop and weed fields, walking along a few feet inside the field to its end, then returning along the same field but a few feet outside the border or hedgerow. Move quietly and you may trigger a close flush.

Since you have no dog to aid you, look for sign. A circular accumulation of droppings indicates a roosting spot, which is likely to be productive toward the day's end.

The biggest problem for the dogless hunter is to find every fallen bird he's shot; and the sec-

A lone bobwhite, perched on a fallen tree trunk, calls to the other members of the covey as regrouping begins.

ond biggest is to locate single birds after flushing a covey. Both problems are addressed primarily by means of sharp observation—marking where a bird comes down, whether it's been shot or merely flown away.

After shooting a quail, I always walk directly to the spot where it fell (or where it seemed to fall, since this sometimes differs a little from reality). Unless I immediately see the bird, I pull out a bright handkerchief or bandanna and attach it to whatever vegetation is handy. This marks the spot where the bird supposedly dropped, and it will be the central point of my search. Even if the bird was stone dead when it

hit the ground, it's apt to be well camouflaged, blending into the undergrowth. If it came down still alive, it may have moved a few feet or quite a few yards before settling into a hiding place.

I begin by searching the ground thoroughly where I've tied the handkerchief, and then I move out in widening circles until I find the bird. If you walk around without first placing a landmark—a hat, handkerchief, bandanna, or whatever—you'll soon lose track of the proper search area.

In the case of unscathed singles that I simply want to hunt up and flush again, I just walk to where I've marked them down. I don't delay

When trying to find a fallen bird, tie a handkerchief or comparable marker to the foliage where the bird was marked down, and then search carefully in widening circles. Don't forget to check the lower limbs of trees. Injured bobwhites, like pheasants, will sometimes alight on a branch instead of the ground.

doing this, as I would when hunting with a dog, because there's no sense in waiting for the bird to start moving about and leaving a scent trail. The bird is apt to have moved very little if I get there quickly and—having just flown—will be reluctant to fly again until I'm quite close.

Theoretically, I then have a sporting chance when the bird does flush. I'll admit, however, that quite often the bird flushes behind me or off to one side while I'm in midstride, too slow to swing on it, and my only hope is to mark it down again. Well, the truth is sometimes I don't bother to mark it down again since any bobwhite smarter than I am has earned a reprieve.

GUNS AND LOADS

You don't need or want much gun for birds that so often break from cover at a distance of five paces. The range may be 20 yards by the time you get a first shot off, but it's seldom much more. My idea of a peerless quail gun is a light, short 20 gauge with improved-cylinder or skeet choke. For that matter, a 28 gauge is fine. A truly light 12 gauge is fine, too, if it has a cylinder or skeet choke, nothing tighter. I believe in the adage that needlessly tight chokes result in too many wing-tipped birds that never enter the bag even when a good dog combs the underbrush for them, and many such crippled birds will be captured and eaten by some predator a day or two later.

What you want is a dense but wide pattern of small pellets. I've used No. 7½ shot but prefer 8 or even 9. I don't believe scatter loads are necessary in most quail habitat, but they can be useful in really heavy brush where you have to make your shots—or just one shot—very quickly.

I'm a firm believer in field loads or skeet loads for quail shooting, whether the gun is a 12 or 20. Some hunters like a little heavier powder charge—an "express" load—in 28 gauge, but even with that small bore, I doubt the need for it. All it adds is velocity, not pellets, and a dense cloud of pellets is what bags quail.

8

Western Quail:
the Crested and the Plumed

Large portions of this continent are unsuitable for the bobwhite but contain excellent habitat for one or more quail species adapted to the rigors imposed by arid or semi-arid climate. All of the four major ones are marvelous game birds, avidly pursued (actual *pursuit* often being the key to success) by wingshooters in the Southwest and Far West.

One of these is a demurely handsome, crested species, the scaled quail. The other three are the so-called plumed species, elegantly beautiful birds distinguished by a feather or feathers rising jauntily from the crown like the plume waving almost upright atop a Victorian lady's hat. These three are the desert, or Gambel, quail; the mountain quail; and the valley, or California, quail. Regionally, other names—descriptive of appearance or locale—are used for each, but those are the most widely accepted names, recognized by all hunters and wildlife observers throughout the areas of distribution. All four of these Western species display behavioral similarities—adaptations to habitat—but there are differences as well.

SCALED QUAIL

The "scaly" is also known as the blue quail, cottontop, Mexican quail, and blue racer. Having hunted this astonishingly fleet little bird in southwestern Texas, I feel that the last-mentioned name, though least common, is most appropriate. Half or more of the challenge in hunting these desert runners successfully lies in chasing or tricking them into flight.

Scaled quail are distributed from eastern Colorado and southwestern Kansas down through the Oklahoma panhandle, the western half of Texas, almost all of New Mexico, lower Arizona, and the lands southward into central Mexico. That, at least, is the historic range. They've also been introduced into appropriate habitat elsewhere, notably in Washington and eastern Nevada. Their way of life has sometimes been threatened by heavy grazing, which rips away nesting and escape cover, but modern arid-country game management includes the provision of brushy shelters and precious waters. Scaled quail have been slowly extending their range for some years now, although I'll venture

Slightly larger than bobwhites, scaled quail are named for the pattern of feather edging on the neck, breast, and underparts. They're also called blue quail and, for obvious reasons, cottontops. Coveys tend to be small in early autumn, but by winter a hunter may see flocks of more than a hundred.

to say that the hunting probably remains best in New Mexico and Texas.

This species is slightly larger than a typical bobwhite, averaging 10 to 12 inches in length and weighing 6 or 7 ounces. Its light, grayish brown head is crowned with a cottony crest, buff on the hen, whitish and higher on the cock bird. The male's cheeks and throat are pale and pearly, the female's streaked somewhat with brownish shafts. On either sex, the back, wings, and tail are gray or brownish gray with narrow white streaks on the wings. There's an overall bluish tone, most pronounced on the neck, upper breast, and upper back. The lower breast and belly are whitish (or chestnut on one southerly subspecies). Both sexes display black feather edging—the "scaled" effect—on the underparts, breast, and lower neck.

In Arizona or Nevada, where the season usually opens rather early in the fall, you might at first encounter small coveys—fewer than 20 birds in a group. As winter comes on, the birds congregate in progressively larger flocks, typically numbering between 20 and 40, and once in a while a desert hunter may be startled to see more than a hundred blue quail galloping about through mazes of sage or cactus.

Like other quail species, they subsist chiefly on seeds. These include the seeds of mesquite, hackberry, cat's-claw, thistle, ragweed, sorghum, snakeweed, deervetch, lupine, sunflowers, and filaree. The birds are addicted to thorny or spiny ground cover such as patches of cactus, Spanish bayonet, and yucca, as well as shady spots under mesquite and juniper. They never have to walk more than a few yards to find grit and dusting places, but they'll travel far in search of water. You'll often find them at small streams, ponds, irrigation ditches, and cattle tanks. They're also attracted to the cover of man-made structures such as fencerows, abandoned buildings, old farm machinery or vehicles, or tangles of barbed wire.

You can't sneak up on scaled quail, though you may be lucky enough once in a while to top a rise and stumble onto a covey within fairly easy shooting range. Where ground cover is relatively dense, it's possible to make good use of a very well-trained pointing or flushing dog. The trick is to control the dog at a considerable distance, sending him around and in front of the area where a covey's presence is suspected and having him work back in your direction. These birds won't hold for a dog, but almost invariably they'll race ahead of him (which, unfortunately, can be the ruination of some pointers) until they're close enough to you to feel pinned—forced to fly. In maneuvering with or without a dog, remember that all Western quail share a trait with the chukar partridge: they prefer to run uphill to escape predators. Whenever possible, get above them.

Where ground cover is scanty—and where thorns and cactus needles (to say nothing of rattlers) are a menace to dogs, most hunters simply do without assistance. A common method is to scout the desert from a vehicle, then stop abruptly, jump out, and load on the run when a covey is sighted. A variation I prefer is to drive on, around the nearest rise, and then walk back and try to surprise the birds into flight. Whether feeding, dusting, or just loafing in a shaded spot, blues make no real effort to hide until they're disturbed. The hunter therefore has at least one advantage—the likelihood of spotting coveys at a distance. Some hunters carry compact binoculars and scan the country as if hunting mule deer instead of game birds.

The boom of a gunshot will usually (not invariably) startle these quail into the air. Since they scamper almost as fast as rabbits, forcing a flush by shooting one on the run is considered sporting. At least some of the birds will go up, so the second shot presents the option of a running or flying bird. Most of us choose the latter.

In South Texas, a friend and I once went out for a mixed bag of scalies and rabbits. Ambling about on the desert, we walked within range of a covey, and as the birds began their ground-running retreat a rabbit bounced out of a clump of Spanish bayonet. Actually, I think the rabbit alerted them, as they started racing like roadrunners just at that moment. The shot that potted the rabbit sent several into the air, giving me an odd double: one rabbit, one quail.

The birds scattered, and I believe they came down running. We could hear their rallying calls, which a Texas friend described as sounding like the name of the Pecos River—*pey-cos*—but it sounded more like clinking to me. My feeble attempts at imitation produced no responses, but we did locate them and bagged a limit by jogging to the sage clumps from which their voices seemed to come.

There are regions in lower Arizona and New Mexico where Mearns quail (named for the 19th-century naturalist Edgar Mearns) and scaled quail might be hunted on the same day. However, the Mearns, or harlequin, quail needs higher, brushier, less arid habitat than the scaled quail and is extremely hard to find without a dog. Since it behaves and is hunted like the bobwhite, a brief description has been provided in the previous chapter.

GAMBEL QUAIL

The Gambel (or Gambel's) quail, also widely known as the desert quail and sometimes called Arizona or Olanthe quail, takes its most common name from the naturalist William Gambel, who explored the Southwest in the 1850s. Its native range in the United States encompasses arid and semi-arid lands in lower California, Nevada, Arizona, New Mexico, western Texas, and small parts of lower Utah, southwestern Colorado, and southern Idaho. The species is also found on the northern mainland of Mexico and large parts of the Baja California peninsula. Small but huntable populations have also been established in Hawaii (on the islands of Hawaii, Lanai, and Kahoolawe).

This is a beautiful little quail weighing perhaps 6 ounces and having a length of about 9½ to 11 inches. Both sexes have a blackish, slightly forward-curling black head plume, somewhat larger on the male, jutting up and arching over almost like a question mark. Both also have a gray or grayish-brown back, tail, wings, and upper breast, but the male's breast (with variations among the seven subspecies) has a strong bluish tone. The male has a black or nearly black face bordered by a white forehead stripe and an almost connected white crescent from the eye around the cheek to the throat. Both sexes have rusty or chestnut bars and thin white streaks on their sides, and both also have white feathering on their underparts. The male, however, has a blackish central patch on the lower breast and belly. Against a contrasting background, these colors are striking; amid sagebrush they become perfect camouflage.

Where the ranges of the Gambel and the scaled quail overlap, coveys of both species may occupy the same desert habitat or semi-arid brush and grass. However, Gambel quail are more dependent on rainfall because they feed more heavily on green and succulent plants. Important foods include lupine, bur clover, mimosa, other legumes, and the seeds of weeds and grasses. They also like cat's-claw and paloverde beans, but seem to prefer mesquite

The Gambel quail, or desert quail, is a small, plump bird with a forward-curling black head plume, usually larger on the male (right) than on the female. Coveys vary from perhaps a dozen birds to 50 or more.

beans over any other kind. In addition, they seek creosote, prickly pear, yucca, skunkbush, sage, desert thorn, hackberry, and ocotillo seeds. In the northern reaches of their range, they like greasewood, rabbitbrush, and saltbush as well. In agricultural areas, they come to alfalfa. And like all of the Western species, they seem to be virtually magnetized by deervetch and filaree.

Coveys of desert quail are often composed of two or more family groups, numbering anywhere from a dozen birds to 50 or more. Like scaled quail, they run hard and flush wild, yet quite a few hunters use pointing dogs to good effect. The dog or dogs will almost invariably bump a covey too far out on the first flush, but will be more successful on subsequent rises or on singles if the birds scatter. (The more abruptly the birds are surprised, the more likely they are to scatter, and that's a help.) After being pushed up once or twice, these quail will hold a bit tighter and provide good singles shooting.

A dog that has hunted desert quail soon learns to check brushy washes, ravines, willows along the rare watercourses, and mesquite clumps. The best general strategy, with or without a dog, is to force birds into the air and break up a covey, then hunt singles. Their rallying call is a querulous, somewhat crowing whistle, not easy to imitate. All the same, some hunters use commercial calls (mentioned in the chapter on

Both Gambel and scaled quail occupy the same habitat where their ranges overlap. Coveys would rather run than fly, but singles hold somewhat better for a point, and increasing numbers of hunters rely on pointing dogs. A common tactic, therefore, is to scatter a covey. Here, the well-known sporting writer Charley Waterman is about to flush a lone Gambel pinned by a favorite hunting companion, his Brit.

Largest of our American quail species is the mountain quail, which often weighs over half a pound. Its nearly perpendicular head plume is composed of two narrow, blackish feathers that sweep back in flight. The bird pictured here is a male.

bobwhites) to elicit responses, and the voices of the birds themselves will help steer you—with or without a dog—toward the next flush.

MOUNTAIN QUAIL

Sometimes called San Pedro quail, painted quail, or mountain partridge, the mountain quail inhabits Washington, Oregon, California, Idaho, and Nevada, plus portions of Arizona and Baja California. It has also been introduced in British Columbia and Colorado. The hunting for this species generally is and always has been best in California.

Largest of the quail species (about a third larger than a Deep South bobwhite), this bird is often a foot long and weighs over half a pound. Equally unusual is its plume, composed of two straight, narrow, blackish feathers that usually stand more or less upright when the bird is on the ground but sweep back in flight. On both sexes, the throat is dark chestnut, blackish at the edges, and set off by a white streak that reaches up to the eye. The breast, head, and neck are grayish-blue or slate-gray, dulling to brownish or olive gray on back, wings, and tail. The belly and flanks are dark brown with wide white bars, edged in black. Sexual identification sometimes is difficult, but the brownish color of the hen's back usually extends to the top of her head, without the predominant gray of the male's neck.

Mountain quail migrate seasonally over longer distances than their relatives, sometimes moving more than 20 miles. They nest in the highlands, but begin to descend in August or early September. By October, a hunter seldom has reason to wander elevations higher than 5,000 feet, and will probably begin to find them in the same habitat where he'd seek valley quail (though they may also be as high as 8,000 feet up in the Sierras).

Promising country is on the foothills of the mountains in pinyon-juniper cover or amid other conifers. They can be found on steep slopes, in canyons, and in thickets, all of which provide good escape cover. Their coveys tend to

This is a female mountain quail, seen in October in a grassy Oregon field. By that time of year, they've usually descended from their highland nesting areas to somewhat lower habitat where valley quail are also encountered. Coveys of mountain quail sometimes number as few as half a dozen birds, sometimes as many as 30, but a group of about a dozen is typical.

be smaller than those of other Western quail species, ranging from perhaps half a dozen birds to 20 or 30. A group of about a dozen is typical.

Preferred foods include sumac, hackberry, grape, serviceberry, gooseberry, mullein, barley, manzanita, elder, snowberry, mountain rye, timothy, sage, clover, wild oats, acorns, and conifer and locust seeds. In fact, they eat a wide variety of nuts and seeds, as well as berries and fruits.

They like to roost and loaf under scrub oaks and other hardwoods, and they'll often come to roadsides to dust or grit, but they don't like to cross open ground and are difficult to find, still more difficult to approach. Many hunters consider them the toughest of all quail species to bag. They tend to feed early and again just before dark. At other times of day, they're more likely to be watering or dusting and loafing in well chosen hideaways.

In the thick canyon cover that attracts them in autumn, I think a flushing dog is a great asset. However, as with valley quail, a pointer that has gained plenty of experience with these birds or with pheasants can often head them off on a ridge or pin them on a flat. Although they'd rather run than fly, they can be prodded up. Since they tend to run upward and then, if forced into the air, fly downhill, there's a last resort that works often enough with or without the aid of a dog. One or more hunters must first move up above where the birds are known (or hoped) to be skulking or resting, while one or more companions must wait downhill or in a gulley. The ridgetop hunters then move downward, driving the birds ahead and making them hesitant to run for the rim. When this succeeds, the birds take flight downhill, and the hunters stationed below may have some fast pass-shooting.

Mountain quail may cackle when alarmed, but when you try to locate them as they skulk through cover you should listen for tremulous whistles—*whew-whew-whew*—which can be imitated pretty easily. Their rallying call as singles regroup sounds more like a rapid *cle-cle-cle*.

VALLEY QUAIL

Valley, or California, quail are also known regionally as Catalina quail, helmet quail, and topknot quail, and they're probably the best known of the plumed varieties. They may also be the fastest-flying, rivaling bobwhites when they spurt across an opening—although all of these birds can go 30 miles an hour. The native range of valley quail extends from southern Oregon and western Nevada down through California and clear to the tip of the Baja peninsula. Widespread stocking programs have also established them in lower British Columbia, Washington (where the hunting generally is excellent), Idaho, Utah, Montana, Arizona, and Hawaii.

Habitat reduction diminished the populations for quite a few years, and more recently a prolonged drought further reduced their numbers, but good management (abetted by somewhat wetter breeding seasons) has stabilized or increased them. I recently read an account of a Baja California hunt on a November day during which a covey of perhaps 40 birds sprinted across a road in front of a four-wheel-drive vehicle carrying five hunters. The hunters parked their vehicle, loaded their guns, spread out in a line, and moved forward into the cactus/sagebrush cover in an effort to flush the covey. Suddenly, birds flushed all about them—obviously far more than a single covey. Within seconds, more than a thousand quail were in the air! The hunters were so flustered that they failed to bag a single bird on that chain-reaction rise, but they followed the scattered quail and flushed enough of them to enjoy the best shoot of their lives.

The valley quail is very closely related to the

These are valley, or California, quail—a cock (left) and a hen. They're closely related to Gambel quail, and the two species are very similar in appearance. However, the valley quail's breast and belly exhibit distinct feather edging like the pattern of a scaled quail.

Gambel quail and, though a little heavier on the average, looks almost exactly like it. The only striking difference is that the valley quail's breast and belly are buff or whitish with dark, distinct feather edging like the scaled pattern on a scaled quail. On the male, the whitish or buff lower breast is strongly tinged with chestnut at the center. The female, like the Gambel hen, has a drab facial pattern with no distinct striping or black throat patch.

Sometimes a chukar hunter puts up valley quail (or mountain quail, for that matter) on canyon rims near grainfields, but the valley birds generally prefer brushy stream banks, oak stands patching foothills and valleys, sage, brushpiles, riverbottom tangles, vineyards, weedy fields, and grasslands. In California, where nearly a million valley quail are harvested annually, mixed oak/grassland habitat seems to be especially productive. Another excellent bet is any edge cover where agricultural fields are bordered by streams, irrigation ditches, or brush.

These birds don't feed in dense woods or chaparral but in fairly open places, usually near water. They like the seeds of filaree, mullein, barley, clover, lupine, sage, deervetch, wild oats, rye, lotus, clover, thistle, pigweed, and bluegrass. Unlike most quail species, they roost off the ground, in thickets of low trees or tall shrubs.

Cast a dog into a food patch or the escape cover of shrubs and brush, and he'll often put birds up out of range—but the scattered singles will hold tighter. In fact, substantial numbers of experienced hunters have the confidence to use skeet or improved-cylinder chokes, the sort of boring associated with bobwhite guns and close shots. Without a dog, driving often works but the shots are mostly longer. Some hunters imitate the rallying calls of the scattered singles—a triple note sometimes described as *you-go-away* or *Chi-ca-go*. Maybe the effort will elicit responses, but the essential tactic is to follow the calls you hear and walk in fast with your gun at high port, ready to mount and shoot.

A cock valley quail perches on a fencepost. All quail and partridges are seed eaters that like to visit weedy fields. In some regions, a hunter combing the habitat near grainfields can't be certain whether he's most likely to put up valley quail, mountain quail, or chukars.

GUNS AND LOADS

For all Southwestern and Far Western quail, a 12- or 20-gauge gun cannot be improved upon, but there are strong differences of opinion about choke. Early in the season (before the birds have learned to stay far ahead of dogs and hunters) and for any situation where relatively close rises may be expected, some hunters prefer an improved-cylinder choke. Others, expecting fairly long shots, favor an improved-modified boring.

For someone limited to a single constriction, modified is the obviously best all-around compromise, but you're better prepared if your gun takes screw-in chokes or has a variable choking device so that you can switch from time to time in the course of a single hunt. Best of all, I firmly believe, is a double-barreled gun with 26- to 28-inch barrels bored modified and full, and with a selective trigger so you can instantly choose whichever barrel is more appropriate in any situation.

For this kind of hunting, the No. 8 shot that I love to use for bobwhites strikes me as just a trifle too small. I therefore have an equally firm belief in the efficacy of No. 7½ shot in high-brass loads for all Western quail hunting.

9

Ruffed Grouse and Woodcock: the Odd Couple

A great many hunters in the East and Midwest regard the ruffed grouse and woodcock as the noblest of all game birds. Ask a hunter what he means by "noble" and he's likely to reply that the honorific is reserved for game so elusive, so challenging to shoot, and so tasty as to be without peer, and that such birds bring out the best in both sportsman and gun dog. Well, grouse and woodcock are, indeed, tasty unless they've been subjected to some sort of idiocy, but so are quail, doves, chukars, and other upland species. Neither are grouse and woodcock in a class by themselves when it comes to bringing out the best—or the worst—in hunter and dog. Both are often but not always elusive, and for a hunter familiar with the woodcock's ways it's a less challenging target than quail or doves.

I submit that a great part of their charm lies in their habitat. No wingshooting is more relaxing and at the same time exhilarating, it seems to me, than an autumn walk along field edges, old orchards, overgrown meadows, logging roads and streamsides, shrubs, brush, and second growth—young "pioneer" trees such as aspen, alder, and birch—interspersed with ancient hardwoods and conifers used by grouse for roosting and cover. Another aspect of their charm is contained in the adage that, within generally good habitat, "grouse are where you find them" while woodcock are somewhat more predictable. Hence, woodcock can often rescue a day when grouse seem to be supernaturally elusive, and the hunter is apt to put up at least a bird or two—or sometimes many—under such circumstances. Both species (but especially grouse) are challenging not so much to a dog's instincts and nose as to his training, and an added exhilaration comes from watching a good dog work the coverts—"covert" rather than cover being the traditional term in connection with grouse and woodcock.

Without a dog, little methodology is involved; it's simply a matter of searching coverts where the birds are likely to be, proceeding slowly in a go-and-stop, go-and-stop sequence, and remaining very alert for surprise flushes. Of course, those surprise flushes are often just as nerve-shattering *with* a dog, and they would give any game bird an aura of magnificence—nobility, if you prefer. The twittering whistle of a woodcock's rise or the thundering whir of grouse wings can be unnerving when the bird has been invisible until that instant. The sound seems to come from no single direction, close though it is, and you're not sure which way to spin for a shot.

Add to that the challenge sometimes presented by the habitat itself as you labor up a steep slope through tangles of wild grape and laurel because you're sure the grouse are up there; or when you "bull" your way through an alder jungle that you probably shouldn't have entered since you can hardly get your gun up, can't swing it freely, and will get no more than a glimpse of the exiting woodcock.

I recall an autumn afternoon in West Virginia when I was hunting woodcock over a German shorthair and was also trying my best to be ready for grouse, the season being open on both. After missing a woodcock that corkscrewed out of tall brush edging a worm-rich meadow (my excuse was that the bird flew far to my left, at an awkward swinging angle), I followed the dog along a steep slope where the brush was equally high. The pointer, walking a lateral bench on the slope, abruptly turned upward, and so did I. He began to act "birdy," I began to tense, and then he pointed.

I heard a thunderous whir from the vicinity of a stunted tree next to a sizable blowdown directly above me on the steep slope, but saw nothing—perhaps the bird went out low over the ridge rather than downhill. Then, with equal suddenness and a far louder crackling sound, a whitetail doe bounded from the blowdown above me and leaped right over my head,

Taking a midmorning rest break, a setter poses for a tailgate portrait with the day's first bounty—a woodcock and a grouse. Throughout most of the Northeast and upper Midwest, woodcock are in residence and legally huntable when and after the grouse season opens.

one front foot grazing my cap as she sailed downhill. I fell over backward and rolled several yards before I regained my feet and my composure. The encounter wasn't *typical* of a day of grouse and woodcock hunting, but was the kind of experience that sometimes punctuates such days and renders them noble.

Despite the overlap of distribution and habitat, and the opportunity to hunt woodcock and grouse simultaneously in many regions, the differences between the two species are vital to understand, and the hunting seasons, like the habitat, overlap rather than coincide. It will therefore be helpful to discuss each bird in turn.

WOODCOCK

The plump, long-billed, stubby-bodied woodcock, with its rounded (hence, short-looking) wings, appears ill-equipped for sustained flight. Moreover, migrational flight isn't often witnessed because most of the traveling is done after twilight. It therefore seems almost miraculous that the species migrates 1,500 miles or more—or rather, many woodcock do. Some nest in the South, but the primary breeding range reaches through eastern Minnesota, Ontario, Wisconsin, Michigan, New Brunswick, Nova Scotia, and Maine. Small but important breeding populations also summer in Ohio and the East, from parts of New England down to West Virginia. They winter chiefly in the Deep South. Immense concentrations gather in Louisiana, while others winter in Florida and eastern Texas.

In years of relative abundance, the birds are hunted in nearly 40 states plus New Brunswick (which is famous for its woodcock), Nova Scotia, Prince Edward Island, Quebec, and Ontario. Annual harvests are often greatest in such states as Michigan, Wisconsin, New York, New Jersey, and Louisiana. The migration is a long chain of short flights interrupted by feeding and resting stops. A frost that hardens the ground against probing for earthworms will prod the birds onward from each stop. Thousands of them gather in the area around Cape May, New Jersey, gathering strength and perhaps awaiting favorable winds for the long crossing over Delaware Bay. Several hundred may congregate for a few days in some little bushy spot behind a Cape May beach where the habitat looks too poor to sustain the birds—and then one morning all are gone.

The hunting seasons are set within federal guidelines (as with all migratory game birds) to coincide with the presence of "flight birds" arriving from the North as well as "natives" that have spent the summer in a given region. In New Brunswick, the season usually and traditionally begins in mid-September, a couple of weeks later in the Lake States and upper New England, and mid- to late October in New Jersey. It opens in Louisiana in early December when the largest gatherings start to arrive, and has generally ended in early February, with the onset of northward migration.

Woodcock need moist, almost boggy uplands, often dominated by such vegetation as alder and birch, with enough brush for ground-roosting and escape cover but open enough for two crucial purposes: probing for the earthworms that are a dietary mainstay and taking off almost vertically to escape danger.

For several decades the birds have suffered a gradual decline, and a steeper decline during the last decade. One factor has been urbanization—and suburbanization. Like several upland species, woodcock have been hurt by habitat reduction. At present, a number of states (notably Maine and Pennsylvania) are conducting habitat-improvement programs. In addition to the management of state-owned lands, assistance and guidance are provided to private landowners and lumber companies for management that will benefit woodcock and wildlife in general.

Other factors have also contributed to the decline. At one time, woodcock were believed to be underharvested, and the seasons and bag limits were simply too liberal. In addition, toxic substances such as DDT, mercury, PCBs, and so on were suspected—probably with good cause—of reducing nesting success. The presence and effects of avian parasites were also studied by dedicated biologists such as Sam Pursglove, who afterward went to work for the Ruffed Grouse Society (see Appendix III), an organization whose work benefits woodcock as well as grouse.

More recently, researchers have confirmed that woodcock populations have been reduced by an avian virus that afflicts domestic poultry and may have been transmitted to woodcock feeding in areas infected by domestic ducks. The virus causes loss of weight and strength, making the birds more vulnerable to cold weather and sometimes leading to starvation. At the time of this writing, researchers cannot say with certainty whether viral infection has reached epidemic proportions, but studies are being conducted to learn more about the disease and ultimately control or eradicate it. With attention focused on these problems, the outlook for woodcock at last seems bright again.

A close relative of the snipe and the European woodcock (but smaller than the European species), the American woodcock is a rotund, stub-tailed bird no more than 10 or 11 inches

Female woodcock (left) is usually larger than the male. Her bill is almost always at least 2¾ inches long, whereas a male's rarely measures over 2½ inches.

long if you include its long, narrow bill. The bill, by the way, is the most reliable means of distinguishing sex (which is impossible until a bird is in hand). A female's bill is almost always at least 2¾ inches long, while a male's seldom exceeds 2½ inches. Most males are also smaller in body. An average cock in early October weighs 5½ ounces or a trifle more, while a hen weighs seven ounces or more.

Both sexes are mottled brown, with a buffy head, a black line from bill to eye, a little black "ear" patch, and wide crossbars on the back of the skull and the nape. The breast is cinnamon, the underparts buff, and the back, rump, and scapulars are mottled and barred. The rounded tail has black and white tipping, and the primaries are slaty. When this bird hugs the ground amid brush or fallen leaves, it's nearly invisible. I've almost stepped on a woodcock that relied on silent stillness for escape. I saw it for only an instant before it finally leaped into the air. Having seen it on the ground, I was unable to shoot it. As one writer has aptly observed, a woodcock in flight is an aerial target; spied on the ground, it's a very fragile living creature, mysterious, fearful, defiant, desperate, and somehow commanding our forbearance.

It's also an amusing and unique bird, sometimes described as having the physique of a bumblebee and equipped with an upside-down brain. In its evolution from shorebird to upland earthworm borer, its legs have shortened, its oversized head has snugged into its shoulders with a consequent loss of neck, its eyes have shifted far back on the skull—with the socket shift forcing the brain rearward and down—and the sensitive bill has developed both a flexible hinge for grasping worms and sensitive nerve endings for detecting their underground vibrations and perhaps "tasting" their nearness.

It drills that bill into the earth right to the hilt. A sprinkling of small, round "bore holes" or "drill holes" in a limited area indicates a good covert (if the birds haven't departed southward

the previous night), as does "chalk"—the white spatters of liquid droppings, an inch or so across.

There's a certain look to the best woodcock areas, and experience will teach a hunter to recognize it. The earth is likely to be soft and fairly dark, and there are shrubs, young trees, and openings. The finest habitat provides foods to supplement worms—insects, seeds, and berries, especially sedge seeds and blackberries. Whether or not these are present, look for trees 10 to 20 feet high, close and more or less tangled (for escape and concealment cover) but with an ample amount of light ground cover to facilitate boring.

A study in Maine showed that during one season almost half of all flushes were from alder thickets. In a similar New Brunswick study, most birds were moved from alder, gray birch, and evergreens. A Louisiana study showed the birds there to be frequenting a variety of alluvial bottomlands and pine woods, while a Pennsylvania study showed them flushing most often from alder bottoms, and from crab apple and hawthorn on slopes.

Long ago I wrote something about those studies that still seems valid: "An experienced woodcock hunter reading of those locations will probably bet that the slope flushes occurred in cool weather. On hot days woodcock rest in deep shade, particularly under evergreens. On mild days they're most often in alders but may also be in overgrown pastures, boggy fields, old orchards where rotting apples have enriched the soil, and sometimes in uncut cornfields next to alder cover."

There's an old belief, almost unshakable, that woodcock feed only at night and are therefore flushed exclusively from hiding and resting coverts. The fact is, they also feed heavily at dawn, again at noon, and again at dusk. Many hunters, and especially those without dogs, plunge into the thickest alder covers and try to penetrate the central portions, figuring that they'll surprise woodcock deep in their hiding places and startle them into flight. They may be there, or almost anywhere in the vicinity, but most flushes occur near the edges of coverts and not in the middle. The birds are attracted to the combination of open places for feeding and the edges of escape woods. A hunter without a dog should proceed slowly and as quietly as possible on a zigzag course, stopping frequently. I've passed by many woodcock without ever seeing them when I was dogless—I know that for a fact—but I've also put up a good many.

A springer spaniel, or for that matter a cocker spaniel (originally named for its ability with English woodcock) will perform well if trained to work really close to the gun. So will a Labrador retriever. Most popular, however, are close-working setters, Brittany spaniels, and pointers (some English pointers but mostly German).

Wingshooters who are inexperienced with woodcock tend to miss as many birds as they hit until they realize they're trying to shoot too fast. In the fall, woodcock are generally silent while on the ground—though once in a great while you may hear a nasal buzzing, chirps, or little quacking notes—but they rise with a startling, twittering whistle, produced by air rushing through their fast-beating outer primary feathers. The natural reaction is to whirl in the direction of the sound and snap-shoot at the target, too often sending the pattern low or to one side.

Woodcock tend to flush suddenly but close, leaping up on a steep, erratic, sideward-veering course sometimes described as corkscrewing. But at the top of the rise there's almost always an instant—just an instant—when the bird seems to hang motionless before departing on a somewhat more level plane. It isn't a fast flyer; though capable of reaching 30 miles an hour, it typically moves at less than 20. Use the rise to track your target and get on it, then fire just as it seems to pause instantaneously at the top of the rise or—if you haven't tracked it quickly enough—after it levels off. Do that and you'll find these birds rel-atively easy to bring down when flushed in the open. Often, of course, you can barely swing your gun when you're among clustered saplings, but frustration is the salt of success.

RUFFED GROUSE

The coveted "drummer of the woods," the ruffed grouse, is the most widespread of nonmigratory native American game birds. It can be hunted from central Alaska eastward through the lower reaches of the Canadian territories and through all the provinces to the Atlantic Coast. Along the Pacific, it ranges down into northern California; and along the Eastern Seaboard, it's distributed as far south as Tennessee and upper Georgia. It's found in the forested Pacific mountains, the middle and upper Rockies, the forests of the Midwestern Lake States, the Appalachians, and the quilted New England landscape of woods and farmland.

There are at least 11 subspecies. Most familiar to Eastern and Midwestern hunters is the eastern ruffed grouse which is usually brownish, but the gray ruffed grouse is wider-ranging, occurring across Canada and down through the Rockies. In addition to these subspecies, there are so-called color phases within subspecies. Red-phase birds (reddish-brown) are most common at low elevations, in relatively dry regions, and in the southern part of the overall range, while the gray phase is bagged in higher, moister, and more northerly habitat where conifers outnumber deciduous trees and the plumage blends with a carpet of needles rather than brown leaves. Northern "silvertails" tend to be slightly larger than the red phase, but both can occur in a single brood.

In size, the average bird is midway between quail and pheasant: about 17 to 20 inches long, plump, and weighing about 1¼ pounds. It's a very handsome, wood-colored bird, mottled on the head and upper body with dark bars and darts, and with black-edged pale "eye spots" on

In the fall, ruffed grouse seldom vocalize, but sometimes the males perch on a fallen log or other slight elevation and drum—beating the air with their wings—just as they do in spring. A hunter can occasionally locate a bird by the ghostly sound.

the lower back and rump. The underparts are pale. A loose crest, more pronounced on males than females, curves back over the head, and a neck ruff (often blackish on the male) runs out to the sides and back around the head like an Elizabethan ruff. Over the eye is a narrow, inconspicuous comb of featherless skin, salmon-colored on most males, bluish-gray on most females. The wide tail varies from reddish-brown to gray and is crossed by six to eleven dark, narrow, pale-edged bars, a broader dark or black subterminal bar, and gray tipping.

A grouse may walk or fly with its tail held straight or fanned out. In the hand, one that can be fanned out to a full 180 degrees is most often a male's, but a surer indication is the subterminal bar. On females, it's nearly always broken by brown on the two central feathers, while the male's subterminal bar is uniform or nearly so. In life, the sexes are generally indistinguishable—and even if they weren't, no gunner would ordinarily have time to differentiate.

The recent evolution of the ruffed grouse can be clearly—and fascinatingly—seen in behavioral differences from one region to another. Next to a logging road in lower British

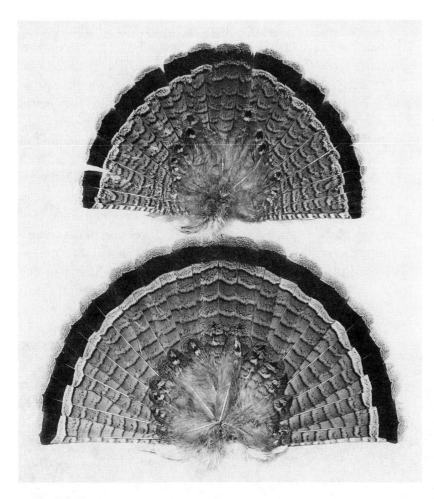

Once a "ruff" is in hand, a hunter can usually determine its sex. The female's tail (top) doesn't fan out quite as widely as the male's, and its black subterminal bar is nearly always broken by brown on the two central feathers.

Columbia, I once spotted a grouse perched on a low tree limb and I walked right up and tossed several pebbles at it to make it fly—which it did reluctantly. When colonists first settled the Eastern Seaboard, they referred to the ruffed grouse as fool grouse, fool partridge, or fool hen. The birds were easy to kill for food, but not worth hunting for sport. Grouse are still very trusting where they're not often hunted. But in the East, the Midwest, and small portions of the Far West, they're justly known as the wariest, most elusive, most quick-witted of game birds. The innocent, trusting ones were all killed a couple of hundred years ago and so, by human intervention into the ongoing process of natural selection, only the wary survived to pass on their genes.

By the late 19th century, several eminent hunting writers stated that ruffed grouse weren't worth a hunt exclusively for them and no other game—not because they were too easy but for precisely the opposite reason. Grouse by then were described as too difficult to find and flush, and then too difficult to shoot. Gunners of that era were accustomed to game birds that presented themselves in large numbers and either flushed close—like quail and woodcock—or flew over within easy gunshot—like doves and pigeons. Oddly, the attitude toward ruffed grouse changed within just a couple of decades, probably in part because hunters were learning to train their dogs for grouse work, and perhaps because grouse in the East and Midwest may have reached one of their cyclical population peaks.

Early in the season, a hunter may occasionally flush a grouse family that hasn't yet dispersed, a covey like that normally associated with quail and true partridges but not with grouse. Shortly afterward, however, the birds will disperse and seek solitude. Thus it's typical to flush only one bird at a time or sometimes two feeding or roosting near each other, but seldom more. In some years, grouse are hard to find for another reason. Many birds and mammals are subject, like lemmings, to population cycles, but in the regions we hunt, these fluctuations are probably most pronounced among ruffed grouse and varying hares. Hunters planning to visit distant states should inquire in advance about abundance, because cyclical timing varies considerably with locale.

In most regions, the second or third year of each decade brings fine hunting, and by the seventh year it's relatively poor. This generalization has significant exceptions, however, because in some places the grouse cycle spans only seven years, in others up to eleven. The ten-year peaks are most widespread, all the same, and are followed by two or three years of decline, then three or four years of recovery and several years of excellent hunting. Scientists believe the cycles are caused by a combination of climatic cycles, plant succession, and competition or crowding.

Northern coverts exhibit the most pronounced cycles. A tract of ideal habitat in one of the Great Lakes States may contain 300

Where aspens are abundant, their buds top the list of grouse foods, but these birds eat a wide assortment of seeds, berries, nuts, and leaves. This Michigan grouse is foraging on the forest floor.

grouse per square mile in a peak year, but only an eighth as many when the population has plummeted. A healthy density is probably one grouse per 15 or 20 acres.

In parts of the East and Midwest, grouse have benefitted from the spread and subsequent abandonment of small farms. Unlike some closely related species, they don't thrive as well in unbroken old forest as in a mix of brush, shrubs, openings, and relatively young second-growth trees such as aspen, alder, and birch—all providing food—situated close to the roosting cover of taller hardwoods and conifers. Farms, logging, and even fires have therefore benefitted them. In some areas, state agencies, private landowners, and organizations such as the Ruffed Grouse Society have improved the habitat by selective cutting (or burning) and planting to establish "grids," a patchwork of feeding and roosting places.

In the regions where I've done most of my hunting, we never overlook old or abandoned apple orchards, and we pay equal attention to aspens since aspen buds are the most important grouse food wherever they grow. But the hunting is seldom that simple. In the Midwest, clover patches are promising early in the season; in the East, wild-grape tangles, blueberries, cranberries, rhododendron thickets, or sumac will sometimes yield more rises than aspens. And grouse also feed on acorns, beechnuts, dogwood, serviceberry, bunchberry, willow, maple, hop hornbeam, thornapple, and laurel. The old folk myth that laurel—or any other poisonous plant, including poison ivy—toxifies grouse meat is disproved annually by the families of many thousands of hunters.

Most autumn foods are utilized through the winter, but late in the season hawthorn, greenbrier, and wintergreen also assume importance. In the Catskill country I used to hunt, preferred foods also include hazelnut, birch, and blackberry. No list can be complete; remember the adage that grouse are where you find them.

Remember, too, that if a covert holds grouse this year, it almost certainly will next year unless the population cycle is on its downward curve.

If my friends and I fail to move grouse in our favorite coverts, we explore all the likely-looking woods—particularly the edges—and when someone finally brings a bird down we open its crop. The contents may tell us where to hunt. With or without a dog, you can improve your chances by identifying the seeds, buds, leaves, fruits, or nuts.

As the season progresses, we hope for snow, which will be a boon to the birds as well as to our hunting. Freezing rain or severe cold and wind without snow can be lethal to ruffed grouse. These birds can walk on snow and (unless danger is perceived) would rather walk than fly. When not searching for food, they burrow under the snow, warmed by its insulation and hidden from predators. If you've marked a bird down on snow-covered ground but your dog fails to find it—or if you're hunting without a dog—you can often track a grouse, following its wide, three-pronged prints, each of them placed precisely in front of the last one.

The trail may lead you to some sheltering rhododendron or other protective tangle where you'll flush the bird. Where a grouse lands in the snow, you'll see a blurred indentation made by its body, with tracks leading away; where it takes off, you'll see wide wing marks in the snow, left by the first powerful wingbeats.

During hunting season, grouse seldom call, but the males occasionally drum, just as they do when proclaiming their territories during the spring breeding season. The sound won't be as loud, long, or common, but is worth recognizing. The male generally stands on some slight elevation such as a log, balanced by his fanned tail while his wings beat the air. The sound, produced by an implosion of air filling a vacuum created by each powerful stroke, has been likened to a ghostly tom-tom beat that quickens into a drumroll.

In winter, a hunter with or without a dog can sometimes track a grouse to where it's tunneled into concealing and insulating snow, or found shelter under low foliage—or taken off. These photos show grouse tracks and the wing marks where a bird took flight.

All the sights and sounds just described can help you locate grouse with or without a dog, but without one you'll walk by many an unseen bird and will be unprepared for surprise flushes. About the best you can do is to meander through the woods just as you do for woodcock, going and stopping, hoping for a rise you can see rather than just hear. The loud whir of a takeoff, from the ground or from a tree limb— all too often behind you, a limb you've just passed under—can make you jump.

One morning in Vermont while hunting whitetails, I seated myself on the edge of a steep little bluff, perhaps 20 feet above the forest floor and overlooking a well-used deer run. I sat there for perhaps 10 minutes in the perfect silence of the winter woods. Not even a chickadee or squirrel made the slightest sound, and I was beginning to nod when a thunderous whir erupted from

the eye-level branches of a fir rising from roots 20 feet below. It was, of course, a grouse, and it rocketed right over my head. Its loud take-off made me jump back from my sitting position. I lost my balance and slid all the way down the bluff. Fortunately, the rocks and ground below were blanketed with six inches of soft snow.

Upon takeoff and in flight, ruffed grouse have an uncanny ability to dodge around trees and through screening mazes of branches, giving you hardly more than an instant to shoot. Except when you put one up in relatively open woods, low brush, or a clearing, you must swing fast and often snap-shoot. This is why the birds are revered by wingshooters as the most challenging of upland game.

Sometimes, having missed a shot or failed to get one off, you can mark the bird down and follow it. It will often hold a bit tighter on the

Ruffed grouse quite often perch in trees and unnerve a hunter when they take off suddenly and loudly from a branch overhead—or worse still, overhead and to the rear.

next flush—evidently grouse tire quickly after the initial burst of erratic speed—and will make shorter subsequent flights. It's therefore worthwhile to follow up missed birds, and this is most easily accomplished (especially if you've failed to mark the bird down and know only the general direction it took) with the aid of a dog. What you want is the same sort of close-working dog used for woodcock, and this is certainly fortunate since both birds are hunted simultaneously until woodcock have departed southward or the season on them closes.

Grouse, however, don't permit as close an approach as woodcock before flushing. A springer spaniel, Lab, or other flushing dog can be used successfully if he works very close to the gun, but most grouse hunters today prefer a pointing dog that not only works close but has such a keen nose that he freezes on point before getting too close and "bumping" a grouse out of range.

There are woodcock hunters who seldom devote much effort to finding grouse—merely bagging one now and again as a bonus to woodcocking. And there are grouse hunters so obsessed with the challenge of their favorite species that they all but ignore the woodcock, or regard it as a distraction. Though woodcock are unquestionably easier for me to hit, I find those attitudes baffling. Each of these birds is challenging in its own way and each has its own unique charm. Moreover, the places most likely to hold woodcock are more predictable than the coverts that will yield grouse; this being the case, woodcock sometimes turn an unproductive day of grousing into a day of tingling action.

GUNS AND LOADS

I dislike anything more cumbersome than a very light, short-barreled gun in grouse and woodcock coverts. A heavy gun can be wearying to carry for a full day in the woods. More important, a light, short, well-balanced gun is faster to swing, and its swing is less likely to be impeded by brush, saplings, or branches. Any gauge from 12 to 28 will serve, but—like most hunters—I regard the 20 as ideal.

If I used a repeater, I'd want interchangeable screw-in chokes or a variable choking device, and the constriction I'd choose most often would be improved cylinder. What I do is use a double, bored improved and modified; the first barrel gives me a desirably wide pattern, the second a slightly tighter pattern for longer follow-up shots. Some hunters like a true cylinder for the first barrel, skeet choke for the second, and that's not a bad choice.

Since the pattern must be dense and uniform as well as wide, I use field loads of No. 8 or 9 shot when and where woodcock are the sole quarry. However, the grouse is a considerably larger bird, heavily feathered and harder to fell. Where both species are present and legal, I use No. 8 field loads. Some of my friends who carry doubles load the first barrel with No. 8 loads, the second with 7½ for the longer, follow-up shots. Where grouse alone are the quarry, 8 is a proper size for dense cover, 7½ for more open cover, and I personally think 7½ is helpful during the late part of the season when the leaves are down and birds may rise rather far out in relatively open places.

10

Timber Grouse and Ptarmigan

Closely related to the ruffed grouse are two crestless, ruffless "timber partridges"—the blue grouse and spruce grouse. Also related are the willow ptarmigan, rock ptarmigan, and whitetailed ptarmigan, all of which turn white in winter. These birds will never rival the ruffed grouse as game to challenge an upland hunter, but there are regions where the only upland game is one or more of these species, and under certain circumstances they can be very sporting quarry.

The blue grouse ranges from southeastern Alaska down the West Coast to northern California and the mountains of southern California. It's found in the lower Yukon, all of British Columbia, western Alberta, and southward through the Rockies all the way to New Mexico.

This is the largest of the timber grouse, and males are often more than 22 inches long. Both sexes have a long, squared, dusky or occasionally marbled tail with a pale gray terminal bar. The male is gray or slaty with brown and black mottling and wavy blue-gray lines, and a whitely streaked or mottled throat and shoulders. Over his eye is a pronounced yellow or yellow-orange comb, and on the sides of his neck are feather-less air sacs, conspicuous when inflated during courtship displays but hardly noticeable during the fall hunting season. On the female, the combs are absent and the air sacs unnoticeable; she's browner, darkly barred and mottled, and has yellowish brown bars down her breast. Slight variations abound, some darker, some lighter, since there are eight races of blue grouse.

The spruce grouse, far more widely distributed, is the smallest of the group. It ranges from Alaska down through coastal Washington and upper Oregon, and eastward though the Yukon, lower Northwest Territories, and all the provinces, as well as through the Rockies of Idaho, Montana, and Wyoming, the upper fringes of the Great Lakes states, and most of New England.

The male is mostly gray, with wavy black markings. He has a narrow scarlet comb, a black throat edged with white, and a black breast patch with a broken white border. The belly is blackish with tawny or white checkering. Both sexes have a brown or blackish tail with a broad orange-brown terminal band and narrow white tipping. The hen is brownish, flecked and

Largest of the timber grouse is the blue grouse, which is often close to two feet long from bill to tail tip but isn't hard to bring down. Both blues and spruce grouse rely chiefly on conifer needles for food and are most often found in high-country timber, where they haven't learned to be particularly wary of hunters.

barred with buff, ocher, and black. Her underparts are dull white, cross-barred with brown. In flight, she's easily mistaken for a ruffed grouse.

Both spruce grouse and blues rely chiefly on conifer needles for food, but also eat berries, buds, and deciduous leaves just as ruffed grouse do. They're most often found in high-country timber, and are a traditional source of meat for mountain hunters camped in the wilderness during the pursuit of deer and bigger game. Although occasionally killed with shotguns,

they're often potted with .22 handguns or rifles, packed along by big-game hunters to harvest small game for the camp. Often the .22 cartridges are loaded with very small bird shot, but many hunters pride themselves on using bullets and shooting for the head, which requires a fair degree of marksmanship.

These two species both tend to wander about in clear view on the forest floor or perch on low branches in clearly visible locations, flushing only reluctantly. The name "fool hen," once applied to ruffed grouse, is still applied to them. They can be bagged pretty regularly without any need for a dog, but some people do use canine assistance—as much for company, I think, as for practical reasons.

My friends Janey and Roland Cheek used to outfit and guide sportsmen on elk hunts, and Jane, as camp cook, provided occasional grouse and other treats. As she led several of us and a pack string of horses toward camp on the first day out, her dog trotted through the woods just a few yards to one side of the trail. I assumed she'd brought the dog along merely as camp mascot and companion until she raised her hand, signaling us to halt, and called back, "Hold on a minute." She dismounted, walked a few steps into the woods, and unholstered her .22 revolver. Only then did I realize the dog had

In the Far Northwest and the Rockies, blue grouse often forage and take the sun on open meadows. With or without dogs, they're fairly easy to find, but dogs are certainly an asset. In this photo the well-known sporting writer Jim Zumbo bags one over a Lab and a Brit.

flushed a grouse. I had neither seen nor heard it.

The dog ran to the base of a tree and stood there, looking up like a hound with a treed raccoon. I still couldn't see the bird, but Janey saw it. A moment later the dog delivered a feathery bundle to her hand and she stowed a blue grouse in one of her saddle bags, the first of several timber grouse she collected for a splendid dinner on our second evening in camp.

Early in the fall, a few hunters in the Rockies may trudge the fir-cloaked ridges and grassy meadows with shotgun in hand before the elk season opens. The rut has begun, and they're likely to hear the bugling of the bulls—especially young bulls yearning for harems and eager to outbluff one another though not to challenge an older, bigger harem master. If you hike the high country at this time, you may even encounter an aggressive elk, in which case there's wisdom in shouting and waving your arms, making it very clear that you're not an elk. Since there's also the possibility of encountering a bear, you don't try to move silently. On the contrary, you talk and make noise, announcing your presence in order to give any bear plenty of time to avoid you. The last thing you want is a surprise meeting.

All you do want is the solitude, the humbling magnificence of the wilderness. Perhaps you'll find grouse tracks crossing a little patch of snow; perhaps you'll flush one and get a shot; perhaps you'll see one perched on a limb, reluctant to leave, and you'll toss a pebble or twig to make it fly, hoping you can then get your gun up in time. Even if you don't, the sights and sounds and smells are worth the climb.

PTARMIGAN

Ptarmigan in some regions can be more sporting in the traditional sense. All three American species are small, plump grouse—extremely tasty, by the way—that turn white in winter and have fully feathered legs, adaptations to high elevations and high latitudes. White-tailed ptarmigan have a relatively limited range, but willow and rock ptarmigan are circumpolar in distribution; in fact, the renowned Scottish red grouse is a subspecies of willow ptarmigan, though few sportsmen here or in Scotland are aware of it.

On this continent, seven subspecies of willow ptarmigan range from northern Alaska down into central British Columbia and across all of Canada, plus Greenland, Baffin, and the smaller arctic islands. Eleven subspecies of rock ptarmigan occupy the same general range but aren't found quite as far south except along the Pacific Coast. Five subspecies of whitetailed ptarmigan range primarily from central Alaska down through the western Yukon and British Columbia to Vancouver Island, and there are scattered populations in the Rockies from Alberta down to New Mexico.

Below the Canadian border, only Colorado has a ptarmigan season, usually in September, and the hunting there can be described as fair even though whitetails thrive only on alpine tundra. The last time I checked, the Colorado harvest was a little under 5,000 birds, in contrast to the 30,000 rock and willow ptarmigan that may be bagged yearly in the Northwest Territories and the 50,000 that may be bagged in Newfoundland.

Ptarmigan males are slightly larger than females. A cock willow ptarmigan may be up to 17 inches long, with a weight of 20 to 24 ounces. His eye is browed with a red comb, his primary and secondary feathers remain white all year, and his white-tipped tail remains mostly dark brown with white central feathers. In winter, however, very long, white upper tail coverts hide the brown. In summer, the rest of his plumage is predominantly chestnut or rusty brown with dark barring and paler underparts. The female is combless and her summer plumage is heavily barred with dark brown and ocher. Both sexes begin to molt in early autumn,

Willow ptarmigan range from Alaska and British Columbia eastward across all of Canada.

and soon look as if flecked with snow, but the male's back remains brownly barred longer than the female's. By the time both sexes are winter-white, their feet are covered with coarse, hairy feathers that help support them on snow.

The rock ptarmigan is slightly smaller and has a blackish tail throughout the year. In summer, the scarlet-combed male is browner—less rusty—than a willow ptarmigan and has thin brownish black markings rather than bars. The female is lighter and more coarsely barred. By autumn, a cock is turning ash-gray, while a hen is browner, with sprinklings of white. After they've turned all white, a black streak can be seen on the male's face from the bill through the eye, but the female sometimes has a completely white head and is hard to tell from a willow ptarmigan,

although she has a smaller, blacker bill.

The whitetail is the smallest of the three; a male seldom exceeds 13½ inches in length or 12 ounces in weight. He's brownish in summer, barred, vermiculated, and mottled with black, buff, and white; his rump is tawny or yellowish brown, his underparts white. The female, more yellowish and spotty, is the only hen ptarmigan with a comb, but it's smaller than the male's and not as bright red—and even his comb is inconspicuous. Throughout the year, both sexes have white tails and wings. In autumn, the birds are pale cinnamon on their upperparts, spotted and lined with brownish black, and speckled white on the breast. By winter, they're pure white except for black bill, eyes, and claws.

The spattered brown and white autumn

This male rock ptarmigan—distinguished from the female by the black streak from his bill through his eye—is in winter plumage, all white except for a blackish tail. Note that the feet are completely feathered in winter, not for warmth but as an aid in walking on snow.

plumage or their white winter plumage camouflages ptarmigan so completely that they can roost invisibly in the open. On the slopes above the timber line, a hunter may hardly notice some patch of lichen-and-snow-specked rubble until it disintegrates into a dozen winged fragments suddenly billowing upward a few feet, cackling, wings beating the air, then sailing downhill in the typical manner of all high-country grouse when flushed in the open.

They don't rise explosively like ruffed grouse but take off about as fast as pigeons. Once in the air, however, they probably have a speed close to 40 miles an hour, making them worthy aerial targets. In country where they seldom see human beings other than a very few big-game hunters, they may behave as stupidly as northern spruce grouse, but where they've been hunted by shotgunners they often dodge low along the ground or flush far out, and they're the major upland game of the North.

Both willow and rock ptarmigan migrate in the fall to lower, somewhat more sheltered habitat, and all three species gather into loose flocks. Hens seem to seek more sheltered—forested—habitat than cocks, and in some regions the flocks become sexually segregated. It isn't unusual, therefore, to bag only cock birds during a day's outing.

Willow ptarmigan feed chiefly on willow buds and twigs, rock ptarmigan on dwarf birch buds and catkins, whitetails on alpine willow, heath, and mosses, and all of them add whatever buds, berries, and seeds they find in their habitat. Willow ptarmigan are bagged, as a rule, at relatively low elevations, on moist tundra with moderately tall shrubs, along the timberline, in openings amid the boreal forest, on muskegs and burns, and among streamside willows. Rock ptarmigan more often flush from shorter, sparser vegetation on higher rocky slopes about at the timber line or above. White-tailed ptarmigan are found in overlapping habitat that extends still higher, and they're often flushed from ridges and steep slopes well above timber line.

Some hunters pursue ptarmigan without a dog, or with a dog trained to stay at heel and then work only at retrieving birds. Where ptarmigan have been hunted lightly or not at all, it's possible to wander the slopes, now and then putting up birds within range. In willows or brush, pointing dogs perform quite well on ptarmigan; amid relatively thick ground cover, the birds hold fairly well, but on open terrain they usually run before they fly. A pointer working the tundra may therefore develop the habit of chasing birds unless well trained and under firm control. In recent years, springer spaniels and Labs have become rather popular for ptarmigan hunting. When the birds begin to covey in willow runs and birch thickets, a flushing dog can perform very well, working close to the gun and putting ptarmigan up within range. A dog of this sort is at a disadvantage on open tundra, but if he's well trained and bird-wise, he may be adept at circling around and flushing birds before they can run and then fly downhill out of range.

My friend Charley Waterman has hunted rock ptarmigan over a pointing dog—a Brittany spaniel—in Alaska, where the season opens in August. As expected, the birds flushed far out from rocky pockets and lee shelters above the timberline, but some were within range. After a first flight, moreover, they tended to hold until Charley was within easy range, and he bagged them about as efficiently as you'd expect to bag nervous chukars. There are stories of ptarmigan killed with long sticks by native Americans, but those were birds that had been exposed only to a few subsistence hunters.

Five subspecies of the whitetailed ptarmigan range principally from central Alaska down through the Western Yukon and British Columbia, and there are additional populations in the Rockies below the Canadian border. They aren't heavily hunted, but Colorado opens a season for them.

When pursued by wingshooters, they learn pretty quickly to employ the evasive tactics of swift game birds.

GUNS AND LOADS

With spruce grouse and blue grouse, the choice of a gun-and-load combination is hardly critical except from the standpoint of the hunter's comfort. Any light, short gun will do, with light loads of No. 7½ or smaller shot. As noted earlier, these birds are frequently killed for camp meat—shot as they perch on limbs rather than on the wing—and the only sport involved is a matter of marksmanship with rimfire .22 hand-gun or rifle, employing either a shot cartridge or standard bullet load.

Ptarmigan, however, are fast flyers that often demand long shots, and I would recommend a 12- or 20-gauge gun in combination with high-brass No. 6 or 7½ loads. On open tundra, I'd choose 6. A modified choke is probably best for most situations. In Canada, where upland regulations limit cartridge capacity to two shells, a light improved-cylinder and modified double may be ideal in the willows, but where the tundra's ground cover is low or almost absent, a better choke combination would be improved cylinder and improved modified, or even modified and full.

11

Grouse of the Prairies

Larger than their timber-dwelling relatives and very different in their habits are America's three unique species of prairie grouse: the prairie chicken (more properly but less commonly called pinnated grouse), the sage grouse, and the sharptailed grouse. Those are the common names, in addition to which each species is known by several regional nicknames. The prairie chicken is sometimes called prairie hen, yellowlegs, squaretail, or bar-breasted grouse; the sage grouse is also known as the sage hen, sage chicken, and even sage turkey; and the sharptailed grouse, or sharptail, is sometimes called pintail grouse or white-bellied grouse.

Few hunters realize that the extinct Eastern heath hen was a pinnated grouse, a bird overexploited along with its habitat for 200 years and finally obliterated during the first quarter of this century. Three subspecies remain: Attwater's prairie chicken, which is rare, limited to the Texas coast, and fully protected; the lesser prairie chicken of the lower plains; and the greater prairie chicken of the upper plains. The lesser averages perhaps 15 or 16 inches long, while the greater may be almost 19 inches long and easily weigh two pounds.

The range and numbers of prairie chickens were severely reduced by the pasturing and plowing of grasslands, developments less detrimental to sharptails and (in some regions) sage grouse. The prolonged droughts of the 1920s and '30s inflicted a further decline, but modern wildlife management has done much to rebuild the populations. The birds are sufficiently abundant and blessed with enough good habitat to permit hunting in six states. In huntable numbers, the greater prairie chicken inhabits the taller grasses of lower South Dakota, Nebraska's Sandhills region, eastern Kansas, and northeastern Oklahoma. The lesser occupies the arid short-grass prairies of southwestern Kansas, the Oklahoma panhandle, northwestern Texas, and eastern New Mexico, but is not sufficiently abundant in Kansas for a season to be opened. Paradoxically, Kansas generally has the best chicken hunting—for greaters only, in the eastern part of the state in November. The hunting is usually good, too, in the other states listed, and South Dakota generally has a very long season. Wildlife-management programs in several other states maintain "chicken" populations, but at present cannot support open seasons on the birds. Colorado, for

The prairie chicken, or pinnated grouse, is a strikingly barred species, varying in length from about 15 (lesser prairie chicken) to almost 19 inches (greater). The air sacs on the male's neck are hardly noticeable in fall but impressive when he inflates them, raises his pinnae (stiff neck quills), and bows and struts during the breeding season.

example, manages them as non-game because the habitat is limited by aridity.

Both subspecies of prairie chickens are yellowish brown or buffy brown, with heavy barring of deep brown and black on the body and scapulars. The underparts are paler but also darkly barred. The blunt tail and primaries are deep brown, but the wings usually have white spots on the outer feathers, and the tail usually has some narrow white tipping. The yellow legs are sparsely covered with pale feathering.

On the sides of the neck are long, stiff, dark quills, or *pinnae* (from which the name pinnated grouse is derived), and these are much more pronounced on the roosters than on the hens. When lowered, they cover a bare orange patch on each side of the neck, but they're lifted above the rooster's head like horns when he puffs out his air sacs as he attracts hens and proclaims his bit of territory on the spring "dancing ground," or *lek*. The sacs inflate to the size of large lemons. Both sexes have a slight crest, and

the rooster also has a pronounced orange comb over the eye.

Sharptails include a half-dozen subspecies. Those in the northern part of the range tend (with exceptions) to be paler than the others, and some are a bit more migratory than those to the south. These birds range from Alaska all the way across Canada to Quebec and from eastern Washington to northern Michigan. The prairies of eastern Alberta and western Saskatchewan provide superb sharptail hunting, and below the Canadian border the birds are hunted in all or parts of many states from Washington to upper Michigan and as far south as upper Colorado. Whereas prairie chickens require vast tracts of grassy prairie—even though they feed heavily in cultivated grainfields—sharptailed grouse are more adaptable to changes in food and cover.

Generations ago, when the wagons of market gunners plied the prairies, the horses flushed birds enough—in some regions including two or all three species of prairie grouse—to fill a buckboard by sundown. Such numbers will never be seen again, and in some years the birds exhibit cyclic declines, but in good habitat they breed prolifically enough to offset attrition and natural calamities. At present, sharptailed grouse remain abundant on the north-central plains, and future prospects are bright.

A sharptailed grouse is about as heavy as a greater prairie chicken and has a typical length of about 16½ to 18½ inches. Its upperparts are tan or buffy flecked with darker brown and black, and the wings are brown with conspicu-ous white spotting. The breast is paler than the prairie chicken's, and it fades to white on the belly, marked with dark lateral rows of chevrons. The tapered tail is white except for two long, dark, spiky feathers. Both sexes have a slight crest and feathered legs. The rooster has a yellow or orange comb and on each side of the neck, an air sack whose color ranges from orange to pink or pale violet. As with the other two species of prairie grouse, the sacs are hardly noticeable when not inflated.

Two subspecies of sage grouse, much alike in appearance and behavior, range from central

These male sharptail grouse are assembling on their lek, or breeding ground, where they dance and occasionally battle in spring as they vie with one another to attract females. Both sharptails and prairie chickens will return to the area of their leks again in early fall to assert their territorial rights.

The sage grouse is an exceptionally large prairie species, with hens weighing up to four pounds and roosters averaging about six. For these birds the author prefers high-brass No. 6 loads in 12 gauge, but a magnum 20 will also serve well.

Washington down into California and eastward across the lower portions of the Prairie Provinces and through the plains states, as far south as parts of Nevada, Utah, and Colorado. In typical years, 10 states have open seasons. Like the pronghorn antelope, the sage grouse has been severely threatened in some areas where cattle dominate the range but—again like the pronghorn—it has been the beneficiary of good modern management and is thriving in many regions.

Traditionally, the sage grouse provides the year's first upland shooting in the West, with seasons opening at the end of August in some states. In typical years, the season may be open in some states for only a week or so in late September or early October but may last much longer elsewhere—notably Montana, which has excellent hunting in the eastern part of the state. There the season on sharptail grouse is also long. A Mon-

tana hunter can scout water holes for sage grouse and on the same day walk the brushy coulees for sharptails—just as a South Dakota hunter can go out for prairie chickens and sharptails on the same day, conducting a classic morning stand-shoot for chickens as they arrive over a grainfield, and later walking up sharptails in wheat or corn or working a couple of dogs through scattered woods on the grasslands.

The sage grouse is the largest of the prairie species—larger, for that matter, than any of America's gallinaceous birds except the wild turkey. A hen may weigh as much as four pounds, and six is about average for a rooster. Females generally measure a little under two feet long, males about six inches longer. Both sexes are grayish brown, mottled on the upperparts, pale on the breast and flanks, with black bellies and feathered legs.

The male has a black chin and neck and a

white V across the throat. Under his white breast feathers are two large, frontal air sacs, varying from dull yellow or olive to reddish brown. Inconspicuous when relaxed, these air sacs are puffed up so enormously during courtship that they often rise above the head; behind the sacs and the white feathering are black, hairy feathers that rise up behind the head during sexual displays. The male also has a fairly pronounced yellow comb. Both male and female have long, pointed tails of brown, marbled and barred with white and black. The tail feathers taper to thin points, and the rooster fans them out to form a sunburst when he struts for hens.

Typically, all three prairie-grouse species fly no faster than about 30 miles an hour, and the big, heavy-bodied sage grouse is slowest, yet even a fat sage rooster can easily achieve a spurt of 40 miles an hour without a tail wind.

Hunters accustomed to bagging the speedier prairie chicken and sharptail frequently miss sage grouse by leading them too far with the first shot, then overcorrecting and firing behind them with a second shot.

When the first hard frosts come to the Great Plains, all three of these grouse make short migrations to areas of easy foraging and some slight protection from harsh weather, and soon they congregate in loose flocks, called "packs" by hunters in some regions. They also gather in large groups in the spring, collecting to breed on *leks*—relatively flat, open spaces, sometimes with considerable ground beaten almost bare of vegetation. This activity usually peaks in March or April and dwindles in May.

Each species has its unique courtship behavior, but in general the roosters' displays begin with rapid stamping and strutting—the inspiration for some of the traditional Plains Indian

Sage grouse on a dancing ground put on a spectacular performance. The air sacs of the competing males are distended enormously, and they fan out their tails to a spiky sunburst shape.

dances. This is followed by leaping, fluttering, fighting, tail-fanning and snapping, vibrating, and the ballooning of the air sacs, all accompanied by squawking, croaking, gobbling and, in the case of the prairie chicken, a three-note booming produced by the sudden expulsion of air from the sacs. The noise of a booming ground is sometimes heard a mile away.

Hunters as well as bird watchers like to scout for and observe the leks (from a respectful distance). This isn't difficult since the same sites may be used year after year. The displays are fascinating, and a knowledge of the locations becomes useful when the fall hunting seasons open. As a rule, birds will be found somewhere in the same locality. And although sage grouse (which form the largest gatherings) congregate on the leks only in the spring, sharptailed and pinnated roosters come there again in early fall, evidently to assert and establish territorial rights.

In some parts of the West, a good many people hold stubbornly to an old prejudice against eating sage grouse—and I've heard the term "sage buzzard" derisively used—but it's just as tasty as the other species. Its chief food is sage, but it also loves dandelions, clover, and alfalfa, and will eat a wide variety of grasses and other soft vegetation. Like other prairie grouse, this bird feeds actively from dawn through the early morning, then rests and seeks water during the warmest part of the day, and feeds again in late afternoon. Good places to hunt include sage flats and basins, especially wide basins cut by gullies; and around midday you should be sure to check any nearby pond, creek, or other water source. If you're hunting on a farm or ranch, always investigate any stock tanks, irrigation ditches, and the edges of alfalfa fields.

Sharptails come pretty regularly to grainfields—particularly corn, wheat, sorghum, and oats—and when they're not feeding on cultivated crops they're likely to be in tall vegetation that provides both cover and food. Poplar groves and rosebush thickets will hold them, as will other clumps of brush or trees, especially near prairie potholes and creeks. Like prairie chickens, they'll feed on such plants as knotweed, wild rose, clover, bristlegrass, blackberry, buttonweed, ragweed, bluestem, goldenrod, and flowering spurge. However, they seem to eat more buds than do prairie chickens after the early part of the hunting season, and they can be flushed from birch, oak, mountain ash, alder, willow, and chokecherry. Sharptails, like ruffed grouse, often roost high, so a hunter who habitually keeps his eye on the ground may be too slow to swing on a bird that goes out overhead.

Sharptails and prairie chickens often jump from the same brush or high grass, but prairie chickens differ in their early-morning feeding habits. These are the grouse most addicted to cultivated grainfields, a habit that provides gunners with a traditional and popular kind of

In parts of the Midwest, it's quite easy to hunt prairie chickens and sharptails on the same day in the same general habitat. A pointing dog is very useful in gunning for either species. This South Dakota hunter is holding a prairie chicken (left) and a sharptail.

hunting that sometimes amounts to a social affair reminiscent of Eastern dove shooting.

STAND-SHOOTS FOR PRAIRIE CHICKENS

Flocks of chickens develop local flyways—habitual flight routes to good feeding spots—and thus they provide a kind of pass-shooting roughly comparable to dove hunting or waterfowling. Often, there are enough birds flying a wide enough corridor to allow participation by a big party of hunters. Before the sun is up, the shooters space themselves out at intervals, crouching along fencerows, in ditches, or in shocks and clumps of vegetation, and they won't have long to wait. Join such a party and at first light you'll probably begin to see loose flocks coming in low—big, blocky, square-tailed birds, beating the air with cupped wings in a series of fast, powerful strokes followed by a long glide. (The glide of sage grouse is shorter since their size and weight require more wing-beating, but the same basic type of flight is shared by all prairie grouse.)

The manner of flight and the size of the birds make their speed deceptive. It's true that a prairie chicken is likely to be traveling at 30 miles an hour or less, but it may also come in over a field at 40 miles an hour. Many of us have to endure a few misses before we learn to judge varying speed and match the length of the lead to it.

Sorghum is the prairie chicken's favorite cultivated crop. Originally an African plant, it's closely related to corn but has smaller kernels which several species of birds seem to prefer. Wheat, corn, and other grains also attract chickens, but choosing a good field for a stand-shoot needn't be a matter of guesswork. By the time the season opens, flocks have been observed visiting some fields regularly and in substantial numbers. It's worthwhile to take a stand in such a field from dawn through early morning, and

then—perhaps after a relaxing coffee break—move into the tall grass.

GENERAL HUNTING METHODS

In brush or high grass, you can walk up chickens and other prairie grouse without a dog, though some of the flushes will be fairly far out. Big, late-fall flocks don't always hold well for a pointing dog, but the smaller groups sit pretty well for a pointer working through dense cover. Upon flushing, prairie grouse may fly clear out of sight, but it's just as likely that you'll be able to mark down a few singles. Although some of these singles may run after landing, a pointer can often pin one while you walk in and put it up.

Some hunters use flushing dogs for these Western grouse, but I prefer a pointer because the birds tend to rise so far ahead of any perceived intrusion. For this kind of shooting, I like a pointer that works close to the gun and has a keen enough nose to make him freeze before getting so close to the birds that they panic—in other words, the same kind of dog that performs so well on ruffed grouse, though in much different cover.

With sharptails and prairie chickens, you want to watch up ahead and off to the sides—looking into the middle distance, as you do when hunting deer in cover thin enough for good visibility. You'll often spot loose packs or even an occasional single in brush or grass. And when hunting sharptails in thickets, don't forget to watch the branches as well as the ground. Sometimes it isn't too difficult for a dogless hunter to get within range, although the birds become progressively "hawkier" after they've been hunted for a few weeks.

In making your approach—with or without a dog—bear in mind that these birds tend to rise into the wind. This direction of initial flight is most consistent with the big sage grouse, which can often be approached from a crosswind or downwind direction so that they won't stretch

When hunting any species of prairie grouse, it pays to know the locations of water holes. These sage grouse have gathered to drink and cool themselves at noon.

the range by the time they get well into the air. They rise rather ponderously before they level off and gain speed, but they can be difficult targets because they tend to fly higher than other grouse. Since a pack usually takes off in a ragged, almost hesitant manner, a few birds at a time, you can sometimes rush forward and get a shot or two at late-flushing birds.

Another method is for a hunting party to form a wide line and drive birds through the ground cover, while a second line of standers waits to take birds that flush too far ahead of the drivers. I've seen this work well with sage grouse, and I've been told it's fairly effective with other prairie grouse.

I like to carry a binocular and scan the country from high spots. While this is especially rewarding with sage grouse, in some areas the cover is thin enough to reveal the other species of prairie grouse at a considerable distance. There are times when loose flocks speckle a whole mile of flat country. Occasionally, you can actually stalk your birds. This, too, works best with sage grouse, which aren't as alert as sharptails or prairie chickens. They do, however,

have good vision and hearing, and may flush too far out if they see movement or hear the scratch of brush against your pants.

Utilizing sign is also most effective with sage grouse, I guess because the ground cover tends to be so sparse in sage country. It pays to search around water holes for mazes of tracks and heaps of mottled droppings. This type of scat weathers slowly, so you can't be certain how recently the birds used the site. However, if you find dark, soft blobs of droppings you can bet the area is currently being used. With or without a dog, you can then walk the vicinity and try to put birds up. My choice, however, would be to wait right there for the grouse to fly in again or feed their way back toward me.

GUNS AND LOADS

Many Western hunters use full-choked 12-gauge duck guns for prairie grouse (and for pheasants, too). Since these are bigger birds than ruffed grouse and many of the shots may be relatively long, the logic of the choice is valid. Personally, however, I think the ideal firearm for plains-country grouse is a double, choked modified and full or modified and improved-modified. Some of today's loads tend to pattern very tightly and thus require no more choke than improved-modified. It pays to test your gun for patterning characteristics with several loads.

I don't believe the 12 gauge is the only choice, but if I use a 20 I want it to be chambered for three-inch magnum shells. The consensus is that high-brass No. 6 loads are best for this kind of hunting, and I agree.

Of course, the very best loads can't compensate for careless shooting. You need to judge distance, bird size, and speed in order to master the length of your lead. In this connection, I have a shooting tip that may prove useful: while prairie-grouse roosters fly fairly straight, the hens twist and dip a bit—but not enough to escape a good pattern. Don't let the slightly erratic flight fool you into wavering or jerking your swing. Ignore the twisting and maintain a smooth swing, giving the low flyers just a little lead and the high ones considerably more.

12

The Americanized Partridges

Introductions of wildlife from foreign lands have sometimes failed, and the successes have often been controversial at best—and at worst damaging to native American wildlife. Barbary sheep brought to the Southwest at first seemed to fill a vacant ecological niche but later proved to be detrimental to native game such as the desert bighorn. The most notorious avian example is the starling, whose aggressive feeding and nesting habits have devastated many songbirds. But there have also been a few unqualified successes. Among our game birds, the most famous is, of course, the pheasant.

Two others have been spectacularly successful although, like the pheasant, they resisted early efforts to establish them in the wild. Their American range is more limited than the ringneck's, owing to their needs with regard to climate and terrain, but hundreds of thousands of wingshooters take delight in hunting them, sometimes making long trips to locales of abundance. Both are true partridges—the chukar and the Hungarian, or gray, partridge.

Textbooks usually refer to the latter bird as the gray partridge since the designation Hun-

garian (or "Hun," as most of us affectionately call it) is not quite accurate. The species acquired its most popular name early in this century because most of the original importations came from the plains of Hungary. The name chukar, on the other hand, is accurately descriptive. It's derived from a Hindi word (in turn derived from an ancient Sanskrit term) describing a cackling call the birds use to keep a covey together: *chuh! chuh! chuh! ch-ka, chu-karr, chu-kar-a!*

Hunting for one or both of these partridges is available on shooting preserves in many parts of the country—and they're worthy of the hunter's attention under preserve conditions—but from the wingshooter's standpoint they achieve their greatest glory in the wild. Each merits a discussion of its characteristics.

CHUKAR PARTRIDGE

Also known as the red-legged partridge, red-leg, Indian hill partridge, or rock partridge, the chukar is native (in the form of one subspecies or another) to southern Europe and large por-

The chukar's name is derived from a Hindi word denoting the sound of the cackle it utters to maintain contact with the covey.

tions of Asia. During the last 60 years or so, most states and Canadian provinces have attempted to establish chukars, originally to supplement dwindling populations of native game birds. Until the 1950s, the majority of game departments considered the experiments a failure, but by then scientific field studies were gaining sophistication. Many of the birds had been released in seemingly rich habitat—lush, relatively flat farm country where so many other gallinaceous species thrive. But chukars can't survive heavy winter snows, and they need more arid, rocky, steep terrain.

As soon as game departments realized their mistake and began stocking chukars in ecosys-tems that looked less hospitable, the birds pros-pered. In their preferred canyonland domain, they've never become detrimental competitors with native birds, yet their range has spread considerably. A population will plummet after an excessively dry breeding system, but unless there's a severe prolonged drought, they regain their numbers in ensuing years. Hawaii, which has plenty of steep, rocky, sufficiently dry habi-tat, added chukars to the game list in 1952, seven years before becoming a state.

Today, chukars are legal (and abundant) game in nearly a dozen states and in British Columbia. They range from the south-central part of that province down to Baja California and eastward through the Great Basin and the Rockies to the edges of the plains. In addition, they're stocked on preserves from coast to coast.

Sporting literature sometimes incorrectly lists America's chukars as the European subspecies so popular among the hunters of Spain—a bird whose call is a ringing whistle. The clucking, cackling chukars on this continent are descendants of Himalayan stock supplemented by a smaller number of Turkish birds. This subspecies averages 13 to 15 inches in length and 15 to 20 ounces in weight—slightly smaller than a ruffed grouse, although I've shot several larger ones on preserves.

It's a very beautiful bird, with a blue-gray upper body, wings, and breast, a wash of brownish gray or olive on the crown and back, and chestnut brown on the outer tail feathers. The lower face and throat are whitish. Beginning just above the red bill is a contrasting black band that crosses the face and the red-ringed eyes, extending almost to the rear of the head and then curving down along the sides of the neck and over the upper breast. The breast below this black necklace is blue-gray, fading to tan or buff on the belly. The pale buff flanks are sharply marked with eight to thirteen vertical black and chestnut bars. The legs, like the bill and eye ring, are red.

It's very difficult to tell male from female, but if you're curious you can sometimes determine the sex of a bird in the hand. The legs of older

Chukar hunting is popularly—and correctly—associated with canyon climbing, but the birds regularly visit cropfields close to their steep escape terrain, presenting an opportunity to hunt the flats in some regions. Here the dogs have sniffed out a single and the bird has risen well within gun range.

This band of chukars has come to a stubble field to feed on rich gleanings. Where cultivated fields lie fairly close to steep cover, chukar hunting is often excellent, but the birds feel vulnerable as they peck about on flat, open ground and will often flush wild.

males usually have slight, blunted spurs, and the distance from the tip of a male's third primary feather to the wing's "wrist" joint is apt to be more than 5¼ inches.

Chukars on shooting preserves don't usually behave as they do in the wild. On a preserve, you're likely to be hunting single birds rather than coveys, and the typical terrain is likely to be flatter and less rocky than wild habitat, with considerably more high brush. As a result, preserve chukars in most regions will hold for a pointing or flushing dog about as cooperatively

as a pheasant will, although—also like a pheasant—these birds will often run before they fly. In such a setting, chukars provide excellent practice for dog and wingshooter, and they're extremely tasty.

In the wild, at least one-quarter of any stretch of really good habitat almost always consists of talus slopes, rock outcroppings, bluffs, or cliffs, and the land will probably be generously sprinkled with sage and cheatgrass, preferably mixed with bunchgrass, ricegrass, or bluegrass. Any additional herbs or weedy forbs—Russian thistle, filaree, or fiddleneck, for instance—will add to the attraction for chukars; and although the birds don't need agricultural crops, any fields of wheat or alfalfa close to escape canyons will make the locale ideal. Sagebrush needn't be dominant if there are other shrubby plants such as rabbitbrush, saltbush, or greasewood. Chukars feed on grasses, forbs, and grains, use brush for nesting cover and shade, and use slopes and rocky shelters for escape and roosting. Some of those slopes should be moderately steep and at least 200 feet high if they're to hold many birds, and since most coveys are found within about half a mile from water sources, there must be a few brushy creeks or other watering places in the area.

The birds roost on the steep slopes, sometimes under shrubs or low trees. In cool weather, a covey often roosts in a circular formation, facing out, like bobwhites. In windy or colder weather, many will roost in rocky niches or hollows, but they'll still try to remain in a loose covey. Around water holes, coveys sometimes come together to form large groups. Elsewhere, the number in a covey can vary from perhaps half a dozen birds to more than 40, but the average is about 20.

It's wise to begin hunting in the early morning by exploring south-facing slopes—warm roosting sites. Feeding activity peaks around midmorning, and on a cool day a covey will move about and forage through most of the afternoon, so there's a good chance of flushing birds in any grassy area. Around midday in hot weather, however, you should check shady draws, watering places, and cool dusting spots where you'll probably find tracks, droppings, feathers, and little hollows scraped in the soil. Grassy hollows high on canyon slopes are feeding places worth checking again as the day cools. Late in the afternoon, chukars usually go to water as they feed their way toward the steep slopes and move up to roosting sites.

When alarmed, these partridges almost always run uphill, and when (or if) they finally take wing, they usually fly downhill. You'll never get within range by chasing them uphill—they've been clocked scampering up slopes at 17 miles an hour—so the usual procedure is to climb to a rim and then hunt downhill, blocking their way. Since they don't snuggle down into concealing grass the way bobwhites do, coveys are sometimes seen rather far off on the slopes, in which event you can circle above them.

Quite a few hunters insist that a dog is no help except perhaps for retrieving, so they locate chukars by sight and sound alone. A feeding covey can occasionally be heard clucking—*took, tu-tu-tu-tu*. And the aforementioned cackling is heard when a covey begins to spread out while feeding and again when scattered singles are regrouping. They'll respond to an imitation of these sounds, and some hunters can mimic the call vocally. It's easier with the commercial calls sold in chukar country, but with or without a mechanical aid you'd better listen to the real thing a few times before trying to imitate it.

Dogless hunters glass the slopes, hunt streambeds, drive along back roads to scout, listen for coveys, and sometimes use calls to elicit a pinpointing response. With that done, the problem is to get close enough. One way—for the young and very fit—is to sneak above the birds and run down at them to force-flush them. For the rest of us, a more practical way is to fire a shot over the covey. It isn't guaranteed, but gunfire very often gets them airborne. Scattered singles and doubles will then hold tighter—relatively speaking. Even if you fail to mark them down, you can locate them by their rallying calls.

More and more hunters are using pointing dogs for this sport. (Partial though I am to springers, I don't think flushing dogs can handle chukars properly.) A good tactic is to keep the dog at heel while you climb to the crest of a slope and then use a binocular to scan the lower ground for little gray shadows moving about in

In the states at the western end of the Great Basin, much of the hunting is on terrain like this Oregon canyon. Since chukars usually run uphill from intruders—and then fly downhill when flushed—the recommended maneuver is to climb to the rimrock and then hunt laterally and down.

the scrub. When you spot a covey, walk downhill toward the birds while you cast your dog off to one side—the idea being that the two of you form a wide obstacle that's harder for the birds to outflank, so they'll be less apt to run uphill on one side or the other. Of course, this is more effective with more than one dog and more than one gunner. Assuming you've headed off the birds with this maneuver, keep your eye on the dog. The moment he stiffens into a point, walk in fast to force the birds into the air before they can scurry past you in an end run. They won't rise high—perhaps no more than 10 or 12 feet before leveling off and swinging down-

hill. Even if you get your gun on one quickly, it may be streaking through the air at 35 miles an hour, and it will gain momentum, sometimes reaching almost 50 miles an hour. Certainly a fair test of wingshooting skill.

HUNGARIAN PARTRIDGE

In this country, the first releases of gray partridges, or Huns, took place in California and Washington shortly before 1900. Those introductions weren't very successful, yet subsequent stocking there and elsewhere during the next few decades succeeded beyond expectations, and in some regions the birds largely replaced native game diminished by the cutting of forests and the plowing or overgrazing of grasslands.

There are five subspecies distributed through most of Europe and three others distributed eastward all the way into Siberia. Although our early importations were from Hungary, America's present populations are derived from several geographic races. Having come from European and Asian plainsland—much of it tilled or grazed—they're adapted to life on open terrain that provides sufficient food and cover. This includes fertile flatlands and gently rolling prairies where grassy expanses are often interspersed with small-grain crops. In the Great Basin, they can subsist amid sage and bunch-

The male and female Hungarian partridge are very difficult to tell apart until they're in hand. In this photo, the male is at the rear. These birds are shaped like bobwhite quail but they're about twice as large.

grass near streams but tend to spread or move to the nearest wheat and hay.

North America has three distinct major ranges. The westernmost stretches from eastern Washington and Oregon down into northern California and across Idaho, northern Nevada, and northwestern Utah. The largest range is mid-continental, covering the central and lower portions of the Prairie Provinces, Montana, North Dakota, upper Wyoming, upper South Dakota, western Minnesota, and northwestern Iowa. The third range is the Great Lakes region, including parts of Wisconsin, Michigan, Indiana, Ohio, and lower Ontario. The eastern tip of this range extends into southernmost Quebec and upper New York and Vermont. Smaller populations occur in eastern New Brunswick, Nova Scotia, and Prince Edward Island.

As with many game birds, regions offering the best hunting may shift from year to year, but it's been excellent most frequently in Washington, Oregon, Idaho, Montana, Alberta, Saskatchewan, Ontario, and Wisconsin.

These are Christmas-card partridges, as round as bobwhites but twice as large. They average 12 or 13 inches in length, and you can estimate the weight at an ounce per inch. In flight, a gray partridge looks pastel brown, but its breast and belly are a finely vermiculated gray. A dark chestnut horseshoe runs across the breast and back along the flanks. The wings are brown, with white scapulars. The face is cinnamon, the crown buffy brown, and the back grayish brown or sometimes gray, mottled near the wings and streaked with buff on the sides. The squarish tail is rusty, barred and vermiculated.

You won't be able to distinguish sex when the birds fly, but the horseshoe marking is occasionally absent on a hen, or more often small and indistinct—or sometimes whitish rather than chestnut. Also, a cock's scapular feathers are yellowish brown with fine, wavy black lines, and they turn chestnut near the outside edges, whereas a hen's are blackish at the base, with light yellow crossbars, no chestnut, and vermiculation only on the outer parts. Many females also have a wide buff stripe along the wing feathers.

Huns are seed eaters. In some of the relatively dry parts of the West they subsist on a wide assortment of forb and weed seeds, but they'll eat cultivated grains wherever possible. On the Canadian plains and probably throughout much of their range, wheat, oats, and barley make up about 70 percent of their fall and winter diet. In Washington, wheat and alfalfa attract them, and in Michigan they feed heavily on corn. They pick grit on bare or relatively bare ground such as trails and back roads, and they roost in hayfields—alfalfa wherever available—and in brushy edge cover.

In windy weather (which makes them "hawky" and hard to approach, incidentally) they find shelter in draws, on lee hillsides, and sometimes on the lee side of farm buildings or other structures. They seem to be less dependent on water than most game birds, but must have some in the general area.

Very deep snow can diminish a population, but these birds can tolerate severe winters. They'll tunnel into foot-deep snow to feed and, like grouse, will burrow into it for insulation and concealment. They winter and then breed

Flat, open country like this is typical of Hungarian partridge habitat. When a hunter flushes a family covey, the birds try to stay together and fly in one general direction, as these Huns are doing. However, coveys composed of two families are common late in the season, and they'll usually split up. The gunner then tries to mark them down and hunt them separately.

in the same vicinity, and since there's no seasonal shift of habitat, hunters in partridge country soon learn where coveys—and succeeding generations of those coveys—feed and roost.

Early in the season, a covey is a family group consisting of one or both parents and about eight young of the year. Much larger coveys—18 or 20 birds—are sometimes flushed at or near the end of the season, and they consist of two families. This may be in preparation for mating, since hens seem to refuse parents or siblings as mates.

When you flush a two-family covey, the birds usually split into two groups which can be marked down and hunted separately.

Unlike most of America's covey birds, Huns tend to stay together when flushed, often flying 300 yards or more and coming down as a loose group. Some years ago in Ontario, I was hunting with a couple of friends and a local guide named John Ouderkirk when a dozen birds rose and wheeled right over us. We happened to bag the two in the lead of the group, and the others

To work Huns effectively, a pointing dog should be wide ranging with a keen nose that stops him far enough from a covey so that he won't "bump" the birds before the hunters can come up. On this Ontario pasture, the author (right) and his friend Pat Smith walk in over a careful point by a fine English setter.

scattered and came down right in the field where we stood. John explained that we'd killed the mates, and the rest of the covey—the young—were still used to following their parents. Deprived of leaders, they broke up and came down close. I've seen no scientific study to confirm this, but I've witnessed it again on subsequent hunts.

We were hunting over Danny, an English setter that had won 23 field trials, but one wet and very windy day when scenting conditions were close to hopeless, we left the dog in the car, walked the fields briskly, and managed to put up an occasional single, couple, or small covey within range. They didn't do any ground-running, but with each subsequent approach they flushed wider. When one covey finally disappeared over a hill and we failed to find them, John suggested returning to the field where we'd first flushed them. They often return after being prodded out of a roost site or choice feeding spot. Sure enough, they'd circled back and we took several.

Normally, this game is best pursued with a pointing dog that has learned to range wide, sometimes pointing coveys from the far side so the birds will feel pinned and won't fly too soon—or if they do fly they may come back in the direction of the hunters. The dog needs a keen nose that will enable him to lock on point at perhaps 20 yards. Huns in stubble won't wait to fly if a dog comes closer. Often they can see the hunters approach, and one day when the wind was making them nervous I watched them rise while we—and the dog—were at least 50 yards away.

They generally rise only 10 or 15 feet high and don't erupt from ground cover as explosively as bobwhites, but they can fly 30 miles an hour and now and then surge faster. You don't have to snap-shoot, but you do have to swing ahead of them quickly and smoothly. Like chukars, they can be difficult targets.

GUNS AND LOADS

Because shots are frequently long, many hunters use full-choked 12-gauge guns with No. 6 high-brass loads for both chukars and Huns. I'm not in complete agreement. For one thing, with today's tight-patterning ammunition I think a modified choke is more practical if you're using a repeater. And I think an even better choice is a double-barreled gun with improved-cylinder or modified boring in the first barrel and a full choke in the second. I also think a light 20-gauge gun chambered for three-inch magnums is just as efficient as a 12 for these partridges, and more fun to carry.

My old friend Charley Waterman told me about his long-ago chukar hunts (to which he used to be addicted) with a 20-gauge European double whose right barrel gave him improved cylinder for close birds while the left barrel gave him full choke for long shots. It had two triggers for instant choice, and that strikes me as perfect. I also agree with his use of No. 7½ shot, but there might be wisdom in using that size in the first barrel and going a size larger—No. 6—for long shots with the second barrel.

Many hunters do that for Huns as well, and it's a sensible compromise. Typically rising 15 or 20 yards from the muzzle and thus offering a first shot at 25 to 35 yards, followed by a second shot at 50 or more, the gray partridge is a candidate for No. 7½ on the rise and No. 6 for a second bird or after an initial miss. This partridge, too, can be hunted efficiently and comfortably with a 20-gauge magnum, and the choke logic that applies to the chukar applies equally to the Hun.

13

Doves and Pigeons

Four closely related species of doves and pigeons inhabit this continent, and from a hunter's viewpoint they have more in common than biological similarities. All of them present interesting problems to the wingshooter, all are commonly hunted without need of a dog to locate them (although a dog is extremely valuable for retrieving), and all are delicious.

The mourning dove is the one that attracts the most hunters and has the most fearsome reputation as a difficult target, yet the whitewinged dove of the Southwest seems to me to demand equal shooting skill. Since the bandtailed pigeon of the West and Southwest is extremely swift on the wing and tends to fly higher than doves or other pigeons, it certainly rivals the others in its demands on the shotgunner. Least demanding—not only because it's slower and less erratic in flight but also because it isn't hunted much except in areas where it becomes an agricultural pest—is the common pigeon, the same bird that accepts handouts in city parks but soon learns evasive tactics when gunners try to reduce its numbers around a farm.

The common pigeon, also known as the rock pigeon or (erroneously) rock dove because it

likes to roost and nest on rocky cliff ledges in rural areas—and building ledges in urban settings—is the only nonmigratory member of the quartet. Many states set no closed season or bag limit because a thinning of the pigeon population would benefit other wildlife as well as man. Because the other three are migratory, states comply with federal migratory-bird guidelines in setting seasons, shooting hours, and bag limits. A typical state in a typical year might permit 70 shooting days between early September and mid-January, usually in the form of a split season of either two or three segments with rest periods between them. The bag limit might be 12 daily in the East, 10 in the West, but shooting hours in Eastern states are generally limited—noon to sunset—while in the West shooting may commence half an hour before sunrise. The split seasons benefit hunters as well as the game, because doves and pigeons become extremely wary after a few weeks of gunning.

DOVE SHOOTING

The mourning dove (named for its cooing call, which strikes many people as mournful) is most

Hunted in a great many states, doves are considered to be among the most difficult aerial targets. They're relatively small, slim birds, and their flight is both swift and erratic.

abundant in the East and Southeast during the hunting season, but there's also a Western subspecies, and in a good year at least half of our states have ample seasons on these birds. In the Northeast, some states classify doves as songbirds and allow no shooting, while neighboring states classify them as game. In rural western New Jersey, where I live, doves are sufficiently overabundant to be pests, but to hunt them I have to drive a couple of miles and cross the Delaware River into Pennsylvania.

The closely related whitewinged dove breeds in Texas, New Mexico, Arizona, lower Nevada, and California (and a few are bagged as far east as Florida). Many of the flocks winter in South America. Whitewing populations fluctuate sharply, but are generally high enough to cause occasional crop damage.

A typical mourning dove measures about a foot from bill to the point of the long tail and has a wingspan of about twice that length. As it comes near in its often twisting, dipping flight, you can hear a whistling, produced by air rushing through the wings. When doves are flying high, en route to feeding or roosting destinations, their manner of flight is direct. Only when they come low enough to be within range do they swerve and dip, compounding the gunning problem presented by a small, slim body and deceptively long tail. Very often the leading edge of a shot pattern trails the bird's gray-brown body and sprinkles harmlessly through the tail feathers.

The whitewing is stockier than the mourning dove and is easily identified in flight by big white patches on the wing coverts, contrasting with the dark brownish-gray primaries and secondaries. It has a blunt tail, broadly tipped with white at the rear corners. It flies silently, without the mourning dove's soft whistle of air through the primary feathers, and it doesn't swerve and dip as much, but it's about equally fast. As with the mourning dove, some gunners wryly refer to a limit of whitewings as "a box of shells."

Where no grain crops lure the birds to the fields, doves of both species prosper on a wide variety of weeds and seeds—bristlegrass, dove-weed, ragweed, pokeweed, pigweed, crabgrass, and so on. But they dearly love browntop millet, sunflowers, barley, wheat, corn, cane, sorghum, rye, buckwheat, peanuts, and peas. It's illegal to sprinkle bait to attract doves, or intentionally reap grain in a manner that leaves excessive amounts in a field, yet it is legal to plant crops with the intention of attracting doves, a sometimes subtle distinction that has occasionally led to controversy—and conflicts between land owners and game departments. Someone who speaks of planting a "dove field" or "dove patch" is probably raising millet or sunflowers.

Doves feed diligently in the morning; rest, dust, and pick grit at midday; visit the fields again in mid-afternoon; go to water in late afternoon; and then fly to roosts, very often in trees fringing the nearest woods—or farther away if they've been pressed by gunners. There are three primary ways of hunting them.

Early in the season (or at the beginning of any segment of a split season) traditional dove shoots are a social affair, especially in the South, typified by substantial numbers of hunters gathering at big cropfields where they take up positions at safely wide intervals and await incoming doves. They stand or sit (many bring folding seats) where they won't be spotted prematurely by the birds—along hedgerows, in the shade of trees edging a field, or even in irrigation ditches. Some wear camouflage, while others rely on positioning themselves inconspicuously. I've seen local businessmen come out during lunch hour, wearing their office attire.

The second method is to walk doves up amid tall, standing crops or in brushy areas—preferably near but not too near the roosting trees. This is effective in late afternoon, but if you fire many shots close to a roost the birds will abandon it and find another location.

The third method is to wait in ambush at a water hole—pond, stream, cattle tank, or whatever, sometimes even a very large puddle—or at the edge of a weedy clearing.

Doves won't hold for a dog, so the only way to walk them up is to surprise them in high brush or crops, and this can be done with fair regularity during the early season. However, I strongly advocate the use of a dog for retrieving, regardless of which hunting method is employed. Without one, it can be exceedingly difficult to find a fallen dove in brush or grain crops, and there's no doubt that many are lost and wasted.

Decoys are often used around water holes and weedy clearings. Although commercial decoys are widely available and excellent, some people make their own out of just about anything from wood to papier-mâché and simply slap gray paint on them. Even the crude ones work well. I've had considerable success with only half a dozen—you don't need many, but a few more can't hurt. Where the ground is clear and open (say, on the bank of a water hole) you can set a couple down, but most should be propped, pinned, or hung conspicuously—on

Doves won't hold for a dog, but a retriever is extremely valuable for finding and fetching downed birds. Too many doves are lost—wasted—by hunters who dispense with canine assistance.

tree or shrub branches or on fence rails and wires. A friend of mine in Virginia has strung a long clothesline high and taut across a clearing and attached long cords to his decoys, which are weighted with fishing sinkers. He tosses each decoy up over the clothesline, pulls the cord to raise the decoy until it just about touches the line, then ties the cord to hold it in place. The rig doesn't look convincing to me, with the fake doves hanging just under the clothesline rather than perched on it, but the birds don't seem to perceive the difference. They're accustomed to seeing birds perched on telephone wires and power lines, and I suppose that's what this set-up looks like from above.

In the Southwest, decoys are used less frequently, but whitewings come enthusiastically to cattle tanks and other water holes, to crop fields, and to wild feeding spots known to the local hunters. In the states I've mentioned, dove hunting is generally excellent early in the season, and a little later there are big shoots below the Mexican border.

My own experience has been with mourning doves, and they've convinced me that their reputation as tricky targets is exaggerated by a single mistake gunners commonly make: trying to take birds before they fly close enough. I suspect this is particularly true at big field shoots where a friendly rivalry induces each hunter to rush

During the first few days of the season, it sometimes seems that no amount of shooting will long deter doves from visiting a field. Later on, decoys are an enormous help. These hunters are using molded commercial decoys supplemented by homemade cut-outs (note the decoy at far left on the fence wire).

his shots—before a bird veers away over some other hunter. Some years ago, I took my older son, who was about 10 at the time, to a shoot in Kentucky. He let a few birds pass him as he watched me and the other shooters, and then, when he began to swing on birds, I watched him. He missed four or five straight, and I could see a look of mingled discouragement and bewilderment on his rather grim face.

"Wait them out," I told him. "They can't see you in the shade of that tree. Wait until they're really close."

People say it takes a good shooter to bring down more than two doves for every five shells, but he then bagged four out of the next five. Their dipping and twisting doesn't matter that much when they're only 20 to 30 yards away. I propped a fallen tree branch upright at the edge of the field, about 30 yards from where we stood, and he and I refrained from shooting at any bird that didn't cross that distance marker. Both of us did about as well that day as any of the veteran dove shooters ringing that field.

PIGEON SHOOTING

The common pigeon is just that—common everywhere—and needs no description. The bandtailed pigeon breeds from lower British Columbia down the Pacific Coast to Baja California and eastward into New Mexico and the southern Rockies. Migration begins very early in September and dwindles in October. The winter range is from Puget Sound southward, with the greatest concentrations usually in California, Arizona, New Mexico, and below the border. In addition to those states, they're hunted in Washington, Oregon, Utah, and Colorado, generally with a daily limit of eight in some states, five in others.

The bandtail has dense, smooth gray feathering with brownish and bluish overtones on the back and wings. Across its fanned gray tail, which is wider than a common pigeon's, is a dark gray-brown subterminal band, followed by a broad, pale gray terminal band. The head is apt to be lilac, with a narrow white crescent, or collar, crossing the nape and ending above the throat. The sides of the neck have an iridescent sheen, often greenish, like the common pigeon's. The feet are yellow, and the bill is yellow with a dark tip.

Unlike the rock pigeon, the bandtail roosts in trees, most often tall ones with dead high limbs that afford a clear view of approaching birds of prey. Generally the most important foods in good habitat are acorns, pinyon nuts, and/or hazels, followed by wild cherries, elderberries, wheat, oats, barley, dogwood, waste corn in stubble fields, wild grapes, various grain sprouts,

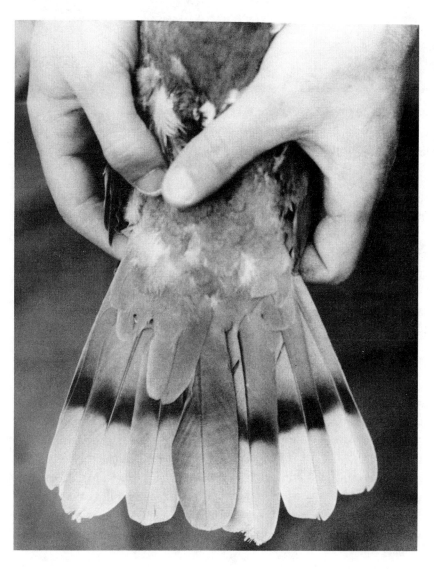

The bandtailed pigeon of the West and Southwest is easy to identify by the broad, pale terminal and dark subterminal band on its tail, which is wider than the common pigeon's.

Typically, bandtails fly high and have to be taken by pass-shooting as they come over the treetops. However, in country where farmland is close to tall roosting trees, hunters can find great shooting.

blueberries, blackberries, mulberries, and manzanita berries. I think nothing is more delicious than squab that's been feeding on pinyon nuts.

Because bandtails are migrating during hunting season, most are bagged by pass-shooting from concealment on ridges or hills near crops or wild foods. They'll begin to descend as they near a feeding site, but because they're such high flyers it's wise to position yourself as high as possible. Early in the season, they're not very wary, but they soon learn to avoid danger. Once they begin to settle into a given locale, they can be taken from ambush or walked up at water holes and grainfields.

Whereas whitewinged doves and common pigeons commonly rise in a ragged cloud when flushed, bandtails flush the way mourning doves do—a few at a time. After bagging one

(or more if you're both lucky and skillful), remain alert for another rise. They generally begin feeding shortly after first light, and by nine in the morning may be dusting or seeking grit or going to water. After that, they'll perch in trees until the afternoon cools. They'll feed again from about four o'clock until they go to roost at dusk.

Common pigeons are much more strongly attracted to decoys—even crude ones—than bandtailed pigeons or even doves. And sometimes they help a hunter gain a hearty welcome to private land. Where they raid crops in large flocks and foul farm buildings, the owner is often glad of an offer to shoot some. About all the hunter then has to do is follow the owner's instructions regarding safe shooting locations and directions—and wait in hiding or at least in an inconspicuous spot for the birds to fly in.

After one or two shooting sessions, they may quit coming within range of a given site. One solution is to try elsewhere. Another is to set decoys on the open ground and on fences. I've seen commercial decoys, but I've seen far more made from ordinary cardboard. All the same, pigeons seem to learn quickly, and crude decoys can lose their allure if they aren't supplemented by something more persuasive. I long ago learned from other hunters to add the pigeons I bring down to my decoy spread. A few can be placed on open ground as if feeding, but it helps greatly to prop a few on fences or other elevated spots.

GUNS AND LOADS

Either a 12- or 20-gauge gun will serve very well for all of these birds. When hunting doves or common pigeons, I prefer no more choke than improved cylinder in a single-barreled gun—remember, I'm an advocate of waiting them out and passing up long shots. In a double-barreled gun, an improved-cylinder first barrel and modified second barrel will be just about ideal. For doves, I generally use field loads of No. 7½ or 8 shot, and I've done very well using trap loads. For common pigeons, I prefer 7½.

Bandtails demand a bit more punch because so much of the hunting involves pass-shooting. Westerners very often use 12-gauge full-choke repeaters or doubles bored modified and full, typically loaded with high-brass No. 6s. I definitely agree with those choices for pass-shooting and for the wary birds seen late in the season. However, during the first weeks and especially at grainfields and water holes, a 20 gauge with a modified choke (or modified and full) can be just as effective with field loads of No. 7½ shot.

14

Crows as Game Birds

Only figuratively have I ever eaten crow, and I no longer go crow hunting because I don't kill what I won't eat. However, if I lived in a part of the country where crows inflict agricultural damage—as they do in some regions—I'd probably set myself up in a natural blind along a flyway and once again scare them away with my attempts at calling. By fairly common definition, game birds are edible, but the widespread bias against eating crow doesn't really disqualify them. Some native American tribes used to eat these birds, although I must say that a crow in hand feels dishearteningly hard-bodied. I must also say that I might be less reluctant to try it if I knew a particular crow had been dining exclusively on grain and not carrion.

Legally, they're game birds. The government includes them among federally regulated migratory game birds, subject to shooting seasons of 124 days or less in the 48 contiguous states. (The Hawaiian and Alaskan subspecies are neither abundant nor really migratory and should not be hunted.) Bag limits are set regionally, and split seasons are permitted, but the birds cannot be hunted during the spring breeding

season. Exceptions to the regulations are granted only where large concentrations of crows damage crops and trees or create a health hazard.

There are half a dozen American subspecies, of which the largest, most gregarious, most migratory, and most hunted is the common crow (*Corvus brachyrhynchos*). In a few regions, care must be taken to distinguish this big black bird from the even larger raven, which is scarce and fully protected. The raven has a shaggily feathered throat and a heavier bill. More important to the gunner is its appearance in the air: it has a more hawklike, measured flapping and soaring flight than the crow, and it soars with its wings held horizontally, whereas a soaring crow angles its wings upward. Also, its tail seen from below is more wedge-shaped, less squarish, than a crow's.

Crows breed throughout the United States and most of Canada, and they winter almost entirely within the United States. In a good many temperate regions, they're more or less sedentary or migrate only very short distances, but those breeding in Canada and the Great Plains migrate long distances. Family groups congregate into larger flocks in August or

The most widespread of America's corvine species is the common crow.

September and begin to move southward, following ripening crops. Sometimes the migration is prolonged into winter, and in most states the birds remain plentiful until at least February.

The best crow hunting to be found anywhere takes place in winter on farmlands from lower Kansas and Missouri through Arkansas and Oklahoma into Texas. Years ago, the Missouri Department of Conservation used to issue an annual guide to the most heavily populated roosting areas. Regrettably, that's no longer done, but you can obtain advice on where to hunt by writing to: Wildlife Division, Department of Conservation, P.O. Box 180, Jefferson City, MO 65102. Write during the summer or fall, because game departments are often so busy that they can't reply very quickly. It may not be essential to enclose a stamped, self-addressed envelope, but I always do as a courtesy.

An especially large and famous roosting site is located at Oklahoma's Fort Cobb Reservoir. The Fort Cobb Wildlife Management Area also contains an abundance of other game—quail, dove, turkey, rabbit, squirrel, and deer. Hunters travel considerable distances to shoot there, and accommodations are available at many motels in and near Fort Cobb. It's wise, however, to make reservations in advance. For information on the hunting, including current regulations and suggestions, you can write to: Oklahoma Department of Wildlife Conservation, 1801 N. Lincoln, P.O. Box 53465, Oklahoma City, OK 73152; and Fort Cobb Wildlife Management Area, 1811 Chisholm, Duncan, OK 73533. For information about local lodging and the like, write to Fort Cobb Chamber of Commerce, City Hall, 100 Block, East Main, Fort Cobb, OK 73038.

Fort Cobb is no metropolis, but adequate lodging can be found nearby. Besides the local motel, there are others within easy driving distance, at or near Anadarko. Oklahoma has a split crow season, and the shooting is generally at its height during the last half, particularly in January. Bear in mind that the Oklahoma quail season is still open then, too. However, you might want to ask the Wildlife Department about season dates for the area's other game species, as well, and plan a trip accordingly.

Of course, you can hunt crows almost anywhere in this country, either on public lands or where you've obtained permission to shoot on private farmland. They gorge on corn wherever they can find it, but preferred foods also include wheat, sorghum, oats, barley, rice, peanuts, acorns, cherries, and apples. A good shooting site is any hiding place between a roost and feeding area or between two feeding areas, and a little scouting—listening and watching—will reveal these flyways. In the North, roosts often seem to be in tall, dense conifers surrounded by fairly open country, but hardwoods and mixed woods are heavily utilized in many areas. Willow clumps are common roosts in the South, and even relatively low shrubs are utilized in parts of the West.

A roost is noisy, and it's easily spotted when flocks of crows crowd the trees. Moreover, they can be seen flying from a roost in the morning, returning in small groups in early afternoon, and then arriving in large clusters shortly before dusk. It's wise to move your blind location from day to day so the birds won't abandon a flyway or feeding area.

Although the largest and most famous seasonal (winter) crow roosts are in the lower Midwest, huge congregations of crows may gather almost anywhere. This roost is in New Jersey.

This plastic owl appears to be resisting the bullying harassment of two plastic crows. Such decoy setups are more effective when combined with realistic calling, and avid crow hunters learn the vocalizations by mimicking instructional audiotapes.

The widespread belief that feeding crows post sentinels is just a myth—each bird watches out for itself and signals any alarm to the others—but there's no doubt that advance scouts, usually a couple of birds, precede a flock on the wing. If the scouts fly close enough to be relatively easy targets, take them. The rest of the flock will probably come looking for them. But if you aren't really sure of connecting, let the scouts go by unmolested; otherwise they'll wheel back to signal the others with alarm calls.

In hunted areas, no birds are more cautious than crows or more alert to colors, reflections, and movements. Many hunters therefore wear camouflage clothing and head nets—or smudge their faces with commercial camouflage "greasepaint" or home-prepared burnt cork.

Decoys are a great help, and a traditional, very effective set-up is the owl-and-crow rig. (Synthetic owls and crows are widely available from decoy manufacturers.) The owl is propped in a tree or tall bush where it's clearly visible from the air, and two or three crow decoys are propped higher, in front or a bit to the sides, as if harassing the owl—a hated enemy. This tableau is intended to show crows trying to bully an owl while calling for reinforcements. To make the scene persuasive, calling is needed—a mingling of wailing caws and short, angry, raucous blasts.

When large numbers of migrating crows have arrived and begun to crowd the roosts, a larger number of crow decoys—minus the owl—is likely to be even more effective. Some of the decoys can be stick-ups, placed on the ground in front of a manmade blind or natural hiding spot, preferably at the edge of a cornfield or other feeding attraction. But the rig will be much more alluring if you set about a dozen decoys on fenceposts or tree limbs, where they'll be seen from the air at a great distance. When birds are shot, they can be set out as additional decoys—with care to make them look alive. In this situation, too, calling is a great help—rallying and feeding notes.

The problem is that a lot of crow vocalizations sound pretty much alike to humans, seeming deceptively easy to imitate. Hungry, excited crows do a lot of babbling and frequently mix the short and long feeding notes with more strident fighting and scolding calls. If your mimicry becomes too choppy or staccato, you may be sounding an alarm call. The tubular, reed-actuated mouth calls sold in sporting-goods stores work very well when properly blown, and a good trick is to alternately use two

Calling crows near the edge of a feeding field, this hunter is using an autoloading shotgun. Pumps and autos are more popular than double-barreled guns for this kind of shooting because an arriving swarm of crows often provides a chance for several fast shots.

that have slightly different pitches or tones. If two or more hunters are adept, duets or group calling can be still better. But my advice is to buy an instructional audiotape and mimic the expert vocalizations (which include the calls of real crows on some tapes) until you can duplicate them. Otherwise you'll scare the birds off instead of luring them close enough to shoot.

They're difficult targets even though they seldom sail over faster than about 30 miles an hour. We're all so accustomed to seeing various smaller blackbirds that we tend to underestimate a crow's size—about 18 or 20 inches long, with a wingspread of a yard if the bird is mature. Swinging the gun through a target as it careens over the treetops, we perceive it as either surprisingly large or closer than it actually is. The tendency, therefore, is to lead the crow insufficiently—firing the first shot behind it. The problem is compounded if the very next bird streaks in straight and low, appearing faster than it really is and causing the gunner to over-lead the target this time. All the same, there are gunners who take pride in their crow-shooting virtuosity and use repeating shotguns not for second or third tries on a given target but for double and triple kills when a swarm of crows flies over.

GUNS AND LOADS

In some regions, particularly in the West, rifles are legal for crow shooting (and are used to kill magpies, as well). Only shots at stationary targets are attempted—birds on the ground or perched low in areas where there's no danger of a long-reaching bullet endangering life or property. The most commonly used rifles are bolt-action varmint models chambered for such cartridges as the .22 Hornet, .222, .222 Magnum, .223, or .22-250, and equipped with scopes ranging from 6- to 12-power or even greater magnification. A high level of marksmanship is required to kill a crow at long rifle range, but I'm not entirely comfortable with this form of the sport. In all but the most remote areas, the question of safety bothers me. Besides, my personal taste favors wingshooting.

I like a 12-gauge shotgun for crow hunting. It's rather like waterfowling in that you mostly remain in one place, waiting for birds to fly over, so the slight extra weight of a larger bore instead of my pet 20 gauge is of no consequence. Moreover, occasional shots are fairly long and an occasional crow seems to be armor-plated, so I want plenty of pellets in the shot string. And I like a repeater for this sport because sometimes there's a chance to take a second and even a third crow as a flock swarms in—or a chance to correct a mistake and still bring down a second bird.

Some crow hunters use full-choke guns, and I won't argue with that choice for those who can and do consistently hit high birds. But such shooters are few. Most of us will perform better with a modified choke. Some of those same hunters who like a full choke also like shot as large as No. 6, while others prefer the denser patterns of shot as small as No. 8 or even 9. I believe in obtaining a wide, dense pattern with the combination of modified boring and No. 7½ pellets, and I'm convinced that efficiency lies in letting the birds swoop close enough for field or skeet loads to achieve their full potential.

15

Wild Turkey: Big Game of the Uplands

There was a time not very long ago when turkeys were seldom included in the literature of upland hunting. They didn't arouse much enthusiasm in hunters who associated game birds with open fields, beloved bird dogs, light guns, and small aerial targets—nor were they abundant enough to be hunted in a majority of states. Owing to unprecedented successes in game management during the last three decades, we now have huntable turkey populations in every state but Alaska—which is simply too far north for these birds, although British Columbia opens a season for resident hunters.

The combined turkey populations from coast to coast now total an estimated four million birds; and as their numbers have grown, so has the enthusiasm of hunters who have learned how challenging and rewarding—as well as unique—is this big game of the uplands.

Almost everywhere there's a spring season (with dates depending partly on abundance and partly on latitude, which affects the timing of turkey courtship and nesting), and only gobblers are legal in spring. At the time of this writing, 36 states also have a fall season. Among

these states, Alabama and Florida allow only males to be taken, while the other 34 permit autumn hunting of either sex.

Some of the most avid and well-traveled turkey hunters may be surprised to learn there are six—not four—subspecies or geographic races. The Eastern wild turkey ranges from New England into the South and Midwest; the Florida turkey resides farther south but sometimes ranges far enough north to interbreed with the Eastern; the Rio Grande turkey is native to the Southwest and Mexico, and has been introduced in states as far away as North Dakota and California; and the Merriam's turkey inhabits the Southwest and lower Rockies, and has been introduced in states throughout the West. For a growing number of dedicated hunters (who presumably have plenty of leisure time and money) the ambition of their sporting lives is to achieve a "Grand Slam" in turkeys—that is, take at least one bearded gobbler representing each of those four subspecies. Those four are, indeed, considered to constitute a legitimate Grand Slam, but a couple of additional races exist: the Gould's turkey, which

The largest of the turkey clan are the Eastern wild turkey, shown here, and the Merriam's turkey.

inhabits parts of Mexico and may occasionally range northward across the border; and the Mexican, or ocellated, turkey, which occurs in huntable numbers in Yucatan and Guatemala.

Admittedly, few of us would travel all the way to Yucatan just to hunt a single game bird, but I remember the delight with which the late Colonel Dave Harbour—an expert and an extremist in his ardor for turkeys—told me about flying down there with three similarly addicted companions just to bag the exotic ocellated turkey. For Dave, I guess that made a Super Grand Slam.

The Eastern and Merriam's turkeys are the largest of the group. A mature gobbler of either variety weighs between 15 and 20 pounds (to the best of my knowledge, the heaviest on record was an Eastern 28-pounder), and a hen weighs between 9 and 12. The Florida turkey tends to be darker and smaller, the Rio Grande race leggy and pale, but geographic differences in size and color are minor.

The legs of adult males have black spurs (occasionally double spurs) that average an inch long and are so hard and sharp that Indians used them as arrowheads. The male—called a jake when immature and short-bearded, a tom or gobbler when mature—has a naked head and neck, mostly pink but with some pale blue on the face, fading to almost white atop the head. Wattles hang from his throat; his neck is lumpy with fatty growths called caruncles; and a fleshy lobe—called a frontal caruncle, leader, or snood—grows just above his bill and sometimes hangs down over it. When a gobbler threatens another male or struts before hens, with tail fanned wide and spread wings scraping the ground, the naked skin flushes quite red.

A female's neck has fleshy folds and bumps, but they're insignificant by comparison, and her head is usually shadowed somewhat by short, fine, whiskery feathers that make her skin look darker, more bluish gray than a tom's.

The chief badge of gender, however, is the male breast adornment known as the beard—a narrow, downward-hanging pendant of stiff, coarse, blackish, hairlike feathers giving the appearance of a miniature horsetail. A bird of the year has a small one, only a few inches long. It grows throughout the gobbler's life but isn't a reliable indication of age since the ends often wear away or break. The beard of a mature gobbler is eight or nine inches long, sometimes a bit longer, and the records include one that dangled down more than 14 inches. Occasionally, gobblers grow multiple beards, but there's little sense in wasting time searching for a non-typical tom.

Fall hunters are typically inclined to try for the first plump turkey they can manage to shoot, but spring hunters are more trophy-oriented and very likely to send a big gobbler off to a taxidermist to have the tail and beard or even the entire bird mounted. They hope for big birds with long beards, and if the gobbler has long spurs, too, that's a great bonus.

Occasionally, a hen grows a beard, making sexual identification so difficult (if not impossible) that such a bird is generally regarded as legal game during gobblers-only seasons. The head of a bearded hen usually exhibits subdued male characteristics, and she may also have spurs.

In some states, particularly in the West, rifles and even handguns are legal and sometimes used to shoot turkeys at considerable distances on the kind of wide open terrain where the birds are seldom seen by Easterners. One cold fall day in Texas, I saw large flocks of turkeys but had no prayer of getting within shotgun range in that low scrub, where they could see

me from far off. On the same morning, a friend who had the good sense to carry a scoped rifle and binocular brought in a nice gobbler.

He'd taken it pretty much the same way he hunted desert mule deer and pronghorn antelope: scouting the open country, scanning the terrain with his binocular, locating a flock, crouching and stalking until he was within rifle range, again using the binocular and then the rifle scope to pick out a big gobbler, and then nailing it at a distance of well over 100 yards.

Unfortunately, the popularity of turkey hunting has led to an increase in the annual number of hunting accidents. Pennsylvania is unusual among Eastern states in that it allows rifle hunting, and this increases the danger. As a result, that state has enacted a regulation requiring turkey hunters to wear 100 square inches of blaze orange while moving. (While a hunter is sitting still in a blind, he may remove the orange.) This law went into effect for the 1992-93 seasons. Whether it will be permanent or rescinded in a few years remains to be seen. Many hunters resent it, since turkeys can see colors quite well and are extremely wary.

All the same, human safety strikes me as more important than easing the difficulty of killing a gobbler. Moreover, turkeys—like other wildlife—pay more attention to movement than to unfamiliar colors. The blaze orange needs to be worn only while the hunter is moving—at which time he's not likely to get a shot anyway. I'm wholeheartedly in favor of the regulation. Next time I hunt in Pennsylvania, I'll wear an orange camouflage jacket, which intersperses irregular areas of orange with a broken pattern of forest colors—highly visible to the human eye but far less noticeable to wildlife. I think it's a good idea in any rifle-hunting state.

For most of us, the turkey is shotgun game and the hunting techniques are different in the extreme from rifle hunting. For that matter, spring turkey hunting differs drastically from fall hunting even though the same shotgun is used.

SPRING GOBBLER HUNTING

Entire books and magazines are devoted to gobbler hunting, and I won't attempt here to describe in detail every possible trick and tactic. I'll provide the basic strategies and tactics, and—right now, before going on—offer the strong opinion that if you're new to turkey hunting you should take three initial steps:

1. Buy at least one instructional videotape and closely study the locating of roosts, the search for sign, the choice of a stand and attention to concealment, and, above all, the types of calls and calling methods. While you're at it, buy a book or two on the subject.

2. Buy at least two types of calls—a box call and a diaphragm—and then practice with both, practice again, and practice some more. It's both essential and difficult to fool gobblers. The diaphragm has two advantages, as it leaves both your hands free—it's held inside the mouth—and it can imitate several different vocalizations very convincingly if you become adept with it. On the other hand, the box call is far easier to master.

3. Make every effort to plan your first couple of spring hunts so that you can go with an experienced friend, or else hire a local guide to help and coach you.

The first strategy is to locate a roost or feeding area—or both—by scouting, exploring, even before the season opens, and then plan where you'll take your stand. Once, during New York's spring season, I found a hen already sitting on her ground nest, incubating her eggs, under a tall pine near the edge of the woods, and I knew there must be other turkeys nearby, somewhere close to water and food. But that was pure luck. It's smart to search for sign: tracks, droppings, and feathers. Once in a while, you might spot a dusting spot—a shallow oval—but it won't be obvious. A gobbler's big three-toed tracks are obvious, indeed, perhaps six inches long. And if he was strutting, you may be able to see drag marks left by the wings on each side of the footprints. A print longer than 4½ inches is probably a male's, and a stride longer than 11½ inches almost certainly is.

Droppings are an indication not only of a turkey's presence in the vicinity but of its sex. Hens and juvenile turkeys of either sex deposit curled or spiral blobs. An adult male leaves a more solid scat several inches long, almost half an inch in diameter, and somewhat twisted or knobbed at one end to form a J shape. The

Turkeys dislike moving through wet foliage, but muddy ground can be helpful to a hunter because it often provides clear tracks. Here, a hen and gobbler walked across the same muddy spot. The print on the right is almost certainly a gobbler's, as it measures more than 4½ inches from the tip of the long middle toe to the little dent left by the hind toe.

ground under a roost often has a noticeable accumulation of droppings and feathers, as may a heavily used feeding spot or a place where a gobbler has been displaying for hens.

Turkeys prefer to roost in tall trees, usually higher than 60 feet and often situated on a ridge or above a clearing to permit unobstructed flight. In the South they often use cypresses over water, a natural moat that stops or slows predators. Elsewhere, they often use oaks, cottonwoods, pines, spruces, or firs. You can't predict whether they'll use the same roost for several nights or go to a new one every night, but roosting sign can be a key to general location at the very least because turkeys often live all year

Droppings, like tracks, can tell you whether a gobbler has been in the immediate area to feed, roost, or seek hens. Young birds and hens leave curled or spiraled blobs. Adult gobblers leave a long scat like this one, twisted or knobbed at one end.

in an area as small as 600 acres. If you've found a roost, you can return (without approaching too close) before first light the next morning. You may actually hear a bird—or birds—fly down. They flap loudly. If not, you may get a response to a locator call (about which, I'll say more shortly).

Near the roosting sites there will be water—ponds, creeks, seeps, or swamps—and plenty of food. Many of the finest hunting areas have sizable hardwood stands that provide such mast as acorns, hazelnuts, or beechnuts. Conifer seeds will also keep the birds well fed, however. Additional preferred foods include dogwood, sumac, wild grapes, chufa grass, berries of all sorts, corn, sorghum, and oats. The birds feed eagerly for a few hours after dawn and again for a few hours before dusk, but they also feed intermittently throughout the day and may be found in woods at any time.

In the spring, hens yelp to let gobblers know they're receptive to mating. They tend to invite the toms uphill—which is what the gobblers expect—to places that permit fast escape from predators. As a rough rule, then, calling is best done from a ridge or knoll. A gobbler will come—very carefully at first—to a group of several hens or just one. When he arrives, he struts and parades, courting any females present and trying to attract others. He'll guard his harem from interlopers, so you'll sometimes hear not only a male's gobbling response to the females but also his threat or fighting calls.

Having found an area that gobblers are using, you then want to locate your bird, and you'll almost surely have to do that by sound rather than sight. In midsummer I've watched a big gobbler pick grit on a New Jersey roadside, and in midwinter I was dumbfounded to see one walk across a friend's backyard, but they're as elusive as Sasquatch when hunters are in the woods. The most common locator-call is an "owl-hooter," a mouth call available wherever turkey-hunting supplies are sold. Gobblers will respond

This is an Eastern turkey gobbler on the roost at dawn. Locating a roost is often a key to success in turkey hunting. You'll find sign under a roost, and you may hear the flapping of birds going to a roost in the evening.

Strutting to court a hen (and simultaneously discourage rivals), a gobbler drags his wings, fans out his tail stiffly, and puffs up his feathers. The hunter's primary spring tactic is, of course, to mimic a hen or a rival male convincingly enough to lure a gobbler into clear view within shotgun range.

The most widely used type of locator-call is an "owl-hooter." Gobblers will also respond to a crow call or a coyote howl, which gives away their approximate location. Some hunters can mimic an owl closely with their vocal cords, but for most of us a mouth-blown locator produces a far more realistic sound.

to a hooting owl, or even a crow call, and they've been known to respond to a slamming car door—perhaps proclaiming that the woods are theirs and trespassers had better beware.

But turkeys instinctively know that human trespassers are not to be trifled with, and they're deathly afraid of the human voice. Be silent in the woods, or communicate with a companion by signals and very soft whispers if you must, and make no sound at all when a turkey approaches, even if the bird is still a hundred yards away. A turkey's hearing is as keen as its vision. After locating a gobbler, you want him to hear nothing but other turkeys.

I've known old hunters who could yelp, squawk, and even gobble with their unaided vocal cords or through a pipe stem or a hen turkey's wingbone from which the ends were cut. Another common homemade call (which is made commercially as well) consists of a thin, chalked slate and a cedar peg which is scraped across the slate.

Probably the most popular commercial call is the diaphragm type, which is worked between the tongue and the roof of the mouth. With practice, it can reproduce just about all the sounds in the male and female turkey repertoire, but it does take a lot of practice, and I dislike its

vibrations in my mouth. Vying with it for first place in the affections of hunters is the box call, usually wood but in a few instances wood and slate. Its lid is attached to the sound box but movable. By rubbing the chalked lid over the box rim, you can make it yelp, gobble, or yodel, depending on how you hold, work, or adjust it. This, too, takes practice, but if you follow the maker's instructions and listen to an instructional tape or experienced caller, you can become reasonably proficient fairly quickly and easily.

The hen's invitational call is a vaguely plaintive yelp—*keowk, keowk, keowk.* Don't overdo it, and if the gobbler stops replying wait a few minutes before resuming. A lot of gobblers have been fooled before and escaped at the last moment when they spotted a hunter. Maybe the gobbler you're conversing with has even been shot at. He may be call-shy.

It's common for a gobbler to respond initially, and perhaps you can tell he's coming closer by the sound of his next couple of gobbles—but then he falls silent, or he continues to gobble but moves off to one side or retreats or simply stays where he is. If further yelping fails, there are two other basic possibilities.

One is to gobble back, imitating him. Imitating what you hear is very often the key. He

Wearing camouflage clothing and sitting against a large beech tree, this hunter probably won't be detected prematurely—if he stops calling and remains very still during the gobbler's final approach. He's using a box call, which can duplicate both gobbles and the coaxing yelps of hens.

interprets this—or so you hope—as the voice of a rival moving in to commandeer the hen he's been hearing. He may then resume his approach, with or without gobbling. He may even rush straight at you, intent on evicting the rival. As I said, he may.

If that doesn't work, an alternative is to do the moving yourself—maneuvering around without alarming the quarry and then calling again from a different location. There are two difficulties. One is the possibility of letting him hear you, or maybe even see you since he can usually see you before you can see him. The other is the problem of finding an equally good stand higher on a slope or off to one side.

It's a good idea to pick an alternative stand

before or as soon as you station yourself at the original spot. Camouflage is a great help, and most turkey hunters wear it. The stand itself should conceal you or serve to break up your outline, yet also give you a wide arc of vision—that is, a more or less clear field of fire. You can often accomplish this by merely standing still against a large tree or sitting against a big stump or rock, but when possible I choose a blow-down, snag, or fallen tree to shield as much of me as possible.

Sometimes you can tell the voice of a jake from that of a mature gobbler. A jake's call is higher-pitched, while the gobbler's is a high but deeper, throaty yodeling—*grrddel, gl-obble-obble-obble.*

When I first hear a gobble, I like to reply with the hen's higher yelp. If the gobbler responds, I wait a couple of minutes before repeating it. For perhaps the next half-hour, I use my box call sparingly, answering every second or third call from the gobbler if he seems to be cooperating. As his gobbling begins to sound closer, I lengthen my silences to as long as five minutes. More often than not, when he's almost close enough for me to see him amid the brush or trees, he'll become silent, too, approaching with suspicion that almost overwhelms his eagerness. I slowly, silently get my gun into position and try not to move again until I get my shot—probably the only shot I'll get.

I've found that box calls sound best in dry weather, but turkeys are most active on overcast or drizzly days, and maybe that's another reason why so many hunters use diaphragms. A hard rain, on the other hand, makes for hard hunting because turkeys seem to dislike moving through wet foliage. On those days I like to find a stand near a trail, road, or clearing where the birds are likely to search for food without drenching their feathers.

Some hunters set out one or several decoys in a clear spot where they hope a gobbler will appear. These are realistic, life-size hens, as a rule, made of durable synthetics. When a gobbler has come

This is the moment of truth for a turkey hunter. He has a clear shot at a gobbler within easy range. Even in this ideal situation, he wants to center his pattern on the bird's head and neck, while also hoping a few pellets will strike the upper body. Any other shot is less than certain to pin a big turkey and prevent its escape.

Hunters position a turkey decoy on clear ground where an approaching gobbler is certain to see it. Most such decoys are lightweight stick-ups like this one, a realistic representation of a hen.

to your calling but is hesitant to take the last few steps that will culminate in a clear shot, the sight of a hen or two may persuade him. Originally designed for spring hunting, the decoys work well in fall, too, when you're calling birds back after scattering a flock. They're legal in many regions, and although they're cumbersome to carry into the woods, quite a few hunters consider the effort worthwhile.

FALL HUNTING

In fall as in spring, turkeys are especially active and vocal right after they leave their roosts, which means that hunting is best during the first two or three hours of light. But their activity differs in fall as some of the hens and their half-grown poults are joined by other families and broodless hens, forming new flocks, while the males begin to gather in small bachelor bands. As in spring, pre-hunt scouting is valuable in locating feeding areas and roosts. Amid screening brush on the hills or in the bottomland woods, you can begin a hunt by moving along slowly, very watchfully, still-hunting. This seems to be more effective in parts of the Midwest, Southwest, and West, where turkeys are often spotted at a considerable distance, than in the woodlots of the East. The Western hunters who use rifles can still-hunt toward hills overlooking relatively open valleys and then go on stand where they can peer down at any flocks that show up to feed.

Even in thick shotgunning cover, it makes sense to begin by still-hunting, but with the knowledge that you'll get a good shot only by chance and your primary purpose is actually to spook the birds. Turkeys have such uncanny hearing and vision that at the moment you become aware of their presence they're already rustling away through the screening timber or brush. You may only hear them or you may get a quick glimpse of one or more, but usually no shot.

Fortunately, if they become aware of you suddenly and not at too great a distance, they almost invariably scatter instead of retreating as a group in a single direction. And that's exactly what you want—because what they want is to return to the same feeding area and, most especially, to regroup. By calling, you can now try to convince some of them that others have returned and are waiting for them to join the flock.

Years ago, it was fairly common to use flushing dogs to locate and scatter flocks of turkeys in the fall. The practice is still legal in a few areas but seldom employed. No turkey will lie to a point or wait for a flushing dog to put it up within range, so all the dog can do is scatter the flock somewhere near you, noisily enough for you to hear it. After that, the dog must be kept perfectly still and quiet, which can be a problem even with a well-trained waterfowling dog that's

In fall hunting, the primary tactic is to find and scatter a flock in all directions, then call them back. Hens are legal game in most states during the fall season, and this is a typical flock of hens and immature birds.

In the fall, careful scouting occasionally leads to a small bachelor band of gobblers like these three. When scattered, they don't often call and they won't return as soon as scattered hens and young.

accustomed to sitting in or behind a blind.

In country well populated by turkeys—and nowadays there's plenty of such country throughout the United States—you don't need a dog to find and scatter a flock. Two of the ways to do it involve deer hunting. In many states an early deer season (not necessarily the regular firearms season but sometimes a bowhunting or muzzleloading season) is open concurrently with turkey hunting. Before you leave your deer stand toward evening, you may hear turkeys flying to a roost—their wing flapping is very audible. You can then return in the morning to scatter them. Even more commonly, a turkey hunter can take a stand very early in the morning in previously scouted, turkey-rich woods, and wait there while the deer hunters move through the area and thus push nervous flocks toward him. In most states, small-game and turkey seasons overlap and can be used to your advantage in the same way when other hunters move through cropfields and the fringes of woods.

The easiest turkeys to hunt at this time of year are the brood flocks—mothers and young of the year. The juvenile birds are far more vocal than their elders, relying on calls to maintain contact with the rest of the flock. As they move about to feed, you can often hear clucking, trilling, and even an occasional gobble.

When mast is plentiful, oak and beech woods are excellent places to hunt, and it pays to look for sign such as feathers, droppings, and scratchings. If you find tracks, you'll probably be able to tell whether the flock is a family group or a gobbler band, and you then have a chance to take a bearded tom. This becomes easier when there's a little snow on the ground to ease the tracking. Regardless of whether other game seasons are open or other hunters are in the woods, you'll sooner or later locate a flock, and with care—and a little luck—scatter them.

In addition to the woods, pay close attention to the edges of cut cornfields or other grain crops. Hunted turkeys are shy, but they'll very often venture into such fields for the sake of good pickings. A bit of wind can help because rustling masks the sound of your movements until you're quite close when you flush the birds, and that will usually scatter them very nicely.

Unlike hens and juveniles, scattered gobblers aren't bothered much by their forced separation so they call very little if at all—and will seldom come back on the day of their scattering no matter how skillfully you call. If you've flushed them early in the morning, it's worthwhile for you to return in late afternoon, close to roosting time, and try some coarse clucking. If you flushed them later in the day, return the next day or even a couple of days later, get yourself well hidden, and do some clucking, beginning with several loud calls spaced a few seconds apart, then silence for a few minutes, then a little more clucking, and then a longer silent intermission. I'd repeat the clucking about every 15 minutes.

Old gobblers yelp and cluck in the fall, but their calls are coarser than hen or juvenile calls and spaced farther apart. Occasionally, a mature gobbler will utter a lost yelp like that heard among family flocks. If so, call back in imitation. If you have no luck after, say, 45 minutes or an hour, move to another hiding spot in the vicinity but not too nearby. Just as in spring calling, repositioning yourself often encourages an approach, and a quarter-mile very often isn't too far to move.

Scattered gobblers are likely to return one at a time, hesitantly—and silently when a bird is fairly close, sneaking in. If you think a gobbler is coming close, quit calling and remain absolutely still and silent.

Scattered flocks of hens and young—especially the juveniles—will return much more promptly. After scattering them, the vocalization you'll most likely hear is the lost, or rallying, call of the juveniles. High pitched and loud, it begins with pleading yelps that sound like *kee-kee*. After a few yelps, it's followed by *kee-kee-kee-owk*. Those are the sounds you need to imitate. As with learning to mimic the spring mating calls, success may depend on listening to and practicing with an instructional tape unless you have the opportunity to hunt with an old pro.

GUNS AND LOADS

Where rifles are legal for turkeys, some hunters use rimfire .22 magnums, but I wouldn't trust one to kill a turkey beyond about 75 yards, and the shooting distances in open country are frequently much longer. A better choice is a varmint caliber (anything from .22 Hornet to, say, .22-250) with a scope of 2½ or 4 power or one with variable magnification.

Hitting a turkey effectively with a pattern of shotgun pellets is often harder than it seems to the uninitiated. It's true that a gobbler sometimes presents himself on clear ground within easy range and struts about or even stands still for a moment. But much more often, by the time you have your gun on him he's aware of the danger and is running or maybe even flying.

A turkey can run at least 20 miles an hour and be hidden by brush as quickly as you can shoot. And a turkey that's taken wing and is flying through the trees is probably escaping at 40 miles an hour. Furthermore, you must center your pattern on the bird's head if at all possible, because a turkey's body is shielded by dense, hard feathers, its vital organs are deep within a large body, its wings aren't easily broken, and the bird is more resistant to shock than the smaller game birds. A turkey that's hit in the lower body sometimes escapes and can't be recovered.

This doesn't mean you must use a 10-gauge magnum, although quite a few hunters do. Most use a 12-gauge or 12-gauge magnum, either of which is sufficient. Some use a magnum 20 with maximum loads, which is also sufficient but isn't my favorite tool for the purpose.

There are a few turkey hunters who carry old-fashioned bolt-action shotguns, which are all right but a little slow in getting off a second or third shot to nail a missed or wounded bird. There's nothing wrong with a double-barreled gun, either, but most hunters prefer a semiautomatic or pump-action just in case there's need of a third shot. A repeater would certainly be my choice.

Some hunters buy special-purpose shotguns with a camouflage or dull matte finish, or wrap their guns with camo tape, and it's not a bad idea. The glint of something shiny or alien-looking can spook a gobbler at the critical instant. Many gunners also use carrying slings, and I agree with that idea, too, since success entails the task of carrying a very big, heavy bird out of the woods.

There are differences of opinion about choke—modified, improved modified, or full. I consider a full choke best because you want a very tight, dense pattern over the bird's head and neck rather than the larger body area. I'd prefer a clean miss to a wounded but unrecoverable bird.

Because turkeys are hard to kill, quite a few hunters make the extreme mistake of using buckshot. Significantly, many states have regulations prohibiting the use of that shot or any pellets larger than a stipulated size—say No. 2 or 4—for turkey hunting. A buckshot load has too few pellets for a dense pattern, and a clean kill most often depends on multiple pellet hits. Most turkey hunters use No. 4, 5, or 6, and a growing number rely on No. 6 because in today's loads they pack more than enough punch combined with plenty of pellets. The major ammunition manufacturers offer turkey loads, specifically tailored for this hunting, and I see no reason to use anything else. They provide more than adequate power combined with accuracy, pattern uniformity and density, and excellent penetration.

16

From Field to Table

Most of us think wild birds taste far better than domestic ones, and that includes the often maligned sage grouse. I'll admit, however, that birds in a given type of habitat will differ a little in flavor from birds of the same species that have been feeding heavily on some other, single variety of food.

It's also true that some of the larger game birds tend to be dryer than a good chicken when roasted. They require longer cooking time than the small ones, and because they're not as fat as domestic fowl, prolonged heat can dry the meat and make it stringy. A pheasant, for example, has fairly large deposits of fat on its back and lower belly, but they're not as widely distributed over the body as a chicken's. When I roast a pheasant, I baste it generously and frequently, covered (regardless of what many cookbooks advise). I set the heat high—about 400°—and hope it will be sufficiently done in an hour. The sooner it comes out, the juicier it will be.

As with some other game birds, I often lay strips of bacon over it to baste it as it roasts. Some people skin their pheasants (and other game), but for roasting I prefer it with the skin on and pricked for the flow of juices. The skin

and fat of game birds have less cholesterol than that of domestic fowl, by the way.

Wild turkey tends to be dryer than domestic turkey, but any recipe you like for domestic turkey will serve very well for the wild bird, just as any chicken recipe works very well for pheasant. The larger game birds can be roasted, stewed, braised, or baked (in small pieces) in a casserole or pie. Do bear in mind, however, that the larger and older a bird is, the dryer and tougher the meat will be. Personally, I consider a large bearded gobbler a candidate for stewing, though some turkey enthusiasts would call this heresy.

In addition to larding and basting the larger birds when I roast them, I like to fill their cavities tightly with a moist, conventional chicken or turkey stuffing. This lengthens the cooking time slightly but also seems to keep the inner meat juicier.

The smaller game birds can be prepared by all of the same basic methods (sans stuffing) and are also delicious broiled, barbecued, or quick-fried in very hot oil. My vote goes to peanut oil for this purpose, expensive though it is. Even with game as small as quail, woodcock, and doves, I often cook the entire bird (usually split in half—not quartered in the manner of larger birds) because I hate to lose a morsel. I even save the tiny giblets for soup or gravy. But most game cooks simply pluck out the two sections of breast meat, which is understandable because that's by far the best part, and the back and legs have hardly any meat on them.

I don't age or "hang" my birds as is often done in England and Europe, because I prefer the milder fresh taste. Americans sometimes produce disastrous results when they age birds because they don't understand that it has to be done at a very cool, pretty constantly controlled temperature. Several days at 39° is plenty, after which a bird should either be cooked and eaten or frozen for later use. This being the case, all you have to do to age a bird is keep it in the refrigerator.

Another misguided tendency is to overmarinate game birds, as if to tenderize them (most are tender already) or mask a gamey flavor. I'm not even sure what's generally meant by gamey flavor, but I suspect it describes meat mistreated in the field or in storage—of which I'll say more shortly. A mild wine, cider, orange, or teriyaki marinade, or even a sweet-and-sour Oriental sauce (best, in my opinion, with small birds to be stir-fried quickly, like Oriental vegetables) is fine. But it's a treat, not a necessity. A couple of hours is enough marinating time at room temperature, and a day is enough in the refrigerator.

I've read that the first thing you must do after shooting a bird is eviscerate it so the meat won't sour. In most cases that's unnecessary and is a mildly annoying interruption of the hunt. I've shot scaled quail in 70° weather, cleaned them three hours later, and had a wonderful dinner. Actually, I didn't really clean them at all, but acted in accordance with my host's wishes by merely parting the frontal skin and neatly slicing out the breast sections.

In cool to cold weather, you'll do no harm by keeping a bird in your game pocket or pouch for most of the day—if you clean and cool it as soon as possible afterward. But hot weather does present a problem. Dove hunters often bring coolers to the field with them, as well they should. On a typical early-season day, every dove goes on ice immediately. If that's done, there's no need for quick evisceration.

You're not about to lug a cooler around on the desert or hot plains when you're hunting such species as desert quail or prairie grouse, but it's smart to have a cooler in your vehicle so you can put the birds on ice as soon as possible. And there's something else you can do as soon as you shoot one of those birds on a hot day. *This* is when quick evisceration makes sense. The better-supplied sporting goods stores carry folding pocket knives that feature a "gut hook" about as long as the blade itself or a little longer. It's just a slender prong, hooked at the end. After killing a bird, you enlarge the vent by cutting a slit, then insert the hook as far up as possible, twist it, and pull it out again, thus removing the intestines and usually the gizzard—and sometimes the heart and liver, too, if you're thorough and feel the temperature dictates extra care.

I've carried one of those knives for years because I like its blade, but I've never used the gut hook. A stiff twig works just about as well, and so will your fingers if you cut a large enough slit. Fingers are best for a really thorough job, and afterward it's easy enough to wipe them clean on foliage.

Having taken out the lower digestive tract, it's a good idea to clean the other end as well in hot weather. In other words, remove the crop. To do this, you simply cut the skin at the top of the breast, where it meets the throat, and pull out the sac, which contains the food that the bird ate most recently. That, too, can sour. If you're not sure what vegetation the birds have been eating—and thus where to flush more of them—the crop contents can often tell you, assuming you can identify seeds, grains, leaves, berries, or whatever.

As soon as you reach your home or lodgings,

you should detach the heads and legs, and pluck or skin your birds (or remove the breast sections if that's your preference), then wash them thoroughly in cold water, paying close attention to the cavities and removing any trace of internal organs or debris. Drain the birds on paper towels and, as soon as possible, refrigerate or freeze them.

Everybody—except me, I guess—knows that a frozen bird must be thawed and used within three months to prevent freezer burn, drying out, and plain inedibility. But I've had guests tell me how delicious a quail or pheasant dinner was, unaware that I'd served last season's leftover birds. The secret is in making the freezer packages as airtight as possible. I wrap my birds in cling-wrap or plastic storage bags tied tightly, and then wrap on an outer layer of freezer paper, secured with freezer tape or masking tape. Using a felt-tipped marker, I date and identify each package so I'll know later what kind of bird I'm unwrapping and how old it is.

Here are a couple of recipes that work beautifully with any of the small game birds—woodcock, dove, pigeon, quail, or Hungarian partridge.

Braised Minibird

Pluck or skin birds, and split them or use breast sections only. Wipe clean with damp cloth. Heat 4 tablespoons bacon fat, lard, or cooking oil in dutch oven or deep skillet that can be covered. Roll meat in mixture of flour and cornmeal moderately seasoned with pepper and paprika. (I never find salt necessary.) Additional seasoning options include garlic powder added to flour, or one small garlic clove minced or crushed and added later, when simmering begins. When fat or oil is very hot, brown meat quickly on both sides, then drain off all but a little fat, add enough water to half-cover meat, turn heat very low, and simmer, covered, for 1 hour. Check water level every 15 minutes; it should remain deep enough to cover at least lower third of meat. If desired, diced onion,

sliced mushroom, or small celery slices can be added to broth after first half hour. Before serving, some cooks whisk flour to thicken broth into gravy. Two bird halves or three breasts are needed per serving.

Minibird Casserole

4 birds, split
1/3 cup cooking oil or fat
2 medium carrots, slivered or chopped
1 medium onion, chopped (or as many very small white, whole onions as you please)
2/3 cup chopped green pepper (sweet bell pepper)
3/4 cup sliced mushrooms (preferably fresh)
2 tablespoons flour
1/4 teaspoon rosemary
2 pinches thyme (or commercial poultry seasoning)
1 generous pinch tarragon
2 cups stock or 4 chicken bouillon cubes (dissolved in 2 cups boiling water)
1/3 cup white wine

Brown birds in oil, and remove to heated casserole. In same oil, sauté vegetables slowly (about 6 minutes). Blend in flour and then, gradually, stir in heated stock. Stir in all seasonings. Remove from heat and stir in wine. Pour this sauce over birds and bake in casserole at 350° for 1 hour. Serves 4.

Here are a couple of equally easy recipes for somewhat larger birds such as grouse, ptarmigan, or chukars.

Grouse (or Whatever) in Sour Cream

4 birds, whole (optionally marinated in white wine)
2 cups sour cream
Thyme and sage or poultry seasoning, to taste
1/2 teaspoon dried dill weed (optional)
1 teaspoon flour

Dust birds with seasonings (except dill) and roast on spit or in racked roaster at 400° until almost done—30 to 40 minutes. Blend flour into sour cream until smooth, then stir in dill (optional) and additional thyme and sage or poultry seasoning (optional). Roast birds for another 10 to 20 minutes, basting frequently with this sauce. (Note: 2 pheasants can be substituted for 4 smaller birds.) Serves 6 to 8.

Pheasant (or Whatever) with Virginia Sauce

2 pheasants (or other medium-size birds) quartered or cut into pieces
½ cup flour
salt to taste (optional)
¼ teaspoon pepper
1 teaspoon paprika
¼ cup butter or margarine
1 clove garlic, crushed
¼ cup ripe olives
½ cup boiled or roasted chestnuts (optional)
½ cup water
½ teaspoon Worcestershire sauce
½ cup white wine

Dredge birds in flour seasoned with salt (optional), pepper, and paprika. In deep skillet or dutch oven, brown on all sides in butter. Add garlic, olives, chestnuts (optional), water, and Worcestershire sauce. Cover (tightly if possible) and simmer 45 minutes. Turn meat, add wine, and simmer another 30 minutes or until tender. Serve hot, covered with sauce. Serves 6.

I'm not about to waste pages giving you conventional roasting recipes for big birds, from pheasants and sage grouse to turkey. Any and all of the recipes for domestic fowl in standard cookbooks will work nicely. But the following roast-turkey recipe contains a basting technique that works wonders in preventing dryness.

Moist Enough Roast Turkey (or Whatever)

1 (15-pound) wild turkey
Melted bacon fat
Pepper to taste
Salt to taste (optional)
1 cup coarsely chopped large onion
2 cups chopped celery with leaves
1½ cups white wine, orange juice, or apple juice or cider
1 muslin cloth or double layer cheesecloth (about 16 inches square)

After washing and drying turkey, brush with bacon fat, then dust with pepper and salt (optional). Mix onion, celery, and ¾ cup wine (or orange juice or apple juice) and stuff bird's cavity loosely with this mixture. (Amounts may have to be adjusted, depending on bird's size.) Place bird on rack in large roasting pan. Dip cloth in melted bacon fat and cover bird with it. Roast at 300°, basting frequently with pan drippings and remaining wine or juice. (Additional wine or juice may be needed.) Roasting time will be about 3 hours for 15-pound bird, but with smaller or larger bird allow at least 25 minutes per pound. Before serving, onion-and-celery stuffing is usually discarded, but it can be reserved for later use with leftover meat in soup or stew. A 15-pound bird will probably serve 8 to 10.

Hunting Preserves

Wingshooters who haven't visited private hunting preserves or have had a less than memorable experience at one often disparage preserve shooting as artificial and unchallenging. At one time, the pen-raised birds on many preserves were a bit tame, and typically you could hunt only one or two species, most often pheasant and quail. I suppose there must still be a few preserves like that, but the vast majority are well-run operations where the cover and terrain are appropriate to the game, the birds retain sufficiently wild characteristics to test your skill, and quite often there are several kinds of game.

Typical in some important ways is an Eastern preserve I visited last year where pheasants, bobwhite quail, and chukar partridges are stocked. The preserve encompasses a lot of acreage, and in the course of a morning or afternoon hunt you'll almost certainly see rabbits and may move a grouse or two—or a few woodcock in the early part of the season. If you can bag them, they're yours.

The owner's policy is to charge a use-fee for a half-day (morning or afternoon) or a full day on his land, plus a fee for each stocked bird released specifically for you or your party, and a smaller fee for any additional stocked birds that weren't released for you but are shot by you. Released birds are often missed by the preserve's guests, and plenty of these left-over birds stay around because the habitat is perfect for them. (Some, of course, disperse to nearby farmland where they benefit all the local hunters.) This means you may shoot the birds released for you and then—perhaps—flush and shoot another pheasant, quail, or partridge that someone missed yesterday or a week ago.

The game regulations governing stocked preserve birds are more liberal than those for wild, native birds of the same species, but the regulations applying to non-stocked species are uniform, so you can't shoot grouse, woodcock, or rabbits out of season on the preserve I've described, or exceed the bag limit. But if the season's open and you shoot one of those species, the preserve operator charges no extra fee beyond those I've mentioned. You've paid for your half-day or full day and for the stocked birds; anything else you bag is a bonus. This isn't unusual, although the policies and fees of preserve operators vary widely. On some large preserves, most of the game consists of wild, native game, but you're using private land and you pay for hunting there and/or for what you take.

That same preserve, by the way, also offers season-long memberships for hunters who plan to spend many days afield. Depending on the game available and the state where the preserve is located, preserve hunting may be legal (for stocked species only) from September all the way into March or April—much longer than the public season. This obviously and enormously increases your opportunities to hunt during any given year. If you plan to do a lot of hunting, a season membership can be cheaper than paying by the half-day. Some preserves are open to members only (and may have waiting lists, since neither the operators nor the customers will tolerate crowding). Regardless of which arrangements you make, preserves provide you with hunting opportunities both before and after the regular seasons.

Before proceeding further, I should explain my earlier statement that stocked birds retain wild characteristics on a really good preserve. As an example, the owner of the operation I've described uses hybrid strains of pheasants known for their wildness and strong flight. He also uses a very large rearing area where the birds grow from chicks to adults in an almost wild environment.

The method of release also affects the wildness of their behavior. When a pheasant is "planted" for the purpose of training or polishing a dog or familiarizing a novice wingshooter with the procedures of the flush and the shot, a preserve employee tries to make sure the bird *won't* be too wild—that it will hold for a point

or flush. To do this he "rocks" the bird—swings it back and forth upside-down. This evidently has a dizzying or stupefying effect but doesn't harm the bird.

The handler then tucks the pheasant's head back under one wing and gently places the bird in high grass, brush, or under a bush where—ideally—it's hidden from view. Occasionally, a feisty cock pheasant will wake up and walk away after a few minutes. More often, the bird remains drowsy for perhaps half an hour and stays put—until awakened by the approach of dog or hunter. Such a pheasant usually holds tight for a point until the hunter walks in and flushes it. When that happens, the bird almost always flies, so there's no need to contend with a runner.

But if a bird with wild characteristics is simply released in natural habitat, it behaves as a wild bird. The method of release depends on the hunter's wishes. When I visited that Eastern preserve last year, I made an advance reservation (which is almost invariably a necessity). About an hour before my partner and I arrived, half a dozen pheasants were released (simply freed, not rocked) along the edges of three different brushy meadows. We had to hunt them, just as we'd hunt birds that had lived their entire lives out there. They behaved like any other pheasants, running and then flushing wide.

We bagged four out of the six, but had to mark down and flush one cock three times before one of us bagged him. The remaining two escaped, and I wouldn't know whether they've fathered chicks on neighboring farmland by now or were shot by hunters who came later. As for my partner and me, after collecting four birds and failing to find more, we hunted another part of the preserve, where we each took another pheasant—birds that had probably been living in the wild for some weeks since that section of the preserve hadn't been utilized during the first part of the season. The preserve owner, a very fair-minded gentleman, charged us nothing for those last two birds. We'd paid for six and we left with six—and two of those released for us would be potential game for other guests.

I'm not telling you exactly how things will be for you but merely how a preserve hunt often goes. It pays to shop for a preserve—phoning in advance not only to make a reservation but to ask about fees and policies.

On a large preserve in good hunting country, part of what you're paying for is the privilege of hunting on private land. It's very unlikely that all the game inhabiting that land will consist of pen-raised birds. Ruffed grouse, for instance, have proved to be extremely resistant to captive breeding, and any you find will be wild ones; yet some preserves list ruffed grouse among the game available. Not only can you extend your hunting season by utilizing a preserve, but you can also gain the experience (and fun) of hunting several varieties of game that aren't otherwise available in your region. The array of species on some preserves is startling: pheasant, dove, quail, chukar, grouse, woodcock, Hungarian partridge, turkey, waterfowl.

Many preserves advertise in sporting magazines and distribute pamphlets or other literature. All the same, when you phone ahead, ask the owner or manager what game is available and what types of hunts are available. If you won't be bringing your own dog, also ask if a dog—and dog handler—will be provided and at what charge. Most preserves provide well-trained dogs for those who need them.

A preserve setting is ideal for training your own dog (with or without the paid help of a pro) or for giving the dog a pre-season or early-season refresher course. Just be sure to let the management know in advance what you want; otherwise the owner may assume you're bringing a polished dog, want no assistance or guidance, and are merely booking time plus birds.

Some preserves are no more imposing in appearance or high-profile services and facilities than the surrounding countryside. Others are lavish. They include Southern quail plantations with on-site lodging, and Western resorts that offer big game as well as bird hunts. Some also include Sporting Clays ranges and/or conventional trap and skeet ranges. Some have ammunition and equipment for sale. And at some, you can get expert coaching either in a particular kind of hunting or in wingshooting.

This kind of service isn't for the novice alone. Several years ago, I experienced an inexplicable slump in my ability to hit anything moving at more than about 10 miles an hour. I happened to be visiting a preserve in the South and the owner, after watching me miss a couple of pheasants and several quail, asked tactfully if I'd enjoy a session with clay targets and an employee who was a masterful shotgunner. By afternoon, I was no longer raising my cheek from the stock, jerking my swing, or committing other atrocities.

You get what you pay for, and it's generally worth more than the price (although some preserves are very pricey). In deciding whether preserve shooting is for you, consider the local hunting opportunities on public land or free-access private land, and also compare the cost in money and time with a trip to a distant region for a particular kind of hunting.

Most preserves invest in at least a little local advertising, and some are also listed in the classified sections of telephone directories. There are, however, two better and more comprehensive sources of addresses and information—annual directories devoted to the subject. I've noticed that some preserves may be listed in one of these references but not in the other, so it's wise to obtain both.

To order the *Directory of Hunting Resorts* (for which, at the time of this writing, there's a $2 handling and mailing charge) write to:

Wildlife Harvest Publications, Inc.
Box 96
Goose Lake, IO 52750

That directory lists the members of the

North American Gamebird Association, and it's reliable but not descriptive of the game or services offered on each preserve. More extensive and descriptive annual listings are contained in *Black's Wing & Clay: The Sportsman's Annual Guide to Wing & Clay Shooting Locations* ($10 at the time of this writing). The 1992-93 edition contained over 1,000 wingshooting preserves in the United States and Canada, plus some 600 Sporting Clays installations and about 30 outstanding shooting schools. For this directory, write to:

Black's Wing & Clay
P.O. Box 2029
75 W. Front St.
Red Bank, NJ 07701

APPENDIX II

Trip Planning

The classified advertising section in a recent issue of *Sports Afield* contained 17 display ads for resorts, lodges, and guide services offering hunts for game birds. Many of these offered combination attractions, including big game and/or waterfowl as well as upland birds. Multiply that number of ads by about 10 to get an estimate of the total number of similar ads appearing in all the sporting magazines in some months—particularly in summer, when many hunters begin planning their trips.

Such ads are a convenient source of addresses to which you can write for further information and literature, although I believe in planning an autumn trip as early as the preceding spring or even winter. Fewer ads appear then, but that's when I begin investigating, either by letter or phone. Some of the lodges and outfitter/guide services must be booked far in advance. They'll respond to an inquiry with information, promotional literature, and the names and addresses of previous satisfied customers (if requested). Since they want your business, they aren't about to supply bad references, but I make a point of calling three previous customers all the same to get a more objective picture than what's in the promotional literature.

State game departments don't always set a given year's open-season dates that far in advance, but they can tell you if it's safe to plan a hunt during a few days, week, or two weeks that you have in mind. I often write to a game department before I respond to any ad. They're extremely helpful. I ask about the cost and availability of a non-resident license in its various forms. Some states don't permit non-resident hunters to pursue certain species. Some offer a short-term license, good for several days or a week, at less cost than a full-season license. And some offer the choice of a combination license or a cheaper license only for small game (including birds). In some cases you must apply and pay for a license in advance, while in others you can get your license when you arrive.

In states where guides are often hired by visiting hunters, the game department can, as a rule, either supply some of their names and addresses or the address and phone number of a guides' association. You can contact them for information and references just as you'd contact those you've found through magazine ads.

The game department can also tell you the best areas for various kinds of game—sometimes as specifically as the nearest town or a recommended Wildlife Management Area. Many states issue clear guides (including maps) to Wildlife Management Areas and the game they offer. I've relied heavily—and with excellent results—on those published by New Jersey and Oklahoma, and I'm sure all the others are equally detailed and dependable.

The address and phone number of the administration office at each Wildlife Management Area isn't always listed in these guides, but you can obtain that information, too, from the game department. It's a smart move to phone the WMA office for detailed information. You can very often talk to a resident wildlife biologist who can tell you whether the population of a given species is up or down and when is the most promising time to plan a trip. These people are friendly—and proud of the wildlife in their charge—and frequently they can give you information about local accommodations, guides, any special equipment, and other valuable details.

Some states maintain information services (separate from the wildlife management and enforcement divisions) just for hunters and fishermen. South Dakota, for example, has one called South Dakota Adventures, a branch of the Department of Tourism. The Canadian provinces have excellent—that is to say, enthusiastic—tourism departments that are usually eager to help and well supplied with detailed information. All of the game departments maintain main offices in the state or provincial capitals, and so do many tourism departments, so you can get a needed phone number simply by asking your local operator for the area code and then dialing the information operator in that area.

I also like to phone or write the chamber of commerce in the sizable town nearest to a prospective hunting area. The nearest town may be so small that it either has no chamber of commerce or has a chamber office that operates only part-time and has no one available to provide information when you need it. But the nearest *big* town or city will have a chamber of commerce that will provide information on the nearest lodgings and quite often on resorts, outfitters, guides, sporting-goods stores, restaurants, and even sight-seeing attractions and evening entertainment. Consult a state map to find the likeliest town or city near your hunting destination, and then write to the chamber of commerce or get the phone number from the information operator.

For many of us, part of the fun of traveling is the planning, but all those phone calls and letters can consume some time and money. If that isn't for you, booking agents—travel agents specializing in sporting trips—will do just about everything for you. They, too, advertise in the sporting magazines, and quite a few are also listed in *Black's Wing & Clay* (see Appendix I for the address of this publication). The edition I've just received lists more than 30 agents who specialize in arranging trips for wingshooting sportsmen. Some of these are worldwide operations, others book trips to certain foreign countries such as Mexico, Argentina, or Scotland (paradises for certain types of game-bird hunting), and still others book trips only within the United States, Canada, or North America. *Bon voyage!*

APPENDIX III

Conservation Organizations

A great many organizations are devoted to the betterment of habitat and wildlife in general or of some particular group or species of wildlife. Such organizations have been and are of incalculable benefit to wild creatures and their ecosystems, and—directly or indirectly—to the future of our sport. Some of those concerned with the whole nation or whole planet (that is, environment and wildlife in general) vie with one another for the allegiance and financial support of the public, and I'm convinced they'd be more effective if several of them merged, combining their fund-raising activities, capital, facilities, services, and personnel. This would reduce the costs incurred for administration, fund-raising, lobbying, litigation, and often strident rivalry, thus leaving a lot more for their stated objectives.

All the same, a number of these organizations have established admirable records in assuring the survival and abundance of many game and non-game species. One of the most admirable, I believe, is the Izaak Walton League of America (1401 Wilson Blvd., Level B, Arlington, VA 22209). Its name leads some people to believe it's concerned only with fishing and fisheries,

which is not the case. The "Ikes" labor and fight in behalf of clean air and water, the environment in general, the wise use of natural resources, and the welfare of game and non-game. A great many of its members are ardent hunters, and the local chapters perform valuable service at the grassroots level.

The National Wildlife Federation (1400 Sixteenth St., NW, Washington, DC 20036) originated as a group of sportsmen and wildlife professionals fighting for conservation with the express support of the federal government. At the national level, it has changed greatly since the 1930s, and the vast majority of associate members (essentially contributors and subscribers to the Federation's magazines) aren't hunters. The affiliated State Federations, however, are still composed largely of conservation-minded hunters and fishermen who continue to work for the benefit of game—and sport—as well as non-game.

Ducks Unlimited (1 Waterfowl Way, Long Grove, IL 60047-0216) is specifically dedicated to waterfowl and wetlands, so its inclusion here may surprise some readers. The fact is, its habitat-improvement programs in Canada, the United States, and Mexico inevitably expand and maintain ecosystems crucial not only to ducks and geese but to all the creatures that utilize marsh habitat or the type of habitat typically adjacent to marshes. Those creatures include many of the upland game birds discussed in this book, as well as an even wider array of non-game species.

At present, there are four other major organizations devoted to the welfare of specific game birds. Most of the conservation groups, both the general-purpose organizations and the more specialized ones (listed below with their addresses), offer attractive incentives for membership. The National Wild Turkey Federation, for example, is outstanding and yet typical in its services, which include *Turkey Call* magazine, *The Caller* newspaper, automatic state membership, information exchanges, local fund-raising activities, caps and other "premium" offers, calling contests and demonstrations, etc.

Some of these organizations are still in their infancy, hardly more than a decade old, but because their membership drives have succeeded they've already been able to improve prospects immeasurably for their favorite game birds. Pheasants Forever was founded in 1982. I've just seen a brief summary of its past and present activities, and take delight in reporting that at this point the organization has planted 4.5 million trees, purchased 15,000 acres of habitat, and planted more than half a million acres of pheasant food and cover. Pheasants Forever presently has 420 chapters in 29 states.

As in all such organizations, some chapters are more active and effective (perhaps because of members who have more leisure time and are more affluent) than others. Nonetheless, I think it's fair to cite an example of one chapter's successes. The Highland chapter in Illinois raises about $50,000 a year—which has made possible the purchase of a truck, tractor, and seeder, among other things. Local members have planted more than 100,000 trees and several thousand acres of clover, alfalfa, corn, sorghum, and native grasses. I'd say pheasants—and other wild creatures that heavily utilize such plantings—have a bright future in Illinois.

I've quoted these statistics merely as an example, not as an implication favoring one organization above the others. All four do comparably splendid work. I strongly recommend joining whichever one benefits your favorite game bird—or more than one, if possible. Here are the names and addresses.

National Wild Turkey Federation
770 Augusta Rd., P.O. Box 530
Edgefield, SC 29824-0530

Pheasants Forever, Inc.
P.O. Box 75473
St. Paul, MN 55175

Quail Unlimited, Inc.
P.O. Box 610
Edgefield, SC 29824

Ruffed Grouse Society
451 McCormick Rd.
Coraopolis, PA 15108

PHOTO CREDITS

Wally Breese, Arizona Game & Fish Dept., pages 117, 119

Gere Brehm, page 148 (right)

Bill Browning, page 120

Denver A. Bryan, page 122

Calif. Dept. of Fish & Game, page 123

Columbia Sportswear, page 80

Judd Cooney, pages 92, 95, 106, 150, 167

Byron W. Dalrymple, pages 171, 172

Robert Elman, pages 39, 41, 43, 44, 45, 48, 67, 71, 79, 110, 177

John R. Falk, pages 59, 164

Luthur Goldman, U.S. Fish & Wildlife Service, page 185 (bottom)

Bob Gooch, page 141

W. Paul Gorenzel, page 124

Haydel's Game Calls, page 112

C.J. Henry, U.S. Fish & Wildlife Service, page 134

Larry Holjencin, pages 183, 185 (top)

Hunter's Specialties, page 88

Johnny Johnson, Florida News Bureau, pages 63, 109

Sid Latham, page 31

George Laycock, page 143

Tim Leary, pages 60, 127

John Madsen, page 94

Neal and Mary Mishler, page 140

Richard Mousel, page 162

Nebraska Game Commission, pages 91 (bottom), 175

North Dakota Fish & Game Dept., page 53

Pennsylvania Game News, page 190

Doug Petty, Columbia Sportswear, page 65

John E. Phillips, page 188

Chuck Post, South Dakota Dept. of Game, Fish & Parks, pages 148 (left), 152

Remington Arms, page 83

Leonard Lee Rue III, pages 61, 62, 70, 72, 81, 97, 100, 133, 136, 137, 144, 158, 176

Len Rue, Jr., page 132

Saskatchewan Govt. Photographic Services, page 149

Art Scheck, pages 15, 24 (top), 30 (top), 54, 75, 82, 88, 112 (top)

Richard P. Smith, pages 184, 187, 189, 191

South Dakota Dept. of Game, Fish & Parks, pages 91 (top), 99, 105, 148, 151

Charles G. Summers, Jr., Leonard Rue Enterprises, page 145

Tennessee Game & Fish Commission, page 24 (bottom)

Russell Tinsley, pages 68, 114, 178

Charles F. Waterman, pages 111, 159, 161, 163, 169

Winchester Ammunition, pages 105, 157, 170, 181

Don Woolridge, Missouri Dept. of Conservation, page 113

Leonard Wright, page 84